BILL CL⎯⎯

Bill Clegg is a literary agent in New York and
the author of bestselling memoirs *Portrait of an
Addict as a Young Man* and *Ninety Days* as well
as the Booker and National Book Award longlisted
novel, *Did You Ever Have A Family*. He has written
for the *New York Times, Esquire, New York Times*
magazine, the *Guardian* and *Harper's Bazaar*.

BILL CLEGG

Portrait of an Addict as a Young Man & Ninety Days

VINTAGE

1 3 5 7 9 10 8 6 4 2

Vintage
20 Vauxhall Bridge Road,
London SW1V 2SA

Vintage is part of the Penguin Random House group of companies
whose addresses can be found at global.penguinrandomhouse.com.

Penguin
Random House
UK

Portrait of an Addict as a Young Man first published in the UK by
Jonathan Cape in 2010
Ninety Days first published in the UK by Jonathan Cape in 2012

penguin.co.uk/vintage

A CIP catalogue record for this book is available from the British Library

ISBN 9781784708191

Printed and bound in Great Britain by Clays Ltd, Elcograf S.p.A.

Penguin Random House is committed to a sustainable future
for our business, our readers and our planet. This book is made
from Forest Stewardship Council® certified paper.

Contents

NINETY DAYS

PORTRAIT OF AN ADDICT
AS A YOUNG MAN

For everyone still out there

Think of light and how far it falls, to us. To fall, we say, naming a fundamental way of going to the world — falling.

— WILLIAM KITTREDGE, *A Hole in the Sky*

Scrapers

I can't leave and there isn't enough.

Mark is at full tilt, barking hear-it-here-first wisdom from the edge of his black vinyl sofa. He looks like a translator for the deaf moving at triple speed — hands flapping, arms and shoulders jerking. His legs move, too, but only to fold and refold at regular intervals beneath his tall, skeletal frame. The leg crossing is the only thing about Mark with any order. The rest is a riot of sudden movements and spasms — he's a marionette at the mercy of a brutal puppeteer. His eyes, like mine, are dull black marbles.

Mark is squawking about a crack dealer he used to buy from who's been busted — how he saw it coming, how he always does — but I'm not paying attention. All that matters to me is that we've reached the end of our bag. The thumb-size clear plastic mini zip-lock that once bulged with chunks of crack is now empty. It's day-break and the dealers have turned off their phones.

My two dealers are named Rico and Happy. According to Mark, all crack dealers are named Rico and Happy. Rico hasn't shown up the last few times I've called. Mark, who makes it his business to know the day-to-day movements and shifting status of a handful of dealers, says Rico's Xanax habit has resurfaced and is begin-ning to slow him down. Last year he didn't leave his apartment in Washington Heights for three months. So for now I call Happy, who shows up after midnight when the $1,000 limit on my cash card zeroes out and I can start withdrawing again. Happy is the more reliable of the two, but Rico will often deliver at odd hours when the other dealers won't. He'll come in the middle of the day, hours late but when the rest are asleep and closed for business. He'll complain and give you a skimpy bag, but he'll come. With Mark's phone, I dial Rico's number but his voice mail is full and not accepting messages. I dial Happy's and it goes straight to voice mail.

Happy and Rico sell crack. They don't sell cocaine to be inhaled, pot, Ecstasy, or anything else. I buy only bags of precooked crack. Some people will insist on cooking their own — a tricky operation that involves cocaine, baking soda, water, and a stove top — but the few times I tried this, I wasted the coke, burned my hands, and ended up with a wet glob that was barely smokable.

Give me the scraper, Mark barks. His stem — the small glass tube packed on one end with Brillo pad wire — is caked with residue, so after he scrapes it out and packs the end again, we can count on at least a few more hits. He folds his legs in a spidery arrangement and for a moment appears as if he will tip over. He looks like he's in his sixties — gray-faced, wrinkled, jutting bones — but claims he's in his early forties. I've been coming to his apartment for over three years, with increasing frequency, to get high.

I pass him the craggy metal strip that had until last night been the support behind the nylon web of an umbrella. Scrapers come from all sorts of things — wire coat hangers mostly, the ones without paint; but umbrellas have long thin metal strips, sometimes hollow half cylinders, that are particularly effective at cleaning out stems and generating a miracle hit or two when the bag is empty and before the need comes to check the couch and floor for what I call crumbs, what Mark calls bits, but what all crack addicts know is their last resort until they can get another bag.

I reach toward Mark to pass him the scraper and he flinches. The stem slips from his hands, falls in slow motion between us, and shatters on the scuffed parquet floor.

Mark gasps more than speaks. *Oh. Oh no. Oh Jesus, no.* In a flash he's down on all fours picking through the debris. He rescues several of the larger pieces of glass, brings them back to the coffee table, lays them out, one by one, and begins picking and scratching at them with the scraper. *Let's see. Let's see.* He mumbles to himself as he maneuvers frantically over each shard. Again, his joints and hands and limbs seem animated not by life but by strings pulling and tugging him — furiously, meticulously — through a mari-onette's pantomime of a fevered prospector scrabbling through his pan for flecks of gold.

Mark finds no gold. He puts down the scraper, the bits of glass, and his movements come to a halt. He collapses back into the couch, where I can practically see the strings that held him aloft now glide down around him. The bag is empty and it's six a.m. We've been at it for six days and five nights and all the other stems are destroyed.

Morning glows behind the drawn blinds. Minutes pass and nothing but the low whine of the garbage trucks outside cuts the quiet. My neck throbs and the muscles in my shoulder feel thick and tight. The throbbing keeps time with my heart, which slams in my chest like an angry fist. I can't stop my body from rocking. I watch Mark get up to begin sweeping the glass and notice how his body rocks with mine, how our sway is synchronized — like two underwater weeds bending to the same current — and am both horrified and comforted to recognize how alike we are in the desolate crash that follows when the drugs run out.

The creeping horror of these past few weeks — relapsing; leaving Noah, my boyfriend, at the Sundance Film Festival nearly a week early; e-mailing my business partner, Kate, and letting her know that she can do what she wants with our business, that I'm not coming back; checking in and out of a rehab in New Canaan, Connecticut; spending a string of nights at the 60 Thompson hotel and then diving into the gritty crackscape of Mark's apartment with the drifters there who latch onto the free drugs that come with someone on a bender. The awful footage of my near-history flashes behind my eyes, just as the clear future of not having a bag and knowing another won't be had for hours rises up, sharp as the new day.

I don't know yet that I will push through these grim, jittery hours until evening, when Happy will turn his cell phone back on and deliver more. I don't yet know that I will keep this going—here and in other places like it—for over a month. That I will lose almost forty pounds, so that, at thirty-four, I will weigh less than I did in the eighth grade.

It's also too soon to see the new locks on my office door. Kate will change them after she discovers I have come in at night. This will be weeks from now. She'll worry that I might steal things to pay for drugs, but I'll go there only to sit at my desk a few more times. To say good-bye to the part of me that, on the surface anyway, had worked the best. Through the large open window behind my desk, I'll look out at the Empire State Building, with its weary authority and shoulders of colored light. The city will seem different then, less mine, farther away. And Broadway, ten stories below, will be empty, a dark canyon of gray and black stretching north from 26th Street to Times Square.

On one of those nights, before the locks are changed, I'll climb up into the window and dangle my feet, scooch close to the edge and hover there in the cold February air for what seems like hours. I'll crawl down, sit at the desk again and get high. I'll remember how excited everyone was when we opened nearly five years before. Kate, the staff, our families. My clients—novelists, poets, essayists, short story writers—came with me from the old literary agency, the place where I'd started as an assistant when I first came to New York. They came with me, and there was so much faith in what lay ahead, so much faith in me. I'll stare at all the contracts and memos and galleys piled on my desk and marvel that I once had something to do with these things, those people. That I had been counted on.

On Mark's couch I watch my legs shake and wonder if there is a Xanax in his medicine cabinet. I wonder if I should leave and find a hotel. I have with me my passport, the clothes on my back, a cash card, and the black NYC Parks & Rec Department cap I recently found in the back of a cab, the one with the green maple leaf stitched on the front. There is still money in my checking account. Almost forty grand. I wonder how I've made it this far; how by some unwanted miracle my heart hasn't stopped.

Mark is shouting from the kitchen, but I don't hear what he's saying.

My cell phone rings, but it is buried under a pile of blankets and sheets in the next room, and I don't hear that either. I'll find it later, the voice mail full of terrified calls from friends and family and Noah. I'll listen to the beginning of one and erase it along with the rest.

I won't hear the tumble of the new locks on the door of the apartment where Noah and I have lived for eight years—how the sound has changed from a bright pop to a low click as the bolt flies free while his hand turns the new key for the first time. I can't hear any of this. Cannot feel any of these things that have happened or are about to as the construction that was my life dismantles—lock by lock, client by client, dollar by dollar, trust by trust.

The only thing I hear as Mark angrily sweeps the glass from the floor, and the only thing I feel as the city rustles to life outside, are the barking demands at the end of the marionette strings. Through the endless morning and the crawling afternoon hours, and after, they grow louder, more insistent; tug harder, yank rougher, shake the cash card from my wallet, dollars from my pockets, loose change from my coat, color from my eyes, life out of me.

Cheers

It's January 2001 and Noah's cousin Letty is giving a small dinner at her brownstone in Brooklyn Heights to celebrate the launch of the small literary agency my friend Kate and I are about to open. Letty is a well-bred daughter of Memphis. Wellesley educated, widowed, and much younger-looking and acting than her sixty-something years, she has the bright, smiling, goodhearted eagerness of an underdog. Unlike her supersleek, wife-of-a-former-ambassador sister, Letty has always seemed slightly at odds with her privileged upbringing. She hasn't needed to work a day in her life, but she talks often about her jobs in the design departments of several book publishers and her many years working for foundations. She has two daughters, Ruth and Hannah, and scads of girlhood friends with names like Sissy and Babs whom she often flies back to Memphis to celebrate birthdays or anniversaries with. Letty is one of the kindest people I have ever known.

It is the end of January, one week before the agency officially opens. We don't have phones, stationery, or bank accounts. I'm anxious that we still have to hire an assistant and a bookkeeper, but I'm more anxious that we will not have money to pay either. Noah and I arrive at Letty's ten minutes late, and Kate and her husband are already there. Letty has arranged for someone to take coats, serve drinks, pass hors d'oeuvres, and attend to the dinner table. He's in his mid- to late thirties, Asian, attractive, clearly gay, and a bit too friendly. His name is Stephen and his flamboyance makes me self-conscious in the presence of Kate and her husband, whom we haven't socialized with as a couple much and who seem now, together, very straight.

Stephen asks Noah and me what we'd like to drink and scampers off to the kitchen. He brings us two glasses of white wine, even though I asked for a vodka and Noah a Scotch. He flusters and apologizes and goes back to the kitchen but does not return. Five or so minutes pass and Letty gets up to look for him. A few minutes later he comes out with the drinks. Letty is clearly embarrassed.

The evening is decadent. Caviar, shrimp, and cheeses before dinner, then roast lamb. I have too much of everything and am full long before dessert is served. Noah and Letty both give toasts—both have tears in their eyes as they do. I shift uncomfortably in the beams of their praise and cringe, not for the first time, at how close I am to a cousin of Noah's and barely know any of my own. At how Noah and I will go to weddings and birthdays of cousins and siblings and nieces of his and I see my family once a year—at Christmas usually—and then for only a day and a night.

On the way to the bathroom, I ask Stephen to bring me another vodka. He forgets and I drink more wine. As I finally catch a gentle buzz, I look around the table and wonder how on earth I ended up here. Nights like these are for other people, people like Kate and Noah who—with their Ivy League degrees and supportive families—seem born for toasts and congratulations. At dessert, instead of drinking the port Letty has Stephen open, I get up and fix another vodka. Stephen sees this, realizes that he never brought me the earlier one, and from then on is very quick to refill my glass.

Noah and I hold hands in the cab ride home. I've had seven or eight vodkas, at least as many glasses of wine, and still feel a few drinks shy of where I'd like to be. I think of all that is left to do in the coming weeks to open the agency, and of the two other parties being thrown to celebrate. One is a cocktail party at the new apartment of a friend of Kate's; the other is a seated dinner for fifty or so clients and publishing colleagues hosted by my friend David, who is also one of the first writers I worked with. I worry that I'll need to address the crowds at both of these parties—say something at least by way of thanking the hosts—and I begin to think about how to make sure I won't have to. I close my eyes and try not to focus on how much I want to call Rico and do a few hits. After four or five drinks, this option usually rises up and floats in front of me until I either call him, call another dealer, or fall asleep.

It's just before midnight, and my mind starts racing with ways that I can break away from Noah and score. A manuscript left at the office? Cash I need to get from the ATM? Nothing seems plausible. As we cross the Brooklyn Bridge back into Manhattan, Noah takes both my hands and tells me how proud he is—of me, of the agency. As he speaks, the lights from the bridge flicker across his scruffy beard, kind eyes, longish sideburns and close-cropped, receding hair. I lean into him and away from the other thoughts. He smells the way he always smells—like Speed Stick deodorant and fresh laundry. I relax a little, think for a moment that there's not so much to worry about, that everything will work out.

Getting into bed that night, I remember Stephen, the guy at Letty's, and how he forgot to bring out several dishes warming in the oven, spilled a glass of wine, and made flirty eyes at me through dinner. I wonder how Letty found him and remember his lingering too long at the table, asking too many questions, and seeming oblivious of his mistakes. I remember that he let us know he went to Princeton and that, when it came up that Noah was a filmmaker, he listed all the famous people he knew—playwrights, activists, actors. I also remember his writing his number down on the back of a napkin and pressing it into my hand when I went into the kitchen for a glass of water; how he held my hand a beat too long when he told me that he'd bartended lots of book parties, that I should call him sometime. And though he'd been a disaster all evening, I know, as I fall asleep that night, that I will.

Over a year later, when Stephen is setting up a small table in our TV room with glasses and ice—something he has now done for us at least half a dozen times—I notice a long burn mark down the side of his thumb. I ask him what happened and he stops what he's doing, looks at me as if he's been waiting for me to ask this question for a long time, and says, *You don't want to know.* But I do know. Addicts have antennae that can sometimes detect the kindred frequency of other addicts, and in this instant I pick up Stephen's. In fact, I've probably been responding to it since the second we met. But it's not until now—when I know exactly how he burned himself—that I fully understand the reason I hired him, why he is now in our apartment working another party, even though he has twice stood us up on the day of an event with some complicated excuse of illness or family trouble. And so I say, *Maybe you need to be more careful what you smoke,* and when he smiles and asks, *Are you?* I know that this will lead to something. That the ball is in play. I'll be amazed later when I remember what I say next. *Not as careful as either of us should be.* And then next: *We should set that up sometime.*

I throw a party at the apartment when Noah is out of town. It's a Thursday night and I've already cleared the decks so I don't need to go into work the next day. All evening I pretend to be tired—yawning and stretching, rubbing my eyes—hoping to encourage people to leave early. I imagine the first hit and the bloom of exquisite calm it will bring and I quietly, invisibly, detest everyone in the apartment for being there. I move through the apartment with my seltzer—what I always drink when I organize anything larger than a dinner party—and as I'm talking and smiling and hugging congratulations and thank-you-for-comings, I'm running down the list of things left to do. Check in with Noah to give him the sense that the night has wound down and I am heading to bed. Run out to the cash machine to get Stephen $300—maybe $400—to go wherever he needs to go to score. I'll also need at least $300 to pay him for bartending, since he accepts cash only. I decide to tell him not to bother cleaning up, that I'll do it so he can get going.

Stephen leaves around eleven fifteen and returns after one. I've just finished breaking down the bar, washing the glasses, and putting away the sodas and napkins. (He'll include those two hours on his bill.) This night is important. Not because it's the first time I sleep with him. Not because I spend another $700 I barely have. But because at some point, around four in the morning, when we have smoked nearly through the bag, Stephen calls his friend Mark, who, in a few swift minutes, is at the door with more.

Mark is a restaurant publicist. Tall, neat, angular. I notice right away how he vibrates. As if some electrical charge shocks through his body at a low but steady thrum. I also notice how he speaks to Stephen. Like Fagin to the Artful Dodger, he has some authority over him, and even though it's clear he's on his best behavior, I can see how their dynamic involves some commingling of brutality and care. As Mark holds up our stems and complains how oily and burnt they are, Stephen flutters around him like a nervous nurse attending a surgeon. Mark gives him a you-should better look and shakes his head. Stephen doesn't tell h they're burnt because of me. That I have, as I always do, scorched each stem with hits that pull too long and flames that are too high. Everyone I ever smoke with will complain about this. And though I will try, each time, to inhale as gently as I can, it always seems like I'm not pulling hard enough, as if the flame is too low, as if I'm not getting enough.

At some point after Mark arrives, Stephen stops speaking to me directly. There seems to be some new rule that Mark is the only one who can address me, and when he does, he is wildly polite, overly complimentary (the apartment, my looks). It's as if I'm in the forecourt of a long con, and instead of feeling hesitant or cautious, I'm thrilled.

The night grunts on until ten or so the next morning. Stephen and Mark amble out into the day, and by Saturday night I have invited them over again. By Monday morning, my bank account is empty and Mark has suggested he and I get together on our own sometime that week. Noah calls a dozen or so times, and I let the landline ring, turn the cell phone off, and don't call him back. On Monday afternoon, my assistant comes into my office and says Noah is on the line, upset and demanding to speak to me. I close the door, and he cries on the other end of the line and asks me to please stop. Could I just please stop. I feel awful and tell him of course and I'm sorry and that it won't happen again. He presses for details and I get mad. Amazingly, he apologizes. I throw Stephen's number away. I throw Mark's card away. But it doesn't matter. Both call over the next weeks and months, and at some moment, I can't remember exactly when or which one, I write a number down. And at some other moment, not long after, I call.

First Door

It's time to go. He's had to pee for hours, but it's always the last thing he wants to do. The problem — that's what his parents call it — *the problem* is that if he goes, meaning, to the bathroom, he won't actually be able to go. In the way he describes it to himself then, it hasn't *built up enough* yet. There isn't enough pressure. He will wait a little while. Wait until dinner is over, when no one will notice if he's gone for too long. Sometimes it takes as long as an hour. Sometimes he can't do it at all. And sometimes it only takes a few minutes. He never knows until he's there.

It's after dinner and he's standing in front of the avocado green toilet. Noises happen behind the closed door — a dropped ice tray, cursing, breaking glass, louder cursing, a phone ringing. The house swells with urgency. From somewhere inside these sounds, a voice that will always remind him of wind chimes calls, *Billy, are you all right?*

Billy . . . , his mother calls again, but her voice fades.

Nothing for a few moments. Just the green toilet. Hurry, he thinks. Hurry. His hands work furiously over the end of his penis. A loud knock at the door. Then two. A different voice. His father's. *Jesus, Willie, don't make a career out of it in there.*

Little-guy cords — usually navy blue, sometimes green — bunch at his feet. Fruit of the Looms wrinkle just below his knees. He's been in there for over half an hour. He's come close at least three times, but each time it doesn't work. Doesn't happen. He knows it's going to sting — like bits of glass trying to push out — but he just wants it over with. He shuffles in front of the bowl — left, right, left, right — and squeezes the end of his penis. Rubs it with both hands. The pressure builds and his brow is sweating. He has a terrified sense that if his parents find out, there will be trouble. His father has told him that he has to stop taking so long in the bathroom. When he asks his son why he jumps around and makes such a big production of it all, the boy doesn't have an answer. *Cut it out* is what his father tells him, and he wishes he could.

He runs the water in the sink to cover the sound. The shuffle becomes a dance, the kneading becomes a fevered pinching. From a faraway room he hears his older sister, Kim, crying. His father yells her name. A door slams. His mother calls out. A kettle of boiling water whistles from the kitchen. None of these sounds have to do with him. But someone—he can't tell who—is knocking at the door now. Just knocking, no voice. The boy is a panicked animal—jerking and jumping and pinching before the bowl. He braces for another knock. There is more shouting from down the hall. The sound of something breaking. His hands, his legs—his whole body riots around the pressure at his middle. He's sure his parents can hear him, convinced they will come bursting through the locked door at any moment. He tries to stop the jumping but he can't. It feels as if the whole house—his parents, his sister, the cats, the whistling kettle—has gathered on the other side of the door.

In a moment—the one he's desperate for but can't create—none of it will matter. In that moment, he won't hear the slamming and banging and yelling. As the stinging pressure crests and his body flaps away from him, he won't hear anything. In that streaking moment when he loses control and everything fades out in a flash of pain and relief, he will spray the wall, the floor, the radiator, himself.

He doesn't see any of the mess until the little oblivion passes and he's able to steady himself and direct the pee into the bowl. He aims toward the back to avoid the ruckus of water and it goes on forever. He sees there's a big clean-up job to be done, and he's already anxious about what to say when he's on the other side of the door. Once he's finally finished peeing, he begins pulling yards of toilet paper from the roll, spools that ribbon around his feet and begin to soak up the pool of urine on the tile. He wipes down the toilet and the walls behind and to the side. He gets on his hands and knees and begins sweeping the damp away in long wide arcs. He pats his pants down with the tissue until it pills and crumbles in his hands. He puts too much toilet paper in the bowl and it clogs and the water rises. He knows to put his hand up the drain and yank the paper free to avoid another mess. He plunges his arm in, tugs frantically at the clog, and, like an answered prayer, the bowl empties. Just as this happens the knocking begins again and now it's both parents at the door. His pants and underwear are still bunched around his ankles. He hasn't pulled them up yet because he knows that beads of blood have sprung up at the tip of his penis and it will take a few dabs of tissue and a minute or two for it to dry before it's safe. Often he rushes through this part and will have to throw his underwear out later as little brown spots of blood bud and dry in the white fabric. He's tried stuffing toilet paper in there, but it usually slips to the side and doesn't work. Sometimes he forgets and tosses the underwear in the hamper and sees the dryer-dried briefs folded and spotty in his dresser drawer days later. His mother never says a word to him about the briefs, about the peeing—about any of it. This has been going on for as long as he can remember. He has no memory of standing at a toilet and peeing when he wants to.

What are you DOING? thunders from the other side of the door. His father again. The boy calls out that he is coming, just a minute. He mutters to himself—*Please God, please*—actually, he's been muttering this to himself since he locked the bathroom door over forty-five minutes ago. He will never be more specific in his plea. His pants and shirt are soaking with water, with urine. He pats himself down one more time with a wad of toilet paper and puts it in the wastepaper basket under an empty tissue box and a used toilet paper roll. He wipes everything down, again, just one more time—the radiator, the bowl, the toilet seat, the floor. He scans the room again for signs of his time there. He wipes, with his hand, the sweat dripping from his brow and pats his hair carefully into place. He breathes in, murmurs another quiet prayer, turns off the light, and hopes the light in the hall is off so his soak-stained clothes aren't obvious.

He calms his breath, palms the doorknob, and braces for what's on the other side. He is five years old.

Flight

Snow is falling outside the Holland Tunnel. Cars aren't moving. Horns sound and drivers yell. My flight to Berlin is scheduled to take off in less than an hour, and there is no way I'm going to make it. Noah is already there, having arrived at the Berlin Film Festival directly from Sundance to show his film two days ago. I call my assistant, who booked a four-o'clock car for a five thirty flight, which I only now realize isn't enough time, particularly with the snow. It is, of course, not his fault, but I tell him it is and that my life is about to change, and not for the better, as a result. I hang up. These will be my last words to him, to anyone in my office.

I have nearly a full bag—three medium-size rocks and a scattering of crumbs—in my pocket. A clean stem and lighter, wrapped in a kitchen towel, are wedged somewhere in my L.L. Bean duffel bag, between manuscripts, a pair of jeans, a sweater, and a pile of Kiehl's products. The driver is a young, deep-voiced Eastern European woman, and I've already sung her my if-you-only-knew-how-important-it-is-that-I-get-there-on-time song to persuade her to work some kind of magic and levitate us past the traffic. She just stares at me through the rearview mirror. I wonder if she can see how strung out I am, how far over the line.

I know this is going to be the last straw. Even if Noah forgives me again, despite the fact that he knows I've been using since I left him at Sundance, Kate will not. I've been out for almost two weeks and canceled three meetings with her to go over our long-avoided partnership agreement and finances. I have told everyone — friends, clients, employees — that I have thrown my back out and am going to doctors, acupuncturists, and masseurs. But the truth is that since I got back from Sundance five days early, I've been rattling around the apartment in a thick cloud of crack smoke. I've left the building only a few times, to run across 8th Street to the cash machine and next door to the deli for lighters and Brillo wire. The liquor store has made daily deliveries of Ketel One, and I've called the housekeeper to tell her I'm home sick and not to come.

At some point before getting in the car, I send Kate an e-mail telling her to do what she needs to do, that I've relapsed and that she should protect herself in whatever way is necessary. Before I press Send, I look out the window at the thick flakes of snow coming down in slow motion between the buildings and think I am doing her a favor. Giving her permission to get out and move on. But

I feel next to nothing as I end our partnership, our business, my career. I regard that nothing the same way you observe a cut on your finger just after accidentally slicing it with a knife but seconds before the blood appears. For a moment it's like looking at someone else's finger, as if the cut you made has not broken your skin, the blood about to flow not your own.

I finally get to the airport and race ahead of the line to the first-class counter. The woman there tells me right away that I've missed my flight. I ask her if there is another and she tells me there is one that goes through Amsterdam in three hours. Without hesitating I buy a first-class, full-fare ticket. I have over $70,000 in my checking account at this point, and I think, barely think, that five or so thousand is nothing. I ask her if there is a hotel at the airport, because I want to lie down and rest before my flight. She looks at me and pauses before telling me there is a Marriott a short cab ride away. I thank her, check my bag through for the seven-o'clock flight, and take my ticket. In the cab, I call Noah and leave him a message that I missed my flight — *The traffic was terrible,* I say in mock frustration — but I'm booked on the next one out.

The cabdriver is a handsome, dark-eyed Hispanic guy, and I immediately strike up a conversation. How I get to the moment when I ask him if he parties, I don't know, but I get there. He says yes and I say, *With what?* and he answers, *Beer and pot.* He asks me with what and I come right out and tell him. He pauses and asks me if I have any on me and I say yes. He asks if he can see it and, without hesitating, I reach into my pocket, pull out a rock, and hold it up between the two front seats. He slows the cab, eyes the drug seriously, but says nothing. When I pull it back, he laughs and tells me he's never seen it before, and I ask if he wants to hang out. He tells me sure, later, after his shift, and gives me his cell phone number. I take it, even though I know my flight will take off before he's done. He doesn't say his name so I look at the driver's ID framed in Plexiglas behind the passenger seat and notice that it's obscured by a piece of newspaper. I ask him his name and he mumbles something inaudible. I ask him again and he says what I think is Rick.

Something in his manner shifts as we pull up to the Marriott. He suddenly cools, and I'll remember, later, that he barely asks for the fare, that when I hand it to him, it seems irrelevant. I hardly register this, since I'm preoccupied with how lucky it is that I missed the flight, that I now have a few hours to get high.

I get to the room and shut the door behind me as if I'm closing the curtain on a great, terrifying stage where I've had to perform a grueling part, the skin of which I can now finally shed. I take off my coat and pack a big hit. Crumbs scatter on the bedspread as I hold the stem up to light, but I don't care. I pull hard and hold the smoke in for as long as I can. When I exhale, the stress of the last few hours disappears and in its place swells a pearly bliss.

I soon become aware of my body and feel restless in my clothes. I take my sweater off between the first and second hits. They seem like part of a constricting costume for the performance on the other side of the door and of no use now. By the third hit I'm naked, though I grab a towel from the bathroom and tie it low around my hips. I will always do this when I get high. I will always think my torso looks lean and muscled and sexy. I will always, many times, clock myself in the mirror and think, Not bad. I will remember some version of the lines from Ben Neihart's novel *Hey Joe,* when the narrator checks himself out in the mirror and thinks smugly that he's *keeping his shit tight.* I will, to be perfectly honest, turn myself on.

I scooch the towel lower down my hips, cinch it a little tighter, and begin to get restless for company. I call the number of the taxi driver but no one answers and it doesn't click to voice mail. I do this thirty or so times in the next hour. I put what's left of the bag in an ashtray and thrill to what seems like an endless amount. I'm sloppy as I pack these hits. The bedspread and floor are soon speckled with crumbs. I know that at some point I will be on my knees picking them up, trying to tell the difference between crack crumbs and other debris. There will never be a time when I smoke crack that doesn't end with me on my knees, sometimes for hours—hunched over carpets, rugs, linoleum, tile—sifting desperately through lint and cat litter and dirt, fingering the floor, like a madman, for crumbs. I know this is where it will end up. As I pack those lazy crumb-scattering hits in the beginning, I will, each time, think of the floor like a retirement account. Little bits neglected into a place where I will seek them out later. It will comfort me to know there is somewhere to go when the bag empties, something to do while I'm waiting for the next delivery. But in the beginning, in the abundant beginning, this will always seem a long way off.

In the room at the Newark Airport Marriott, as in most rooms where there is crack, porn flickers on the television. This time it's straight and soft and on Pay-per-view. I pay for all six movies and flip between them as one scene disappoints or dulls. I have drunk the small bottle of white wine, the two beers, and both small bottles of vodka from the minibar by the time I realize I need to get back to the airport and onto the plane. Since there is still a large pile of drugs left in the ashtray, I wonder whether I should go at all.

But I do. I let my stem cool and wrap it in a wad of tissue paper. I gather the two rocks and the remaining crumbs from the ashtray and put them back in the mini zip-lock they came in. I ditch the towel, scramble into my clothes, and shove the pipe, bag, and lighter into the front pocket of my jeans. I scan the room a dozen times. Clean every surface and pick up whatever crumbs I can from the floor. I unpack the bag and pipe and lighter at least three times to smoke just-one-more-hit before leaving, to get just the right high to face the lobby and the airport. I leave less than an hour to check in and get on the plane. Noah has called three or four times, but I have not picked up, nor have I listened to his messages.

I don't bother checking out. I go straight to the taxi stand and get in the only cab there. The driver is a big black guy — fat but muscular, linebacker-style. Forty, maybe fifty. The stem, still hot from heavy use in the room minutes before, burns in my jeans pocket like a little oven. Of course I ask him if he parties. He says he does, and I ask him if he ever smokes rock. *Sure do,* he says, and right then, within the first minute of getting into the cab, I know that I am not getting on the plane. That I will probably never make it to Berlin.

So let's hang out, I say to the linebacker behind the wheel, and he says, *Sure thing.* As we edge up to the Continental departures drop-off, I tell him to head back to the hotel, that I'll catch a later flight. He doesn't question or hesitate, just pulls away from the terminal and says, again, *Sure thing.* I call Continental's 800 number and tell them I'm sick and can't make the flight and could they transfer the ticket to the next night. Unbelievably, they can and they do. I am booked in a first-class seat the next night at eight. Acres of time, a bag of crack, company lined up, and a hotel less than a minute away. I've just missed two flights, e-mailed Kate and relinquished any say or stake in our agency, tossed my career down the chute, and stood up my beloved and no doubt frantic boyfriend. I've done all these things and I couldn't be happier.

I leave a message on Noah's cell phone saying they canceled the second flight and that I will be flying out tomorrow. I speak slowly and calmly, with just a little can-you-believe-it annoyance so as to seem normal and not high. Once I've left the message, I turn the phone off so that I don't have to hear it ring when he calls back.

Later, the taxi driver and I sit in his cab behind a 7-Eleven somewhere in Newark. He's anxious about being seen in the hotel
because he picks people up and drops them off there every day.
I pack his hit — small because there is precious little left — and
as he lights up, I tell him how horny I get when I smoke. He nods
in agreement as he exhales, and soon zippers come down — mine
first, then his. I take a hit and he holds himself and talks about
his wife, how she blows him but never wants to fuck. I inhale so
hard that I burn my forefinger and thumb. I should be over the
Atlantic right now, I think, but instead I'm behind a 7-Eleven, in
the shadow of a Newark, New Jersey, overpass. What I want is the
blurry oblivion of body-crashing sex, and instead I get a gloomy
jerk-off session without enough drugs to get either of us high. As
the bag empties, I start to feel shaky and it occurs to me that I've
gone nearly a week without sleep. It's ten thirty p.m. and my flight
tomorrow evening isn't until eight. I ask the taxi driver if he knows
where to score more and of course he doesn't. I hide one last rock
in the small front pocket of my jeans so there will be something
when I get to the hotel room. I start thinking about whether I
should go back to the city — to Mark's, or to a hotel somewhere in
Manhattan where I can call Happy. But the city seems time zones
away. And if I go there, I know there will be no turning back, no
chance of making it to Berlin.

The taxi driver drops me off at the Marriott, and I call Happy the
second I get to the room. After much haggling, he agrees to drive
out to the hotel, but only if I will spend at least $800 to make it
worthwhile. I say no problem.

It is just after eleven when Happy and I speak. At eleven fifty he calls me from the parking lot to say he's there. I can't remember his ever delivering this quickly in Manhattan. I leave the room, take the elevator down to get cash from the ATM in the empty lobby, walk as slowly and calmly as I can, past the check-in desk and out into the parking lot, where his red minivan idles. My heart slams in my chest and my throat is so thick with fear I can barely speak as I hop into the front seat. Happy, as usual, is wearing his white sweatpants and plain black hooded sweatshirt. The only thing missing are the large earphones that usually ring his neck. He's Dominican, in his early thirties, and we never say much to each other beyond amounts, addresses, and number of stems. He is always calm, and even though he's driven all the way out to an airport hotel from Manhattan, tonight he's no different. His movements are slow and patient as he counts out the sixteen bags, and he asks no questions as he hands me two clean stems. I shove it all in my front two pockets, thank him for coming out so fast, and head back to the hotel.

If anyone had stopped to watch me go to the cash machine and withdraw stacks of bills, several times because of the $200 transaction limit, then head out to an idling van with tinted windows, and return minutes later with bulging pockets, it wouldn't take much imagination to understand what had just transpired. As obvious and sloppy as I know the whole operation is, I know that once I get back to the room and take a big hit off one of the crystal-clear new stems, everything will be okay. That all the grim and alarming truths barking loudly around me will vanish in a blast of smoke.

And so they do. It's one o'clock and I have a spectacular pile of crack in the little ashtray on the nightstand. This is the most I have ever had on my own, and I know I will smoke every last bit of it. I wonder if somewhere in that pile is the crumb that will bring on a heart attack or stroke or seizure. The cardiac event that will deliver all this to an abrupt and welcome halt. My chest pounds, my fingers are singed, I fill my lungs with smoke.

Bringing Down the House

He's six. Diminishing the value of the house. That's what he's being told. Bringing it down with piss-splattered heating vents in the bathroom coated with rust and stink. Making it more difficult to sell by scrubbing the pattern off the wallpaper next to the toilet each time he sprays there and tries to clean it up.

They are in the green Volkswagen, and it's not the first time his father has told him these things. That his piss is costing the family thousands of dollars is a fact as old as memory. He is quiet, as always when his *problem* comes up. His father talks in sharp, lean bursts that usually end with *C'mon, Willie. Just get it together,* or *Jesus, kid, fix it.* And then long stretches of silence. The only sounds in the car are the low hum of 1010 WINS on the radio and the click of his father's pipe against his teeth.

They are on a highway heading home from Boston. They drive uncomfortably fast until the traffic congeals and the swearing and the steering wheel pounding starts. As his father turns the radio down and adjusts the heating vents, he imagines him before the great panel of lights and gadgets in the cockpits of the planes he flies. The ones filled with passengers who trust him to take them across the ocean, to London and Paris. There are times — like this — when he can't imagine anything his father cannot do.

The traffic gets worse and his father grumbles at the cars in front of him. The boy stays quiet. He's relieved that the attention has shifted away from him, from the reason they are in a car together today. They have gone to see a doctor — the one the Boston Red Sox use, his father said — to find out what exactly is wrong with him.

What precisely goes on at this doctor's office, he will forget. Maybe he remembered in the car, ran it over in his head as they rode home, or maybe it had already slipped away. In any case, he will spend years trying to remember, but the only part that ever comes back will be the car ride itself. He'll remember the old lines about wrecking the house and the strange, nearly sexual air of the day — so much talk about penises and pissing. Something clandestine and shameful about the whole trip, which had begun with his mother's pinched announcement at breakfast that he and his father would be going to Boston to visit a doctor. He'll remember how worried she looked and how far away. He'll remember wishing the car would rattle at high speed right off the road and go up in a blaze. He will persist with that kind of wish for years—in school buses, planes, vans, trains. He'll also remember—and this most vividly—a prediction his father makes. That very soon his friends—Timothy, Derek, Jennifer—and their parents will stop letting him into their houses for sleepovers or playdates. That it's just a matter of time before they catch on, and once they do, there will be no way they'll allow such a mess, such a monster, in their houses.

This last bit will stick. It will expand into a belief that they already know and are complaining to his parents and warning their children, his friends. He'll worry, until they move away a few years later to a smaller town farther north and deeper in the woods, that secretly his friends and their families and even his teachers know about his problem and that there will come a day when they'll make a spectacle of that knowing. He will imagine and sometimes think he'll hear them say *monster* under their breaths.

And so they drive. His father presses on with talk of declining house values, promises of banishment. The radio mumbles low on the station that will still, years later, remain for him the source of the gloomiest, most desolate sound, and be the station playing in every car his father owns. As they get off the highway and begin to snake along the winding Connecticut roads toward home, there is silence and the occasional click of pipe against teeth. The world outside seems to be in on all of it: the trip to the doctor and the warnings afterward part of some long-considered, collectively agreed-upon plan of action. *There is nothing physically wrong with you,* his father eventually shouts, exhausted no doubt by the whole day. *It's just a matter of willpower. Of choice. God only knows what kind of permanent damage you're doing down there. What kinds of things you won't be able to do, later.*

This last part must have been said on the way up the driveway or sitting in front of the garage because he will remember hearing the word *damage* as he looked up at the charcoal-colored ranch house, knowing that a new radiator and fresh wallpaper were nothing compared with what would be needed to fix him.

Complicated Theater

There is a bar in the Newark Airport Marriott. It's almost midnight and I phone the front desk and find out that last call is at one. I shower and shave and clean up as best I can before going down for a drink and company. I put in a new pair of contacts because when I'm getting high, no matter how much water I drink or how many eyedrops I empty into my eyes, the lenses dry up and pop out. I have packed four boxes of contacts for this trip, and since I've been in the hotel, I have already replaced the left one once and the right one twice. I know I will have to be more careful but as with everything else — drugs, money in my bank account, time — at this point there seems more than enough to last. I wear my navy cashmere turtleneck because it's thick and cabled and hides my rickety frame; it is also expensive and, I think, obscures the cracked-out truth of me. I wear my jeans, and even though I am now cinching my belt to its last hole, I still need to tuck the front of the sweater in to keep them from falling down. I know I will have to find a leather shop in Berlin to punch new holes.

Once I get dressed, I pace through the routine of taking a hit, guzzling a glass of vodka, going to the mirror to make sure I look okay, messing with my hair until I give up and put on the Parks & Rec Department cap. I start to get warm and a little horny and restless in my clothes, and I take my sweater off, lie down on the bed, turn on some porn, and jerk off. I wallow in the little patch of dizzy pleasure for a few minutes, and as it fades and I pour another vodka to cut the speedy buzz and mellow out the high, I think, Just one more, a big one this time to kick up my courage. And so one more. I put my sweater back on, fuss in front of the mirror, squeeze a few eyedrops in, pat down my hair, put on my cap, yank on my jeans, and before I know it I'm on the bed again, shirtless and shimmering and enjoying the short while before I need my stem, another drink, and just a little more time before I leave the room.

I finally make it downstairs to the bar and am immediately disappointed that the place is nearly empty and dotted with a few couples and business colleagues traveling together. I don't see the vulnerable and restless loner I'm looking for—that magical kindred partner in crime, game for a long night.

I slam three or four vodkas and begin to get shaky. More than twenty minutes without a hit is pushing it, and I've been downstairs for at least half an hour. Vodka usually eases that jittery feeling, smooths the little wrinkles of horror that slip in as a high teeters toward a crash, but it's not helping much now. In any case, I've got the largest pile of crack I've ever seen waiting in the room and there is no good reason to stop. I signal the waiter as calmly as I can, leave two twenties and a ten with the $35 tab, and make for the elevator.

The night swirls with thick smoke, and I go through nine of the sixteen bags by early afternoon. I have never smoked so much in such a short time — two bags, shared with at least one other person would normally be a big night — and my skin tingles with heat and I'm aware of every breath and every heartbeat. All my clothes and toiletries are scattered around the hotel room and still I have too much left to smoke to make leaving the room seem like a good idea. I call the cabdriver from last night and leave a dozen messages. He doesn't call back. It takes hours to pack and clean up, with hundreds of pit stops to smoke and drink along the way.

With three hours before the flight, I finally make my way down through the lobby. As I check out, I notice, near the door, five or six men between the ages of forty and sixty. Each has some distinct but unspecific quality — gray slacks, grim shoes, Windbreaker. Head-to-toe JCPenney. They mumble to one another and it seems — though it's not exactly clear — that they all have earpieces with wires tucked discreetly into their shirts. There is no one else in the lobby. Only one cab waits at the taxi stand. I hear, *That's him,* from one of them, or I think I do, as I make my way through the electric doors to the breezeway outside. As I get into the taxi, I notice all five or six of them leaving the hotel and heading toward two or three cars parked in front of the building. The driver gives me a knowing look and states more than asks, *Continental,* which is of course my airline, but how does he know? I ask him and he says, *It's Newark, everyone flies Continental.* I look at his ID displayed in the Plexiglas partition and see that the photo, just like the one in the cab yesterday, is obscured by a piece of cardboard. I begin to panic. He starts the car, pulls away from the hotel, and as I watch the cars filled with the JCPenney guys follow us, I know I am, right now, crossing over from one world into another. I can already imagine myself remembering this cab ride, how it will signal the end of the time when I was free.

I'm about to be arrested. I have a bag of crack and a very used pipe folded in tissue in the front pocket of my jeans. I don't see how I can get rid of it. Throw it out the window? No, these guys, whoever they are, are right on our tail. Stash it in the garbage when we pull up? No, same reason. Stuff it in the seat cushion of a car that is probably being driven by an undercover DEA agent? Obviously no. Swallow it? Maybe. But the glass pipe... what do I do with the glass pipe? These solutions flash and burst, one by one, again and again, as we crawl toward the terminal. None are possible.

Before I left the hotel room, it seemed like a good idea to bring along enough crack to get high in an airport bathroom just before getting on the plane. As the terminal comes into view, I realize, too late, how insane this idea is. We pull up to the drop-off zone and

I notice that one of the cars is directly behind us. I look away as I get out of the cab and pay the driver, who seems indifferent to the fare.

As I make my way into the building, my only thought is when. When will they tap my shoulder and ask me to empty my pockets and open my bags. At the check-in counter? In the security line? The gate? It doesn't seem possible that I'll ever make it to the gate.

Pilots in their uniforms walk in their particular way toward their flights. I imagine their sunny families in the nice but not so affluent suburbs of Connecticut, New Jersey, and New York. Their sons who collect little model airplanes and show off by knowing all the names — Cessna, Piper Cub, Mooney, 747. I can see my father's TWA captain's uniform and hat hung up on the old-fashioned coatrack in his den and remember how handsome I thought he was when I was young. How he looked like a movie star in those dark pressed pants and crisp white shirts. My father. *How did this happen,* I imagine him asking when he hears about what is about to go down. *How did it come to this, Willie?*

There is little distance between the check-in counter and security. I have no idea what to do or where to go. If they're going to arrest me, why haven't they done it by now? I think of getting back in a cab and heading into the city, but I begin to doubt my perceptions. It must be the drugs, must be paranoia. I'm too small in the grand scheme of things, I reason, to warrant a battalion of JCPenney guys and a hotel stakeout.

I need to ditch the drugs and the pipe. I see a bathroom to the left of the security area and quickly make a beeline there. As I enter, it's empty. Two stalls and three urinals. I go to a stall with the intention of flushing the bag and the pipe, but when I get in and close the door, I see the toilet has only a trickle of water and seems to be running without stop. It won't flush. I check the next one and it's the same. I think maybe they've disabled them so I can't flush my stuff. I feel like a trapped animal. I hear someone enter and quickly pull down my jeans and sit on the toilet. Minutes pass and I barely move. I try not to make a sound at first but then realize that of course he can see my feet and that I should pretend to behave normally. As if I am going to the bathroom. Whoever entered doesn't leave and I begin to imagine there is actually a whole SWAT team of DEA agents and police silently filling the room. It's almost impossible not to peek under the stall to see if there are, as I fear, a sea of boots and shoes. But part of me also wants to prolong not knowing as long as possible. To my left is a toilet paper holder and I slowly tear off some sheets and go through the motions of wiping and the audible pantomime of actually using the toilet. At some point it occurs to me that the only thing I can do is wipe down the pipe and bag for fingerprints, wrap them in toilet paper, and place them under the plastic casing of the dispenser. It crosses my mind to throw the crack in the toilet, let it dissolve in the water and hope the residue disappears eventually; but there is something in me that holds back, that can't bear to watch the drugs erode to nothing. I start imagining the difference in jail sentences — ten years with a bag of crack? probation with just a pipe? Still, I wipe down the pipe and bag, wrap them carefully in toilet paper, and stash it all in the dispenser. I do this as quietly as I can and then pull up my jeans, buckle my belt, and open the door to the stall as if it is the last free second of my life.

Standing against the wall, next to the entrance, is an airport security guard. He looks right at me as I walk to the sink to wash my hands. As I head out past him, he moves from the wall toward the stalls and our arms brush lightly against each other's as I pass into the terminal and away from security, toward the escalator.

I try to keep calm as I descend into the baggage area. There is no doubt in my mind that the security guard has headed straight for the toilet dispenser. I don't look back, but I can feel the eyes of a hundred cops and agents on me as I move past the carousels and up toward another escalator. I wander for twenty minutes or so before making my way back to the security area. I stand next to the stairs going up to the third floor and watch the long line of tourists and businessmen and students waiting to take their belts and shoes off before passing through the metal detectors. I see a man wearing gray slacks, a nylon pullover, and plain shoes. He's one of the JCPenney guys from the hotel lobby who got in the car, and now he's here, several feet away, looking right at me. Just past him, back toward the check-in counter, is an older woman, walking slowly, pulling a suitcase on wheels and talking into a cell phone. I notice the blandness of the suitcase, her shoes, her jacket. It's kindred somehow with his. And then, in the minutes that follow, like seeing one water tower in a city skyline and then suddenly seeing them all, I see dozens of these people. Blandly dressed, middle-aged, suitcase-pulling, cell-phone-clutching zombies whose slow, deliberate movements all appear choreographed in response to mine.

I wander the airport for what seems like hours before getting in the line for security. I occasionally get brazen with some of the people I think are following me, look them squarely in the eye and smile, even joke several times that this must be a tedious assignment. They usually respond with a smirk or a rolled eye. At one point, when the tension is great, I imagine jumping from the third-floor balcony next to the escalator to avoid the arrest I know is coming. But the height looks too meager, not capable of causing more than a broken leg or two.

Later, bone-tired from hours of pacing the airport in a state of sustained panic and crashing from nearly a week of getting high, I finally turn to one of these guys, a younger one, and ask, *Why don't you just get it over with?* to which he chuckles and says, *It's much more fun later, once you're somewhere else. Just wait.* I am certain he says this. I freeze at these words and decide finally to get in line, take my shoes and belt off, and go through the metal detector. It's not possible that I will make it to the other side, and I'm now so wrung out that I just need it to be over.

But I make it through. I make it through and feel, briefly, cautiously, elated. Maybe it's all in my head. Maybe it's just the drugs, whose good effects have all fled, leaving the body that held them shattered and its mind delusional. I make it to the gate and the flight is already boarding. I hesitate a few times as I see, again, a few of the JCPenneys wandering around the seating area near the gate. The words of the younger Penney ring in my head but I am desperate for a vodka and somewhere in my bag are over-the-counter sleeping pills. If I can just crash in that big plush seat and pass out, I will be okay. If I can just get on that plane and away from these goons, I know I will be safe. So I march over to the check-in, hand the ticket agent my boarding pass, and get on.

My seat is on the aisle, in the second row to the right. Never has anything looked so welcoming. I sit down and begin to feel the high panic of the last two and a half hours slowly fade. I exhale and look out the window to the tarmac and ground crew loading luggage. This is the first time I realize that the bag I checked the day before was on a flight I never boarded. Worrying about a lost bag now seems like a lucky luxury and I decide not to think about it until I get to Berlin.

I stow my tote bag under the seat, sit back up, and close my eyes for a few minutes. Finally, I think, safe. And then, when I turn around to find a stewardess, the wind knocks out of me. I see them. The Penneys. One, two, three, four, at least five of them are sitting all throughout the cabin. At just this moment, one of the stewardesses leans down toward one and speaks softly. About me, no doubt. About the arrest about to take place in Amsterdam or Berlin. Or right here. Right now. The entire cabin suddenly seems to me like a set, like some elaborate stage prop created to replicate the first-class cabin of an airplane. The napkins seem to be flimsy fakes, the stewardesses actresses, and the Penneys androids—half human, half robot, emotionless and menacing.

One of the stewardesses is suddenly at my side. She asks, in a tone that sounds mocking and insincere, if I'd like a drink. I'm frightened by the Penneys, but I'm agitated by her. Angry, even. I ask her if the plane is, in fact, actually going to be landing in Amsterdam. She looks confused, but not as confused as I think she should look, so I ask, *Don't you think this is an awfully complicated piece of theater for just one person?* She looks at me for a few seconds, excuses herself, and walks away. Moments later she returns with the captain, who politely asks me to gather my belongings and follow him off the plane. I can barely move. And even though I know this is the long-awaited arrest that's been coming since I got in the car at the hotel, I am relieved when the captain puts his hand on my shoulder and says, *Let's go.* Like a scolded kid, and with everyone in the cabin watching, I grab my bag and follow him off the plane.

But there is no arrest. Instead, the captain explains to me that after 9/11 they need to be cautious and that what I said to the stewardess alarmed her enough that they don't feel comfortable having me on the flight. I notice his jacket, its hokey military mimicry—epaulets, stripes. Like everything on the plane, his uniform—shabby compared to the memory of my father's—looks like a flimsy, slapped-together costume. He asks if I have been drinking, to which I answer yes, that I get nervous before flying and drank some to calm my nerves. How I form these thoughts and words, I have no idea. I apologize for alarming the stewardess and just as I am about to make my way back toward security, a man in a white shirt with a binder filled with papers arrives. He says he is the head of operations for Continental at Newark and instantly apologizes to me for the confusion. He asks the captain to reconsider and it's immediately clear that, for some reason, this guy really wants me on the flight. The captain respectfully declines and begins to get visibly annoyed when the operations guy presses him further. I stay very quiet as this plays out. The operations guy finally gives up and the captain wishes me luck and heads back to the cockpit. I watch him disappear into the jetway and have to suppress the sudden urge to call out to him. I have no idea what I'd say if I did, but I know that when he's gone, I want him to come back.

The operations guy asks to see my passport and continues to be apologetic. I tell him it's fine, that I'll just go home and fly out tomorrow. He tells me not to worry, that he'll have me on another plane tonight. He steps away, makes a few phone calls on his cell, just out of earshot, and comes back to say that he's booked me, first class, on an Air France flight that goes to Berlin through Paris. It's all taken care of, and the flight departs in forty-five minutes from a nearby gate. Another person with binders arrives. The little group escorts me to an Air France counter, where a ticket is produced, and then to the gate. I am there for less than ten minutes when the flight begins to board. At this point things have moved so swiftly that I've barely been able to keep pace. I do, though, have a strong sense that someone—not just the operations guy from Continental—wants me on a flight tonight.

And then I see them. Three Penneys standing near the gate. Glancing my way, holding tickets, huddled together like the Three Stooges of badly dressed espionage. At first, I'm angry. And then the last words of the young Penney from before roar through my head.

Just wait.

The people continue to board the plane over the next fifteen minutes until the waiting area around the gate is nearly empty. A few last-minute stragglers wander over, and several people rush to the ticket agent with their boarding passes, relieved not to have missed the flight. Finally, there are just the three Penneys and me. The ticket agent speaks to them. They remain near the desk but don't board. One of the ticket agents comes up to me and asks if I have a ticket for this flight and tells me that it's the last call for boarding. I tell her I get panic attacks and am not sure I'll be flying tonight. I ask if everyone is on board and she gestures to the Penneys and says there are a few left to get on but the flight is nearly fully boarded. I tell her I need a minute. Again, as before, I feel as if I am at some terribly important juncture. If I go, I might get arrested in Paris or Berlin. If I stay, I might get arrested here. If I go and don't get arrested, all might be fine after a few rough days with Noah. If I stay here and somehow don't get arrested, I will keep using. This I know.

So I stand up, turn away from the gate, and expect to get arrested. I look back once and see two of the Penneys walk over to see if I'm walking back toward security. I don't turn back again and start heading out toward baggage claim. I know that I won't make it to the taxi stand. I'm about to be swarmed with Penneys, police, airport security, and God knows who else. The last lines from a novel I worked with years ago somehow surface through the panic. *It would be now,* they read. *It would be now.*

I fish for my cell phone and see that it's on its last bar, which is blinking red. I call David. It's after eleven and his wife, Susie, picks up. I apologize and tell her it's important and ask if David is there. They are clearly in bed. He picks up, asks what's going on. I tell him I'm about to get arrested for drugs at Newark Airport and that I need him to find a good lawyer. I'm probably shouting when I tell him he has to move fast because he shushes me and tells me to calm down. He asks where I am in the airport and I tell him I'm about to pass out of the departure gate into the baggage claim area. He says to just stay on the line and get in a taxi and come home. I tell him I'm not going to make it to the taxi and then the line goes silent. The battery dies. I keep walking. No one is stopping me. I cross the departure terminal and into baggage claim. Suddenly the Penneys have all disappeared. I'm convinced they've raced out of the terminal through the upper level and are waiting at the taxi stand. I walk out of the baggage claim area, through the automatic doors, and cross the street. A taxi comes up. I get in. The driver asks, *Where to?* I say, *One Fifth Avenue in Manhattan,* but because I expect we'll be pulled over before we leave the airport, I warn him it's going to be a short ride. He grumbles and pulls away from the curb. I look at his ID and the photo is unobstructed and shows the same gray-haired, bearded Indian man driving the cab.

I'm floating in a state of shock. Every second that passes, every inch the taxi moves forward without sirens and the glare of flashing lights seems like a miracle. Then it occurs to me that they're all probably just waiting at the apartment. I ask the driver if I can use his cell phone. He passes it back and I call David. *I'm in the cab,* I tell him, *but I don't know that we'll make it to the building.* He says he'll meet me in the lobby and to calm down. I agree as the taxi speeds toward the tunnel, back into the city. I can't believe I've made it this far. I can picture the spectacle of police cars and unmarked DEA vehicles surrounding One Fifth, lights strobing and tenants' faces lit with appalled interest. I wonder if Trevor, my favorite doorman, is on the desk tonight and what he'll think when I get cuffed and carted off.

But there is no spectacle. Just David, with bed hair, bundled in a coat, waiting in the lobby. He looks exhausted and annoyed and says he's spending the night. In the morning we go to breakfast and he asks which rehab I want him to take me to and despite the grim concern I see on his face I answer, *None.*

We sit in the front window at Marquet, on stools, and the day outside and everyone in it flashes like a taunt. This is a shiny world, I think, for the Davids and the Noahs, for people whose lives I can only see as unblemished and lucky. A place where I've been allowed a visit but cannot stay. A place I've already left.

David walks out of the restaurant and doesn't look back. Whatever his last words are, I don't remember, but they are quick and clear and sad.

Under Control

He's ten. It's dinnertime. He's a little more excited than usual because he has a friend over, Kenny, and his uncle Teddy from San Diego is visiting for a few days. He loves Uncle Teddy. He has a pool, asks lots of questions about school, and is one of the only people who can make his father laugh, lighten him up. His mother makes hamburger gravy—a dish that takes ground beef and stretches it out with canned cream of mushroom soup and onion soup mix and is poured over biscuits or rice or mashed potatoes. Or maybe she's made creamed chicken. Same idea as the hamburger gravy but with a bag of frozen vegetables—peas, carrots, pearl onions. These are the dishes she makes—the ones she learned in Youngstown, Ohio, when there was little money, after her father died, the ones she made as a stewardess living in Queens with four roommates. He loves these dishes; will eat them as if there is never enough and have seconds and thirds. His father calls them slop. Tonight he says he can't believe she wanted to feed shit like this to his brother. When he is home from one of his trips, he usually cooks something else — a piece of fish on the grill, a boiled lobster — which is what he's doing tonight.

The kitchen is crowded. His mother fusses at the stove. His older sister, Kim, is setting the table, and his younger brother, Sean, and younger sister, Lisa, are watching TV in the next room. His father's large crystal tumbler is full of Scotch, and his uncle Teddy holds a bottle of beer.

The boys are taunting the lobsters in the sink, making up names for them and running commentary on their crustaceal movements the way sportscasters would a wrestling match. Kenny names the runt Mama-Pet, their nickname for Kim, and the two of them giggle as the bigger lobsters climb all over it. *Oh noooooo...Mama-Pet!* Kenny turns to Kim, who is doing homework at the dinner table, and says, *Run, Mama-Pet! You're getting crushed. Run! Mama-Pet, run!* The two boys can barely speak they are laughing so hard. It goes on and on until Kim storms off with a slammed book and a bloodcurdling *I hate you two!* They love it and are dizzy with laughter. Uncle Teddy laughs, too, and gently tells them they're terrible, but it's clear he is amused.

Dinner is served and his father is quiet. Teddy is younger, but someone outside the family would probably think he was the patriarch, the eldest of the seven brothers and sisters, the leader. Maybe this is why it feels safe to talk at dinner. Maybe the easy laughter in the kitchen and Teddy's smiling approval gives him just the confidence he needs to open his mouth. And so he does. He tells Teddy about his soccer team. How they travel to nearby towns; how he plays right inside, sometimes center. He tells him about Joe, the heaviest kid in the class, who is also one of the fastest, and how he plays halfback and scores the most goals. His father is quiet through this but gets up a few times to go to the kitchen to refill his drink. Kenny talks about their classmate Dennis, who, he says, doesn't bathe and lives in a house without running water. Dennis has a deformed eyelid, one that folds over half his left eye even when open, and Kenny explains how this was caused by malnutrition when he was a baby. That his family is so poor they couldn't afford to feed him.

His mother says something nice about Dennis's family. Kim tells Kenny to shut up.

The boys keep chattering—about school, Kenny's sisters, who knows what—and Teddy listens to both of them, patiently, and laughs his quick rat-a-tat-tat laugh, which only eggs them both on.

Lisa plays with her food, and Sean is in the high chair.

From a distance it looks like any other family. From a distance, he looks like any other boy. Laughing with his friend. Talking about soccer. Dressed in cords and turtleneck like all the other boys his age. Even if you looked closely, you couldn't see how he is a boy who prays at night not to wake up.

He says something, something now long forgotten, and his father finally speaks up and says, *Oh, yeah, Willie, is that so?* He challenges whatever was said, whether it be about soccer, Dennis, school, the moths flapping madly against the porch lights outside. It doesn't seem so harsh, but he knows his father is just getting started. Still, he feels emboldened by the hour before in the kitchen — Uncle Teddy, Kenny — he feels in league with them and, so, safe. He talks about something else. It doesn't matter what. His father then says something that no one else understands, but he does. *Looks like you've got it all figured out, Willie,* he taunts. *Looks like you're really on top of things.* As his father speaks, he knows he's gone too far and not to say another word. *Have your act together, do you, Willie?* The voice is all Boston, all Scotch. *All your problems under control? Any problems you want to talk about? Or should I? How about that?* By this point no one will be speaking or understanding what's going on. But he understands. And he's praying that his father will stop and that he won't, not this time, finally start spilling what he knows, what he'll always have over him. He wonders if he's told Uncle Teddy, because Teddy's looking at him oddly now. Is it pity or disgust? He can't tell. His face grows hot in the tense air and finally Uncle Teddy starts to talk about Chris, his son, and how he's in a play or on a team or building a tree house.

The dinner winds down, and the awkward patch is ignored and forgotten. His mother asks for help in the kitchen and complains about how her back is acting up again. *Could be a slipped disk,* she says and sighs. His father rolls his eyes, Kim rushes to scrub dishes at the sink, and he and Kenny carry a few bowls into the kitchen and take off upstairs.

At some point before sleep he heads to the bathroom, and it takes longer than usual. His mother knocks once, Kenny a few times; he runs the water, does the dance, makes the mess and cleans it all up. It's done, but when he returns to his room, where Kenny is already asleep, it seems far from over.

Morning

I've been at the Gansevoort Hotel for almost two weeks. There have been other rooms, in other hotels. They are all near One Fifth — SoHo, the West Village, Chelsea — but feel worlds away, in neighborhoods I've never visited. I check in under names from childhood — Kenny Schweter, Michael Lloyd, Adam Grant-West — and explain that I'm in a fight with my girlfriend and am not looking to be found. No one ever blinks. They simply look at my passport, run the debit card, and hand me a key.

I've been at the Gansevoort the longest. I've stayed only a night or two, four tops, at the other places, 60 Thompson, the W, the Maritime, the Washington Square Hotel. These were after Newark, after the nights at Mark's, and after New Canaan, Connecticut, where my friends Lili and Eliza checked me into Silver Hill, a rehab I immediately checked out of. After I scored from the driver who picked me up, he dropped me at a Courtyard Marriott hotel in Norwalk, where I stayed until the drugs ran out—romancing the prospect of dying a few miles down the road from the hospital where I was born.

I've changed rooms a few times at the Gansevoort and am now in a suite that the manager says, because I am staying at least a few weeks, he's giving me for nearly half price. It didn't just occur to him; when I changed rooms, I asked the person at reception what sort of extended-stay discount they could offer.

Every night I hear shouting from the street—*Billy, keep it up. You better enjoy it while you can. You're lucky you've lasted this long, Billy.* There are vans parked along Gansevoort Street with metal boxes on their roofs that I'm convinced are surveillance vehicles. There are bland American sedans everywhere, and each one, I'm sure of it, is driven by a DEA agent or an undercover cop. Still, each night after midnight, I put on my black Arc'teryx jacket and black Parks & Recreation cap and shuffle out through the lobby and up to 14th Street to a cash machine at the corner bodega. The place has two of them, side by side, and only once am I able to run my card and key in the codes and amounts fast enough to get them to dispense more than the $1,000 limit. Usually I have to wait and get no more than five batches of $200. Night after night I do this and then load up on lighters. I wonder how many others like me the people behind the counter have seen. Hundreds? None?

I make my way back to the hotel, carrying whatever drugs and stems I have, because I'm terrified someone will raid the room while I'm gone. Twice I have dropped bags of crack in the lobby. My belt at this point has seven holes in it. It began with four. I've carved out one with a knife and two have come from leather shops that I've passed between hotels and cash machines. Still, my jeans are falling down around my hips.

I'm not alone in the room. Malcolm has been with me for four or five, maybe six, days. He turned up with Happy one night and jumped on board for the ride. He went to Dartmouth, he says. He's black, lives in Harlem, is probably no more than thirty, and is beautiful. Doesn't seem gay and can do enormous amounts of drugs without appearing shaky or anxious.

There is a night when I am convinced the room is about to swarm with cops and we race out of the hotel as if it's on fire. We leave everything there—everything besides the drugs—and check into the W near Union Square. I pace the room like a madman, and Malcolm is patient and keeps fixing me glasses of vodka with ice and lime. He distracts me with stories about being on scholarship at Dartmouth and playing football. He dropped out a year ago but plans to return when he's saved enough money or he can get a better break on tuition. He's getting his real-estate license. When I ask, he says he knows Happy from the neighborhood, and when I remind him that Happy lives in Washington Heights, he says that he used to live there, too. Not much of his story seems to hold up but I don't care. He's gentle and sexy and being by myself right now would be unbearable. Being with him makes all the other nights that came before and the prospect of the ones to come seem unspeakably lonely. During some of those nights, I call numbers for escorts listed in the back pages of the *Village Voice* and *New York* magazine. None ever do drugs with me and most stay just exactly one hour. Their skin and their compassion—most at some point say I should slow down, that I might hurt myself—are never enough, never quite what I had in mind, and when they leave, I'm almost always relieved and disappointed.

The room at the W is small compared with the one at the Gansevoort. It's cramped and the ventilation is worrisome since the smoke we make seems to just linger and not cycle through the vents. I'm terrified a fire alarm will go off as it once did at 60 Thompson. I think about checking into a third hotel, but I'm getting worried about money—there is twenty or so thousand left and I've already gone through more than twice that much—so it's the Gansevoort or here.

We gather up what little we have and leave. Heading back into the Gansevoort is terrifying, and yet, as certain as I am that we are about to be busted, I stomp right back into the elevator, down the hall, and into the room. It's precisely how it was when we left it hours ago. I head straight to the window to see if cop cars have pulled up in front of the building. Nothing. No one but the doorman and a few passersby. Then to the closet and the bathroom to see if anyone is lying in wait to ambush us. All is clear, but it takes a few big hits, half a bottle of vodka, and thrashing on the bed with Malcolm for the panic to fade.

Later, as the sun comes up, Malcolm steps out onto the little balcony. *I'm going to have to split soon*, he says. His cell phone has died and he says that he has to go back to his life. I convince him to stay one more night. We have enough to carry us through to early evening when Happy goes back on call, and I promise to really load up. The day clicks by as it usually does, the routine of sex and drinking and hits and ordering food that we barely eat repeats itself from the day before.

Malcolm's talk of his life out in the world makes me think of mine, and I quietly pray for one of these hits to finish me off. I pack each one thicker than I had before and hold the smoke in my lungs a beat or two longer than it feels like I can. My neck throbs and my arm aches and I wonder when. Again, the lines from that novel. *It would be now.*

Malcolm packs up his things in the morning while I doze. I hear the toilet flush in the bathroom and notice he has nearly emptied the ashtray on the bedside table where I keep the drugs. He has left a few rocks and taken many. I let it go. Not because I don't care, but because I knew he would steal, and the night before, while he was in the shower, I hid two whole bags in my blazer jacket to last me through the day until midnight, when I can get more cash. Our good-byes are brief.

The day grinds on. I try to listen to my messages—something I have avoided for days—but my cell phone produces a text message I've never seen before that seems prophetic: *Memory Filled. New Text Rejected*. The message keeps buzzing into the little screen, making it impossible to listen to voice mail. After a few minutes of trying, I give up. As evening comes on, a nerdy boy from room service brings a plate of nachos that I don't eat. The truth is, I order food to have human contact. He is flirty and talks about NYU, where he is studying political science, the five guys he lives with in Williamsburg. As he speaks I am shamed by the youth of him: the pink skin, the clear eyes, the voice that doesn't get snagged on sarcasm or exhaustion. He steps closer as he talks and I can almost smell the Ivory soap he must have used in that crowded loft in Williamsburg early that morning as he showered for work. He could not be closer now, and I could not feel further away. He is a boy at the beginning of everything, untarnished and lovely in a way he does not yet even know. And I am something else, not a boy, with hands covered in burn scabs and black soot from changing the screens on the crack pipes all night. I had, at first, thought about seducing him, but when he finishes talking, I can only scribble my signature on the bill and shrink away. When he leaves, the voices from outside begin to bark louder than usual. I finally am able to listen to a voice mail from Noah that tells me he loves me and is not angry but terrified I am dead. *Just come home*.

I get high and drink, and when the voices outside get too loud and I'm convinced I see a man in the opposite building with a video camera trained on my room, I do a huge hit and decide to go home. To face the music and rush into Noah's arms. I gather up my drugs and stems and clean the crumbs off the table surfaces and head out the door.

A cab pulls up alongside me as I walk out onto Gansevoort Street. It slows, gently, and I hop in. *Home?* the man with a craggy Eastern European face and matching accent asks with a kind smile. I say yes. The music playing in the cab is Louis Armstrong's "What a Wonderful World" and it is calming and magical. The atmosphere twinkles, as if the cab is enchanted. The panic I felt in the room just minutes ago has disappeared. *You're one of them, aren't you?* I ask, as I have a few times to cabdrivers who seem to know where I am going but who only ever smile in response. I check the driver's photo, which, like all the rest since the airport, is obscured by cardboard or paper. I look into the passenger seat up front and see, as I've now seen at least a dozen times, carefully laid out ziplock bags filled with money — single dollars in one, larger bills in another, and coins in yet another. Like all the cabs with knowing drivers, it is immaculately clean. I ask him who he works for and he chuckles and says he can't say. I press and he just laughs. *But you do work for someone and you're not a cabdriver, right?* He laughs more and says, *You're the first one to see.* I can't believe he's crossed the line and acknowledged that he is not a New York City cabdriver. *I knew it!* I say, relieved that these strange encounters with taxicab drivers have not been drug-induced delusions hatched from my paranoia.

The driver seems kind. When he turns around to speak, his eyes dance with light. He is grandfatherly and appears amused. I press on with more questions. *Why don't they just arrest me?* He answers, because they want to watch me. That they have been observing me for a long time, before my recent craziness even, and that it's only now that I've been able to notice. *Is it good?* I ask, and he says, *Yes, it is good. Someone is taking care of you. You are going to be fine.* I ask him who it is and he says he cannot say. But that I am lucky and, again, not to worry. I ask him if they are listening to me in the hotel and he says yes. I ask him to prove it and he says, *Well, you know, you get very upset sometimes. Very nervous and very upset.* I ask him if they hear and watch me have sex and he laughs and says they do but not to worry, they've seen it all before. We pull up to One Fifth, and as we do I feel calm and strangely blessed. *No fare, right?* I ask and he smiles and waves me away. *Don't be so upset, it will all be okay,* he says as I climb out of the cab in front of the building.

I am overcome with a wave of relief, and as I stand there, two people walk by — they are wearing the shoes, the coats, the earpieces, the complete JCPenney outfit — and they smile as if I have finally been let in on some great secret. I can now see that all of them, every last Windbreakered one of them, has been looking out for me the entire time. *They've been protecting me!* I say out loud. This is why I have not been arrested. I look around the street, across Fifth Avenue and up 8th Street and see several people looking my way as they walk at that unmistakable pace, that deliberate and performatively normal gait.

In the lobby, Trevor is at the desk and does not seem alarmed to see me. This is still before Noah notifies the building management to call him if any of the doormen or porters see me and before he has the locks changed. I run past Trevor and he shouts hello. When I enter the apartment, it is empty. It hadn't occurred to me that Noah wouldn't be home. I pour a drink and do a hit in the bathroom and pace the living room for what seems like forever. It is strange to be home after being gone these weeks. Benny, my cat, eyes me warily and disappears into the bedroom. The apartment seems smaller than I remembered, more precious, as if each pillow and book and photograph is part of some meticulously arranged exhibit of The Life Before. I wait, and as I do, I play out the scene that will unfold after he returns. He will want me to hand over all the drugs I have on me and agree to go to rehab. I am desperate to see him. Want to hug him and be hugged by him and somehow blink away the last weeks and resume our lives. But the longer I'm there, the more impossible this seems. I don't know how long I stay that night, but it is too long, or not long enough, and I leave.

On the street outside, a cab pulls up and whisks me back to the hotel without instruction. I look at the driver as we pull up, and he shrugs as if to say, Nice try. He puts his hand over the meter and waves me away and, again, I leave another taxi without paying.

The night passes swiftly and I'm awake for every moment, alone. Not long after midnight, Happy comes and I spend all the cash I can get, $1,000. He doesn't say a word as he hands me the bags and the new stems. Doesn't comment on the increasing orders or the fact that I am making them every day. That he has been coming every night for over three weeks.

I have two liters of vodka delivered at a time with buckets of ice, and I always seem to be running out. I do hit after hit and drink heavily in between. I burn my hands badly from pulling, again and again, too hard on the stems. I shower three or four times. Lather up the shampoo as thick and luxuriously as I can, wash my face with the fancy face soap from the hotel, rinse off and feel clean for a little while.

At some point I am convinced one of my contacts has folded up behind my eyeball. I pull on my lid with one hand while the other scratches and pokes into my eye, trying to feel the difference between the flimsy edge of the contact and the slippery surface of my cornea. After an hour or so of this, my eye is stinging from the assault and the entire area is red and swollen. The stinging has gotten worse, and I'm sure it's because I neglected to wash my hands, which are covered in residue. I take a break to clean them off and instantly see the contact lens stuck to the hot-water knob. I face the mirror and it looks as if someone has poured acid into my eye. The agitation of the last few hours boils over and I yell, loudly and to no one, and storm through the room, throwing pillows, clothes, whatever happens in my way. I throw a water pitcher and it smashes on the dresser. The noise stops me. I instantly worry that I've made too much of a racket and that the management will come. I peek through the peephole and under the door off and on for the next few hours. There will be another shower, another hit, another drink, more shampoo, more soap, more water, more peeking under the door and through the peephole.

Around six in the morning I notice that the sun, east of here, across town, is casting light into the sky above the Hudson. It streaks the palest pink behind the low-rise buildings of the meatpacking district. I hadn't noticed when exactly the fury of the night began to ebb, but it has now vanished. As I step out onto the small balcony off the bedroom and inhale the still, chilly air, I feel relieved, depleted, as if some great thrashing has ended. The closing lines of *Sophie's Choice* sound from some far memory: *This was not judgment day, only morning. Morning: excellent and fair.* I speak the words out loud. I laugh at how the word *morning* sounds now like the most beautiful, consoling word I've ever heard, when it has been what I have dreaded so many times. *Morning!* of all things, excellent and fair.

Birds, hundreds of them, circle above the river. They dive and swoop against the barely lit sky. Are they seagulls? I wonder and immediately dismiss the possibility. But what else would they be? They multiply as the pink light expands and mingles more with the lightening blue. Hundreds become thousands, and the sky is a gorgeous riot of wings. It seems as if some panel of the world has been removed and a glimpse of heaven is being allowed. I wonder, for the first time, if I am still alive.

I hold the rail and see two black sedans circle slowly in front of the hotel, one behind the other. The one in front is just below me, and I can see the driver's hands on the steering wheel. Beyond them I notice there are people walking on the sidewalks. Mostly in pairs, several on their own. They are, of course, dressed in the same slacks and shoes and Windbreakers I have seen since Newark. Their footfalls and movements all seem timed to some very particular choreography of urban surveillance. Like the Penneys last night, they do not seem threatening. The birds above them wheel through the sky, and I step back to watch what seems like a meticulously staged theatrical performance. I remember Newark Airport and all the cabs that have miraculously appeared just when I've needed them. I remember the driver the night before and his words as I got out of his magical cab—*it will all be okay.* As I did standing in front of One Fifth, I think perhaps I've been running from something that has been, all the while, on my side. That maybe, if there is an organized system of observation, it might possibly be designed to protect instead of trap. I flush with the idea that something so elaborate and so stealthy could have at its heart concern, maybe love. For several minutes I lean against the railing and face the gentle morning wind.

Eventually I notice the driver in the car below fiddling with a large white card. He is scribbling something with a black marker. His movements are unbearably slow and with a small white cloth he keeps erasing what he's written only to begin writing again. I go back inside the room and smoke a large hit and pour another vodka. When I return to the balcony he is still scribbling. I can see only his arms and torso and hands. His head and face are obscured by the visor. Finally, he places the card on the dashboard in the front window. It says *BARBER*. Now that he is through with the card, his hands begin to move over a small, shiny black box. His fingers blur from the rapid movements and they maneuver there mysteriously for several long minutes. I am sure he is packing a stem of crack. He then removes a lighter from his blazer pocket and begins sparking it. Again and again but not to light or burn anything, just to spark it. He holds the flame a moment and then begins sparking it again. I'm now leaning as far over the railing of the balcony as I can, certain he is signaling me in some cryptic language that I'm just on the verge of understanding. Suddenly everything depends on my understanding what he is communicating to me. I yell out, *What are you trying to tell me?* but he does not make any indication that he's heard.

After a while, he stops sparking the lighter and carefully removes the white card from the dash. Again, he starts wiping and scribbling. Again, slowly. After a time, he begins, even more slowly than before, to write out another word. Once he's finished, he places the card again on the dash. *TORCHER*, it reads, and my mind reels with the connection between this word and the sparking lighter. *What do you mean?* I yell from the balcony. The driver puts the marker away and carefully folds his hands in his lap. I watch him for a long time and he does not move. One by one and pair by pair, the people strolling outside begin to disappear. Slowly, they round their street corners, or fade away behind buildings and trucks.

The driver is as still as a statue, and it is now almost seven o'clock. I am awake and calm, free of worry or loneliness. My body feels light and relaxed and for once doesn't shake or jitter. I have been up all night but feel well rested. There is still pink in the sky, and I have this great urge to go out into the morning and walk. Unlike following the usual routine of wiping down the counters and getting high and then dressed and undressed, I just throw on my jeans and sweater and shoes and head out.

Both cars are gone from the front of the hotel by the time I leave the building. The streets are empty and I walk down Little West 12th Street toward Washington. I only make it a few blocks before I start getting anxious and the magic air that glowed between the buildings just minutes before vanishes and is replaced with the stench of meat and the low grind of delivery trucks.

I make it up to 14th Street, and as I turn back down toward the hotel, a guy my age in a jogging suit and a trucker hat says hello. He is scruffy and cute and fit and looks like just the right thing to lift the descending gloom. He asks if I've been partying and I say yes, and before you know it he's back in my room, getting high. We take off our shirts and kiss awhile. He isn't there very long when my phone rings. I step away from the bed and after wrestling with several rounds of *Memory Filled, New Text Rejected,* I listen to the message. It's from Malcolm, whom I have completely forgotten about and now hear as I would a long-ago friend from summer camp. He sounds serious and his message begins *Hey, Bill, I really need to tell you something . . .*

I hang up the phone and never hear the rest of that message because it is at that instant that someone knocks on the door. It is loud and urgent, and when I go to the door and look through the peephole, it's Noah.

Where

Grammar school: Nurse's bathroom. Bathroom is at the end of a hall, away from the nurse's desk, has a locked door. Downside: it's the bathroom the principal uses. Upside: no one is ever in the nurse's office. Not even the nurse.

High school: Nurse's bathroom. Dodgy at lunch. Second choice: boys' room next to French class, on the second floor, in the old building. Almost always empty except in the morning before homeroom.

Home: Best is bathroom next to Dad's den at the end of the house, on the other side of the front living and dining rooms (only when Dad is away). In spring, summer, and fall, during good weather, and when Dad is home: the woods. In winter or bad weather when Dad is home: kids' bathroom upstairs, but hurry.

FRIENDS' HOUSES

Derek's: Basement bathroom.

Jenny's: Behind the horse barn or basement bathroom.

Michael's: Upstairs bathroom between Michael's and Lisa's rooms, above garage. If parents are gone or out in the barns, their bathroom at the far end of the house. If house is full, behind barn.

Adam's: His father's church across the street, downstairs bathroom.

Patrick's: Abandoned bathroom downstairs, in the part of the house that's been under construction for years.

Kenny's: THE TOUGHEST HOUSE. Only two bathrooms, both near where people always are. Choose one and pray it's over quickly.

BEAR IN MIND

1. Try to use first-floor bathrooms (people below can hear you jumping).

2. Place rugs, bath mats, and towels in front of toilet to cushion footfalls.

3. If you have no choice but to use an upstairs bathroom: avoid bathrooms above rooms where people are, use extra towels, bath mats, and rugs.

4. Don't overuse toilet paper when cleaning up. It clogs the toilet.

5. If there is a wall near the toilet, pee with your back to it.

Another Door

His family moves when he is seven. It is the summer between second and third grade and it is to a house at the end of a long driveway, near the end of a long road, and fifteen long minutes from a town in the hills of Connecticut that doesn't have a stoplight. The house takes years to renovate, and his parents add bedrooms and porches and a living room and dining room with the most beautiful wood floors that never get used. Money runs out and the upstairs floors, where the bedrooms are, will never be carpeted or finished with proper flooring. They scatter carpet samples and throw rugs over the plywood to keep from getting splinters. From a low, rambling one-story farmhouse, it becomes a large gray Dutch Colonial, and sits at the top of a hill, *one of Connecticut's tallest,* his father says, and there are forty acres of woods and field.

There is a new landscape of doors—another nurse's bathroom

at school, woods to disappear into, barns to go behind, different friends' houses with various pitfalls and out-of-the-way places for jumping and panic and eventual relief.

His third-grade class is small. Twenty or so in the whole grade, ten or so in his class. He is there only a few months when a new kid shows up, a girl. She is small and blond and birdlike and instantly familiar — like a sister or a little mother. She has immediate authority over him, but it is gentle and hard to notice. He understands that she is finer and wiser but also that she is part of him. From the moment she joins his class, he defers to her, looks up to her, and even when he is ignoring her, he worries over her approval. Katherine.

She reads. She is always reading. She asks him what he thinks about the books they read for school. In fourth grade, a book about an immortal family and a girl who falls in love with one of its members after she stumbles upon him in the woods behind her house, drinking from a spring; in fifth grade, a big, sprawling allegorical series of books about a handful of English children who must battle the rise of evil in the world. Later, too soon, she leaves Brontë and Dickens in his cubbyhole. He devours them and worries about the words he doesn't understand and loves them because she does and often sobs at their endings, because for a while he is away, out of time, somewhere he can't remember himself, and it is a shock, always a sad shock, to come back. She talks about these books, and each time, with each book, she sees more and better and has words that dazzle him to transcribe what she sees. He will steal all those words and use them. To himself, in his reports for school, talking to adults, teachers.

With each word he feels a click into a finer self, one more wrinkle smoothed. Her words have a kind of magic, like the garments that carry storybook characters out of their lives. A dress that changes a chimney-sweeping urchin into a princess, a shoe that returns her to the castle after it's all been taken away. She uses the word *desultory* in the eighth grade, and to this very day he works it into conversation the way a swimming champion casually mentions his medals.

They find out their families moved to their small town from towns very close to each other. They find out that they were born in the same hospital, seven days apart. He was born first but he inhaled vomit into his lungs and remained in the nursery for a week longer, so they imagine there was some kind of connection forged in those early, fragile hours when parents didn't exist, only nurses and other October souls screaming to life.

She agrees to kiss him in the eighth grade. It is the day before his thirteenth birthday, and a group, the same group as always — Kenny, Gwen, Adam, Michael, Jennifer — spend the day at the trampoline behind the health food store. Behind the trampoline are the woods, and a long, dark path where they go to make out. On that day she agrees to kiss him, to go down the path, into the woods. It has been discussed during the week and now it is that day, a Sunday, and they're all there.

She stalls. Or hesitates. Or something. He can never remember. He is frustrated, and he and Kenny and a few others go over to the

Nutmeg Pantry to buy candy and soda. She stays, and he's worried that even when he gets back she'll refuse to go down the path with him. The little gang leaves, they cross the shopping center parking lot and then Route 7. They buy whatever they buy and head back. He's slow to keep up, worried that she's changed her mind or chosen someone else. That he'll be the only one who won't go into the woods that day. Everyone crosses back across Route 7 and he trails behind. He makes it to the other side and then everything goes white.

Later, he remembers an ambulance and the voices of the town comforting him. The feeling of being nowhere—between land and sea, life and death, asleep and awake—everything fuzzy at the edges, and coursing through him a great sense of relief, a feeling of flight. Being pulled out, spirited away. He surfaces only briefly from this nowhere and is disappointed when he wakes the next day, fully conscious, in a hospital room, covered in casts.

People talk. They say he and Kenny were playing chicken with the cars. They pass it along as fact and it reaches his mother, who gets very upset. He doesn't find out about the talk until later, but when he does, he silently agrees with the worst things said, even though he has been told they are not true. He never remembers what happened, but a man from the next town gets arrested for driving with heroin and alcohol in his system. He never finds out what happened to this man.

Katherine comes to the hospital with the others and she brings him books. He reads them — all of them — but which ones, he won't remember, except for the tale of children who pass through a wardrobe into a world of unimpeachable good and terrible evil, of ice queens and lions; he will remember that one always. Like in so many of the other books she gives him, there is a magic door to step through — a gurgling spring with water that enchants a family into immortality, a golden ring that turns an ordinary Hobbit boy into the hope for all good in his world, a wardrobe that allows children to escape an unhappy house — some ordinary everyday object that acts as a portal into a world humming with wonder.

Because he can't move yet on crutches, a bed is set up in what his family calls the Backroom. It is a TV room at the end of a long open space that extends from the kitchen and the dining area. The room is two stories high and has a loft with books and games that one can access by a wooden ladder. The far wall of the Backroom has an enormous window that looks out onto an old maple tree that scrapes against the pane and the side of the house. Beyond that, a lawn. And beyond the lawn, the woods. The bedrooms of the house are up the stairs and away from him, and at night he is very much alone. The tree scratches the window, sounds crack from the woods, and a red light blinks on the smoke detector like some kind of evil bead. He will read more and more during this time. Retreat further into himself and feel, in the small bed at the bottom of the large windowed room, breakable.

Friends come and stay the night, teachers bring homework. His mother plays nurse and is attentive to his casts and the physical therapy he's supposed to do every day. She brings him food and wipes his face, and during the day, when she is around, he feels safe. There is a part of him that wishes this time at home with her would last forever. A month or so later, he returns to school, on crutches, and while he's relieved to be able to move again, he's also a little resentful that his old life has resumed, that no one is fussing over and looking out for him.

But before he gets home, before he leaves the hospital, in fact on the first day he gets there, the nurse brings him a bedpan that he is meant to pee into. He is immobile, cannot get himself to the bathroom, and in a flash sees the broken bones as something good, something lucky. A way to somehow shatter the always pattern of fiddling and jumping and upset and relief. Newly thirteen, and there is a little crack in what has up until now been an immovable door. There is, miraculously, hope. He pees into the bedpan and it feels like he's pissing a thousand shards of glass but his hands don't fly to his penis. While he is in the hospital he is able to pee without touching himself, every time.

A year and a half later, chubby, hairless, too pretty, and often mistaken for a girl, he goes to Australia as an exchange student. Between that time and the time in the hospital, there are many moments of triumph when he stands before a urinal and pees without the old ritual. There are also many setbacks, times when he has to retreat into a stall and wrestle with himself for nearly an hour. It goes on like this until the spell that will forever remain a mystery to him begins to fade. It starts when he is still in Australia, when hair finally arrives under his arms and crotch, when muscles gently bloom under his baby fat and inches happen, height happens. These developments occur so quietly and incrementally that he doesn't notice them until he comes home and is at once aware that the energy around him has changed, that people react to him differently. And as all these prayed-for things appear and happen, his old nemesis quietly slinks away. He returns after six months in Australia and never again, not even once, panics before a toilet.

It will all be forgotten: every locked door, every hour he fretted in bathrooms, every flight into the woods where no one could see. It is not until he is twenty-six years old that he remembers that he ever struggled. And then, when he finally does, he remembers it all.

There will never be any explanation for his childhood affliction. Nothing beyond theories, some commingling of psychology and pediatric diagnosis, but nothing concrete or definitive.

Katherine and he will date and kiss and go out and not go out and avoid each other and have dramatic reunions all through grammar school, high school, college, and after. She will go to Scotland to an illustrious university in an ancient town by the sea and read a trilogy by a great Scottish writer about a girl and her family — about everything — that she will quote from often. She will eventually drop out and drift to Montana. A few years later, he will go to a university in Scotland in an ancient city — this one in the hills and not nearly as illustrious — and read that same trilogy and never in his life stop quoting from it. Boyfriends and a husband of hers will refuse to let her see him. Girlfriends and boyfriends of his will eye her warily. As adults they keep their distance. They write many letters. He reads all the books she ever cared about. He carries her opinions and interpretations around as if they are his until at some point, sometime after Scotland, he begins to find books of his own and to shape, slowly, opinions of his own. He graduates from her and both know it, she long before him.

But before that happens, the summer before he goes away to a small college on the eastern shore of Maryland, they drink a bottle of very expensive wine from one of two cases his mother is holding for a dear friend in a bitter divorce. They eventually finish off both cases and find out years later that it was very expensive indeed. They drink that first exquisite bottle of wine, with a griffin on the label, as they sit on a mountain called Indian. She throws pebbles into his shorts until it is clear that she wants him to take them off. She takes hers off, too, and he does the thing he had not done before but she had. It feels like a miracle that it is happening at all, but that it is with her makes it feel blessed, meant to be, but also something like incest. For years he will think it happened in a field her father owned, one night on the way to a play. But it will be her memory, her story, they agree on.

Uptown

How can he be here? How? I look back through the peephole again and again, and each time I am hoping that the paranoid fantasy that Noah is at the other side of the door has vanished and there is no one in the hall. But each time I look, there he is. And not alone. A large man in a heavy tan coat is standing behind him. He is talking into a cell phone and I'm sure he's a cop or a DEA agent.

It's okay, just let us in, Noah calls out. *Don't get upset, we're here to help.*

Jesse, the guy on the bed, tenses up and asks what's going on. I whisper for him to get dressed as quickly as possible, that it's my boyfriend. He moves like lightning and is up, fully dressed and with his coat on in seconds. He heads for the door and I tell him to wait. Wide-eyed and jumpy, he spits, *Only a second, I'm not sticking around.* As quickly as I can, I grab the ashtray on the nightstand and dump the remaining drugs in a plastic bag and stick it, along with the remaining stem, inside my jacket pocket in the closet. I grab a cloth and sloppily wipe down the crumbs and residue on the nightstand and scan the room for other evidence of what's been going on. Jesse moves toward the door as I grab my sweater and jeans from the floor.

Jesse opens the door, does not look back to say good-bye, and pushes past Noah and the man in the tan coat. I'm sitting on the bed as Noah steps into the room. *Let's go,* he says, without even mentioning the guy who has just fled.

The man in the tan coat is named John, and he tells me he is a former DEA agent, that he's pulled a string and called into *the agency* to find out that there is a file on me. Noah then tells me the police have shown up at One Fifth, asking to question me. That my name came up in a drug bust. Mark? I wonder. Stephen? My heart, which is already beating wildly, begins to pound hard with new dread. I'm getting arrested, I think as I eye John, who looks no different from the Penneys.

How did you find this guy? I ask Noah. I'm convinced he's lied to Noah about who he is and that he does not mean well. Noah says a lawyer recommended him and I ask who. I don't know the name, and the more I look at John, the more I think he's snared Noah in a complicated sting to haul me off to jail.

We have to go, John says. *We have to get you out of here.*

It takes over an hour for me to get ready and it still feels like we're rushing. I ask for privacy and load and smoke two huge hits in the bathroom. I let the stem finally cool and put it in my jacket pocket and load the remaining drugs in the stem so I won't have to pack it later should I be able to peel away and take a hit. The high pushes away some of the immediate dread, and I wash my face and hands and run my fingers through my hair. I put on my turtleneck sweater, realize the bathroom is filled with smoke, and switch on the fan. Noah knocks on the bathroom door and I tell him to hold on. The dread returns as the smoke rises up through the vent. I sit on the toilet and take a deep hit off the stem and pray for a heart attack.

We leave the hotel without checking out and jump into a cab on Gansevoort Street. John tells me I'm lucky I haven't been arrested yet. I look up at the driver and the obscured photo on the panel behind him. Jesus, I think, of course. I explain to Noah that nearly every cab I've taken over the last weeks has had a strip of cardboard or paper over the driver's ID photo. That I suspect the drivers are undercover cops or agents of some kind. I try to explain to him about the cabdrivers and the Penneys and that this John here is one of them and the driver, too, and he doesn't know what he's just done to me by putting me in their hands. *You don't know,* I whisper desperately to him as he pats my hand.

I finger the stem in my pocket and know it's good for at least a few more big hits. I also think it probably holds enough to get charged with Intent to Distribute and immediately start worrying about where I can stash it if it looks like they're taking me to a police station. Then I remember the cabdriver is undercover, and as I watch the city streak by outside the window, I start to shake with panic.

Noah puts his arm around me and says we're going somewhere safe to talk. I ask where and he and John signal each other. They don't seem to know what the next beat is, so I ask if we can get something to eat, and by that I mean, though I do not say it, something to drink. I need alcohol in my system to calm down.

We end up in the Seventies off Third Avenue and find a Chinese restaurant with a basement dining room that is nearly empty. I immediately excuse myself to go to the bathroom and take a hard long pull on the stem. After several moments I think I hear full-blown conversations about when to *haul him in* outside the door. I still keep pulling on the stem. It broils in my hand and I dab the edges with cold water to cool it down.

When I return to the table I ask the waitress for a vodka and she says they only have wine and beer, so I ask for a bottle of cold white. Noah begins to object but John turns to the waitress and says fine. It comes and I drink it down like water. I order food of some kind but when it comes I don't touch it.

John explains that I need to check into a psych ward immediately to avoid arrest. Noah nods as he speaks and I'm not sure what to believe. John goes on to say that there is a psychiatrist whom he knows and works with who has secured a bed in the psych ward at New York–Presbyterian Hospital. With these words an image of white sheets and kind nurses and locked doors flashes behind my eyes, and for the first time since Noah and John showed up at the hotel, I feel relief. I can imagine a long sleep there and drugs to calm me down, and without thinking anymore about it, I agree to see the psychiatrist.

A few blocks away we enter a building that looks like an abandoned elementary school. We walk down wide empty halls before arriving at a door straight out of a forties detective movie—frosted glass, stenciled letters. Again, the sense that John has rigged an elaborate sting operation to arrest me rises up like bile. The wine had calmed my panic but it's now back, and at high volume. A frizzy-haired woman in jeans and paisley top comes to the door and greets John with a wide smile. Undercover cop, I think instantly. She gives my arm a tender squeeze and asks us to follow her. *He's just finishing up with someone now,* she calls over her shoulder as she guides us past a room of empty desks and toward a corner office.

I ask if there is a bathroom and she offers to show me the way before John and Noah can say anything. I walk with her back into the hall and to a door marked *MEN*. It's empty, and as fast as I can, I turn on the water in the sink and jump into a stall. The stem is still crammed with drugs so as soon as I find the lighter I fire up a hit, inhale as much smoke as will fit in my lungs, hold it there for as long as I can, and blow the thick cloud out the open window by the stall. Light comes in from outside and dapples the black-and-white tile floor, and for a moment I forget all the people waiting for me. There's a knock on the bathroom door as it opens, and it's Noah.

Everything okay? he asks, and his face registers the smell of smoke in the room. *Have you been getting high?* he asks, and I say, *No, let's go.* He hugs me and tells me how relieved he is that I'm alive, and I'm tempted to fall into his arms, let him sweep all this mess away, but I suspect he is only pulling me close to pat down my jacket and jeans to find the stem and lighter. I wriggle away from him and head to the hall.

The psychiatrist looks like he's from the eighties. Striped red-and-white shirt, suspenders, big horn-rim glasses, wide-wale cords, yellow socks, and tasseled loafers. His hair is curly, and from the half smile he uses with me, I get the feeling he's done a fair bit of drugs himself. He tells me there's a bed ready at the hospital but that it won't be there for long. He signals Noah and John to leave his office and we sit there for a while without speaking. *You high?* he asks, and I tell him yes. *Good,* he says, *enjoy it while it lasts.* He asks what I do, he talks about the books he likes, and then cuts the meeting short and says, *Take it or leave it.*

I'll leave it, I say as I get up from the chair. John and Noah jump up as I come through the door and ask what went on, and I tell them I'm done with this, that I'm leaving. John tells me that I can expect to be arrested before the day is over. His tone is severe, and at this point he genuinely seems alarmed. I shuffle in place and don't know what to do. I'm panicked but I still have money in my account and think if I can just get a pile of sleeping pills and a gallon of vodka I can probably keep this going a few more days and then end it. I am in the waiting room of a psychiatrist's office surrounded by people most of whom I don't know and I begin to sway from the many nights without sleep, the hit I just took in the bathroom, and the wine from before. My head roars with the talk of cops at the apartment, DEA files, getting arrested. I freeze. I stand there and have no idea what to do. I want to run. I want to collapse. I don't want to be arrested. I want Noah to hold me. I want to get high and wipe all this away. I want to be wiped away.

John finally says, *Why don't you just hang on, let's slow down. I know a guy at the Carlyle Hotel a few blocks away who can secure a safe room for you to rest in and think about what to do. Let's just dial this down a little and get you somewhere safe.* Somewhere safe sounds good, and for the first time all day I trust John, have a new sense that he is who he says he is and that he's just trying to keep me from taking off into the city and getting arrested. I agree.

Within an hour I'm in a large, old-fashioned-looking room at the Carlyle with John's colleague, Brian. Brian is quiet and tall and in his midtwenties. John asks Noah to go rest at home and says we will all convene in the morning. Noah's eyes are worried as he gets up from the bed where he's been sitting. *Call me if you need anything,* he says, and leans in to give me a hug. I squeeze him lightly, with my body held away, careful not to let my jacket pocket, where the stem and lighter are, graze his hands. The second he and John walk out the door I am relieved. I walk over to the phone, call room service, and order a large bottle of Ketel One and a bucket of ice. I am crashing and it's time for vodka. Brian says nothing, just sits in a chair and watches quietly.

The vodka comes right away and I stuff a big water glass with ice and fill it to the brim. I ask Brian if he wants any and he laughs and says, *No, thank you.* I swallow down two drinks swiftly and pour a third. I tell Brian I need to take a shower and he says to go right ahead. I bring the drink into the bathroom, lock the door, and turn the shower on. The bathroom is tiny and there is no switch for a fan. But there is a small square window above the shower and I'm soon in the shower, naked and smoking what I think will be a smallish hit, but it turns out there are two or three big hits still left. I suddenly wish I'd brought the bottle of vodka in with me. I pack hits, blow the smoke out the little window into an airshaft, let the steam rise, and soon I am loose. Brian comes to the door once and asks if I am good and I say, *Just unwinding in the shower.* A few minutes pass and, as in the bathroom at the psychiatrist's office, the panic of the day melts away. I decide to save a hit in the stem for later and begin to towel off. I am humming with good energy by this point and the vodka has balanced out the jittery side of the high. *Fuck it,* I think as I walk out into the room with just the towel cinched low on my hips. I put my coat and jeans next to the bed and bring the vodka and the ice bucket to the nightstand. I fix another drink, find the remote control, and lie down.

Brian, who I now notice is curly-haired and green-eyed and has a heavy five-o'clock shadow that reminds me of Noah, seems unfazed as I flip through the channels and drink. I ask him some questions about his job (mostly fishing professional athletes and celebrities out of hotel rooms and getting them into rehab) and what he did before (cop) and find out he has a girlfriend (nice girl, a nurse) and a small house upstate where he goes on weekends. I scooch the towel a little lower on my hips and ask if he minds if I look at porn. He says, *Be my guest,* and I find the Pay-per-view and hit Play. He sits there for a few minutes, laughs at my ridiculous gestures to seduce him, and says he needs to make a phone call.

As he leaves the room it occurs to me that I can get Happy up here and score a bag or two. I need cash but I don't worry about that part as I dig the cell phone out of my coat and dial Happy's number as fast as I can. He picks up, I say *Three hundred and two stems,* the name of the hotel and address, and for him to call me when he's downstairs. Happy sounds unfazed, and I wonder if he's delivered here before. When I hang up, I begin pacing the room, worrying about Brian coming back. Now or never, I think or say, and quickly get dressed, leave the room, get in the elevator, and step out into the lobby of the hotel. I know I have only a few minutes to score the cash and get back to the room before Brian returns. How I'll make the exchange of money and drugs with Happy I can't yet imagine. As the elevator doors open I panic. I think Brian must be somewhere in the lobby and is sure to see me. I head over into Bemelmans Bar and up a flight of steps into a bathroom. It's empty, and I duck into a stall and quickly light a hit off a pipe that is charred from so much use and finally running thin on drugs. But still I pull a decent hit and decide to smash the glass in a fistful of toilet paper and flush it. I take one more big, oily burnt-tasting hit before I crush the thing under my shoe and throw it in the toilet.

The Carlyle's dark bars and various ante-lobbies are a tricky maze, and I cross and recross the sitting area near a bank of phones several times and can't find the exit. This goes on for a while, and as it does, my panic rises. I finally break out onto Madison Avenue and ask a nicely dressed woman if she knows where an ATM is. I worry she'll think I'm mugging her or that she can tell I'm high, but she casually points to a Chase Bank across the street. I take out $800 and run back into the hotel and up to the room.

Brian is still out when Happy calls, and not knowing any other way, and dreading the prospect of leaving the room again, I tell him to come up but that it's going to have to be fast. A minute later he's in the little foyer—white sweatpants, huge earphones, wordless—and though I called for $300, I ask him if he has six and he says he has four and hands me eight bags and two stems.

The tide of relief that passes over me when the door shuts is almost as powerful as the enormous hit I pack in the shiny, clean new stem. I shove the extra stem and bags into my coat pocket, get undressed, wrap the towel around my waist, hop back on the bed, and fix a new drink. By the time Brian returns I am smoking openly and the porn is flickering on the TV screen. *You scored, didn't you?* he asks, and I nod with a wicked smile on my face. *Do you have any idea how close to being arrested you are?* he asks, and I tell him to please relax. That I have one more night of freedom and I promise to stay put if he kicks back and lays off the talk of psych wards and cops. He agrees and sits in the chair next to the dresser.

I go through two liters of vodka and almost three bags of crack as I lie on that bed and talk to Brian and watch porn. I steer the discussion to his girlfriend, sex, and porn, and, for hours, he will manage to keep it clean on his end without disengaging.

At some point in the early morning he falls asleep. I oh-so-gently get off the bed and into my clothes, pack up my few things— phone, stem, drugs, lighter—and tiptoe out of the room, into the hall, and back to the world.

Idiot Wind

It's a small college on the eastern shore of Maryland, and four of us are renting a house twenty minutes away from campus, on the Chesapeake Bay. It's a blue raised ranch with aluminum siding and a deck in back, and to us it's paradise. Ian is a dark-haired, wild-eyed boarding school hellion from New Orleans; Brooks, my roommate from the dorms, is a Cary Grant type from Maryland — Waspy, strangely old-fashioned, friend to all and enemy to none; and there's Jake, a blue-eyed, curly-haired blond peace monkey who bartends in the summer and plays harmonica and sings in a Baltimore band called The Moonshiners.

There is always a keg on the back porch, and in the fridge piles of lamb chops and choice cuts of beef that we steal from the grocery store in the next town. The stealing begins one afternoon when Ian and I are walking through the meat section. He stops and points to an assortment of wrapped packets of lamb chops and whispers, *Billy, c'mon, unzip the pocket on the back of my coat and drop a couple of those beauties in there*. Ian scrunches his face with urgency, his eyes bulge, he pleads in his particular way, *Jesus, Billy, c'mon, what are you doooin'?* and though I'm sure I am going to get caught, I unzip the coat, grab the meat, and slip it in. The coat is an expensive ski jacket with a wide zippered pocket on the back. It holds the meat vertically, and as Ian walks through the store and we check out, there is no sign that he's carrying our dinner on his back. From that day on we never pay for meat. When we go shopping we take Ian's coat.

I read during the day, when I'm skipping class—Hardy and Fitzgerald mostly that year, *Jude the Obscure* a few times. On the weekends I read in my room, the one at the end of the hall, tucked away from the ruckus of the house. There is no one at school or in the house whom I talk to about what I read. I reread Salinger and Knowles and the books of my adolescence. Some of these copies still have Katherine's scribbles in the margins, and I treat them like museum pieces.

Every once in a while someone has coke or acid but for the most part it's pot-around-the-clock. Ian has a red Graphics bong he cleans and recleans and strokes like a pet. I keep a constant stash in my room and smoke off a short plastic bong and listen to Rickie Lee Jones and Bob Dylan and when I'm not reading just stare at the maroon-and-brown tapestry tacked to the ceiling. We road-trip up and down the eastern seaboard—Philadelphia, Baltimore,

Washington, Roanoke, Boston, New York—to see The Dead, Dylan, Neil Young. Mostly it's me and Ian, and mostly it's Dylan.

Brooks is the only one with a steady girlfriend, Shirley, who goes to school in Virginia. I hook up with two or three different girls on a regular basis—all of whom make Ian's face wrinkle with disgust. *Jesus, Billy, what are you dooooin'?* he'll say at the end of the night when it's clear whom I'll be taking back to my room. Jake has girls in Baltimore or in town who don't go to college. We'll never meet them. Ian will hook up with only one girl that I know of—a girl I have made out with a few times and whom I've told Ian I've fallen for—and it will be in the backseat of a car on a trip back from Boston while Brooks and I are in the front. We'll see the whole thing. I'll be mad and he'll say he was asleep and didn't know she was making the moves on him.

One night Jake withdraws money from an ATM and notices a lucky bank error for a sum that makes it seem like a good idea to buy a fresh keg and have some people over. We do and we drink and it gets late and someone notices that Brooks is not with us. Someone else says he's on campus and we decide to go find him. Ian drives, I ride shotgun, and Jake takes the back. We stop at Newt's, a grim honky-tonk bar that has all sorts of specials to lure college kids. Fifty-cent beers to get them in the door and tipsy so that they'll start buying shots. Which is what we do. Tequila. Ian is always several shots ahead of us, but Jake and I are eager to keep up. After last call, we put up stools and chairs and get more free shots. We are all lit in the same way, have the same streaking comet inside us, and agree that heading over to one of the girls' dormitories is the thing to do. Find Brooks. Drag him home. And so we go. Ian blares "Idiot Wind" in the car and shouts the lyrics, *You're an eeeediot, Babe, It's a wonder that you still know how to breathe.* He rocks back and forth against the steering wheel as he wails, and his black hair and red eyes gleam demonlike in the green glow of the Volkswagen dashboard.

It's at least two by the time we get out of the car. We are roaring drunk from the tequila and there is an unstable voltage humming in each of us. Our breath clouds and shimmers in the freezing cold March air, and we move from the car to the dorm like a three-headed monster hell bent on mischief. We tiptoe through the halls and Ian finds a fire extinguisher to bring along for the journey. He pretends to squirt us and at some point it goes off. Glorious plumes of white cloud billow out of the red canister, which is, in that instant, the most extraordinary thing we've ever seen. Ian points his new weapon in the opposite direction, squeezes the handle, and again, a majestic slow-motion miracle blooms out into the hall. Jake and I need to have one, too, so we race upstairs to find two more. Jake finds one and I somehow don't. They go on to spray each other, the halls, the doors, the floor, a girl who is sleeping. We get split up, but there is a sense that we're still connected by some invisible electric tether and only a shout away.

I enter a common area where someone has left a nearly finished quilt. Blue and red squares of fabric sewn together in a groovy mosaic. It reminds me of my mother, and the quilt she made me out of scraps of fabric in high school. Without thinking I gather it in my arms and book into the hall. It's about now that I hear Ian yelling my name. *Billeeeeee, c'mon, Billeeeee.* Occasionally I hear him bark Jake's name. *Jake. We gotta split. Jake, c'mon.* I head back to the hall. Suddenly we all run into one another, and as we do, I see girls coming out of their rooms, shouting. We race for the exit. Someone—one of us? one of the girls?—pulls the fire alarm and almost immediately we hear a siren. The car is parked up behind the bank, and we run through the side parking lot of the dorms and up through the backyard of someone's house. Ian is in full combat mode and pushes us down behind a hedge and barks in a whisper for us to *Stay the fuck quiet.*

And so we do. Police sirens, fire engines, and the fire alarm sound through the town while blue and red lights streak around us. It's now between three and four in the morning and the campus and the surrounding neighborhood are awake. Lights flicker on in the nearby dorms and houses, people pull curtains aside and lean their heads out to see what is going on. We stay there for at least an hour and finally, when things seem to quiet down, we sneak over to Ian's car and drive back to the house. Brooks is there and has already been called by everyone we know who heard Ian screaming our names.

As we walk up to the front door, Brooks looks at me in horror and says, *What the fuck is that?* I look down and am embarrassed to realize that I have been clutching the nearly finished quilt the whole time. I'm so nervous the cops are going to show up any minute that I stuff it into a black garbage bag and shove it under the empty house next door.

We stay up that night, get high, worry, and wait for the phone call from school, which comes, and a day later we are thrown out. Jake never comes back. Ian and I plan to go to UC Boulder together the following fall. Brooks moves into a house with friends in town and finishes the semester.

That spring I go down to Bedford, New York, a few times to visit Ian. His mother moved there from New Orleans when she divorced Ian's father. I'm landscaping with a friend at home, and he's working in a sporting goods store in White Plains. His mother is often away and his brother Sam is in the eighth grade and generally around. Usually Ian scores coke from a friend in Rye and we smoke pot and throw a Frisbee in the afternoon, and at night do lines, drink good beer, and play caps—a game where two people sit on either side of a room and throw beer caps at empty cups placed between their legs until their thumbs bleed from pressing too hard against the serrated metal edges.

One weekend in Bedford we drink so much Guinness and smoke so much weed that by the time the lines come out I've already vomited. We stay up all of Saturday and most of Sunday night and on Monday I am supposed to meet Miho, my family's former Japanese exchange student, in Manhattan. She's in town for the day, and my mother has asked and I've agreed to take her around.

Monday at noon seems a lifetime away as we blare Dylan and do line after line on the breakfast table in Ian's kitchen. We run out around five o'clock Monday morning, take sleeping pills with a few more beers, and head to bed. I'm in a guest room, and at eight o'clock I wake up and suddenly feel wrong. It takes a minute or two to realize that not only have I peed and shit the bed but vomited all over myself. Ian's mother is coming home that day. My head is stinging, and I panic that Ian will find out. I creep from the bed, take off my soiled underwear and T-shirt, and go to the bathroom to rinse the more substantial mess off. I take a shower and then, sheet by sheet, pillow case by pillow case, dismantle the bed and put my clothes on from the night before, which reek of pot and are covered in beer stains. I flip the now-stained mattress, gather up the soiled underwear, T-shirt, and linens, and tiptoe as gently as possible out into the hall, down the stairs, and into the basement, where for some reason I know there is a washer and dryer. I empty the load that's in the washing machine, put it in a basket, and replace it with the horrible load.

Every button I push, cleaning product I open, and door I shut sounds like a rifle shot, and I'm convinced Ian will rumble down the stairs and bellow his trademark *What are you doooing?* Ian could load that phrase with an empire of disgust and contempt. This is a guy who loved Bob Dylan, thought every other musician was a fraud, couldn't stand the state of Maryland, any fat girl or woman, and most everything else that wasn't from Louisiana. I am his friend, but it generally feels like that fragile status is only one wrong band or shitted bed away from being revoked.

I don't want to make any more noise on the stairs, so I sit down there while the clothes wash and dry. Eventually they dry, and by this time it's nearly eleven. I make the bed, gather my things, and call a taxi. I wake Ian up to say good-bye and he scrunches his face and says, *Jeeeesus, Billy, you look like shit.*

This is the last time I see Ian. He won't get into Boulder. I will, but my father will insist that I go back to Maryland and face the wreckage there, which I do. Brooks and I will be roommates until I graduate, and Jake will go back to Baltimore, where he will — and I suspect still does — bartend and play guitar.

I arrive at Rockefeller Center over an hour late for Miho. My clothes reek and the black Aspen cap on my head — one of Ian's, one I wore nearly every day then — is covered with lint and detritus of all kinds from the night before. There is bile rising up at the back of my throat, and I have already thrown up twice on the train.

Miho looks annoyed and impeccable. She has on a yellow Chanel-like suit, red pumps, and a blouse that is so white I can't face it without squinting. She is nineteen but looks like a seasoned executive or a newscaster well into her thirties. She eyes me warily and asks if I am okay. I tell her, *Sort of,* and ask where she wants to go. I should have known: Saks Fifth Avenue, Tiffany, Cartier, Bergdorf, Bonwit Teller, Gucci. We spend the day in places where the security guards keep a close eye on me. It is one of the longest days of my life, and I pop into several delis along the way for aspirin and water.

The city seems like an animated cartoon that I have entered through some great cosmic accident. The security guards are the only ones who notice me: to all others I'm invisible. The ragged shorts, the Aztec cloth belt, the Snowbird T-shirt, and the Aspen cap (neither are places I'd been) are a uniform for another world altogether and not one I'm even comfortable in. People seem so sure of themselves, so securely in their lives as they march up and down Fifth and Madison avenues. Some don't look that much older than me, but they seem carved from matter and shaped by forces I can't even imagine. I will remember them later, often, and they will seem as the city does: golden, magical, daunting.

I don't return to New York for another three years. This is after college, and I'm with my girlfriend Marie, who is nine years older than I am. She sets up an informational meeting with a friend of hers, a book editor at a publishing company—one of the few I'm aware of because it is the house named on the title pages of the Salinger and Dickinson books I've read and reread. I resist and she insists that I at least explore book publishing, which she seems to think is where I belong. I play along a little with her fantasy, but it's as if I were five or six, talking to the big kids at the town beach about diving off the high dive: fun to pretend, impossible to do.

The meeting is one block from Rockefeller Center. The book editor looks at my résumé — the one Marie helped me put together — and frowns. He points to the assistants on the floor outside his office and lets me know that most of them went to Ivy League schools, some of them for both undergraduate and graduate degrees, and that my academic career and job experience are a far cry from anything that would get me in the door at a publishing house like this one. It is exactly as I feared and I am nauseous with shame. Marie is waiting for me by the ice-skating rink, where they light the big Christmas tree each year, I think. I lie and tell her the editor was encouraging, that he thinks there may be something there down the line, just not now. She says, *See, I told you so,* and I agree.

As we have coffee later that day and run an errand for her mother at Brooks Brothers, I am again aware of the security guards, as I was years before with Miho, and believe they can see what I know and Marie seems blind to: that I don't belong here. That this is a place for a sleeker, smarter, better-educated, and altogether finer grade of person. I get on the train that afternoon in Grand Central, thinking the same thing I thought that hungover day three years ago: This is the last time. And: What if it's not?

Beginnings of the End

His first drink is his father's — Scotch — from the bottle, in the woods, with Kenny. They are twelve. It's fall and the leaves are bright around them and everywhere there is the sweet smell of mulchy decay, of rot. They swipe a bottle from the liquor cabinet and scamper down the logging trail with a pack of his mother's cigarettes and a *Playboy* calendar Kenny has gotten from the pharmacy in the next town over.

It tastes bad but he loves it, loves the strange warmth in his chest and the sting in his throat. He has only three or four swigs but it's enough to make him woozy. Enough to give him a toehold in a blurry, blissful place. A place where he doesn't have to bring himself along. What he also loves is the dark project of it. The sneaking into the woods. The stealthy plans, the covert moves.

The intimacy of an illicit collaboration. They giggle, the way they always do. Kenny stops at one swig, wincing at the taste. They barely smoke a cigarette and they howl at more than ogle the naked calendar girls. They will do this together only a few more times. It is, however, just the beginning of his stealing from his father's liquor cabinet. Instead of the woods, he'll bring it to his room, sip it in his window seat from a red-and-orange-striped thermos, and listen to the crickets outside, Bob Dylan, Cat Stevens, Neil Young. He'll barely hear the racket of the house below. This will go on until he leaves for college.

His first drug is a line of crystal meth when he's fifteen. It happens in a cooler in the little market where he works in high school and, later, on breaks from college. The place stays open until ten and sells things like sandwiches, cereal, cigarettes, and gas. A guy named Max who works there gives it to him. Max is older, a sort of bad boy with a dealer girlfriend, someone he's talked to about drugs and inhaled cases of Reddi-wip with ever since they started working nights together. Max offers to give him a try one night and goes into the cooler to set it up — a short, thin line on a box of mozzarella sticks, with a rolled-up dollar bill — behind cases of eggs and soda and half and half. It stings his nose and at first he feels nothing. But then he gets the jolt, the speedy lift Max talks about, and soon he wants another.

They do this off and on for years. Setting up lines in the cooler, ringing up customers, and sipping beer that he keeps under the deli counter. Sometimes it will be cocaine, sometimes crystal. He never really knows the difference, or cares. It passes the time and gives the job a fizziness and sheen that make it bearable.

Pot comes a little later and then it's always around, until he's thirty or so. He'll smoke it nearly every day in college and off and on in his twenties until one night it will taste funny, make him antsy and queasy, and after this it will hold no appeal.

The first time he smokes crack. He never tells this story. Instead he usually says he tried it at a party, that he was pulled into a bedroom by someone he knew, a couple, a friend, someone he didn't know. It's someone different every time. The phony story always sounds less shameful to him, less weird, more normal, even glamorous. But that's not how it happens.

There is a lawyer from his hometown, let's call him Fitz. He's a big fish in the small pond of that small town. His house is large, old, and, in the eyes of those who care about such things, important. He and his wife are social. They belong to the country club, drive beat-up old Volvos and Mercedes, carry monogrammed Bean tote bags everywhere. Everyone knows Fitz.

One early evening in New York he sees Fitz. Fitz sees him. They are somewhere near the small literary agency where he now works, somewhere in the East Fifties. He'll always think it's in the bookstore in the Citicorp building but he's never sure. He is twenty-five now, maybe twenty-six. Fitz says hello first. He's in his sixties, well over six feet tall, silver-haired and handsome in the way the headmaster of a boarding school is handsome. Fitz wears a striped oxford shirt rolled at the sleeves, and liver spots speckle the skin of his hands and forearms.

Why don't we grab a drink at my place, Fitz suggests. And so they go. Soon, twenty blocks away, they are at Fitz's apartment. Both have vodka—he talks about his kids, this one in the Midwest, that one in Bermuda, and one finishing law school in DC. The apartment is in Murray Hill, a large two-bedroom in an old co-op. It smells faintly of mothballs and is decorated like the office of a college admissions officer. The busy print on the simple couch and chairs is navy and burgundy, the curtains are beige, and the dark wood coffee table, its hinges tarnished brass, is covered with family photographs.

A few drinks in and they're talking about college and sex and booze and drugs, and though it should have been perfectly obvious before, he suddenly realizes that Fitz—despite the important house, the kids, the wife, the tote bags—is hitting on him. He's rubbed his neck a few times on the way to the kitchen to fetch more drinks; has moved from the opposite chair to the couch next to him and squeezed his thigh a few times as they talk.

Fitz is telling him now about how every once in a while he likes to get high. Pot mostly, but occasionally something stronger. Fitz asks him if he's ever free-based and he says, without hesitating, yes. He hasn't, but it's occurred to him. He's wondered about it, imagined what it would be like, but it didn't seem to be something he'd ever encounter. Free-basing meant crack, and crack was the stuff of gritty drug busts written up in the Metro section of the *New York Times* and, he thinks, confined mainly to projects and jails. All through the eighties, when he was in high school, crack made headlines for ruining neighborhoods, driving up crime, being famously addictive. A hideous, monstrous scourge, utterly taboo. Something he has always been drawn to, something he has always wanted to try.

He has known only one person who smoked crack: Jackie DiFiore. He and Jackie grew up in the same town where Fitz lives and works. She was four years older and always getting into trouble. She eventually dropped out of high school and, it was rumored, moved to Albany, New York, to live with a black man and became a crack addict. Jackie's story was the most popular cautionary tale parents in their town used to illustrate What Happens When You Use Drugs.

Many years after the night with Fitz, he will remember Mrs. Parsons, his piano teacher when he was twelve. A heavyset Irishwoman who lived down the road who it seemed had at least eight children. She smoked and drank and gossiped and lived with all those kids in a small green house at the edge of a swamp. It looked like a witch's house and sort of sagged into the hill behind it. One day he showed up for his lesson and it became instantly clear that he hadn't practiced. Again. After he'd fumbled a little over a simple étude, she grabbed his hands and told him to stop. *I can see it now,* she thundered. *You're going to grow up and be a crack addict, just like Jackie DiFiore. No doubt in my mind. You are two peas in a pod.*

Fitz goes into the bedroom and comes back with a small vial of what look like chunky milk-colored crystals. He pulls a clear glass tube from his pocket, something he calls a stem, and packs one end with small wire mesh and then a few small bits of the drug, or crumbs, as he says. Fitz carefully hands him the stem and tells him to put it to his lips as he pulls out a lighter. The glass tube is delicate and his hands are shaky. He's afraid he'll spill the drugs but somehow he does not. Fitz flicks on the lighter and passes the flame close to the end of the stem. He draws slowly as he sees the white substance bubble and pop in the flame. A pearly smoke makes its way down the stem, and he draws harder to bring it toward him. Fitz tells him to go gently and he does. Soon his lungs are full and he holds it the way he would hold pot smoke. He exhales and is immediately coughing. The taste is like medicine, or cleaning fluid, but also a little sweet, like limes. The smoke billows out into the living room, past Fitz, like a great unfurling dragon. As he watches the cloud spread and curl, he feels the high at first as a flutter, then a roar. A surge of new energy pounds through every inch of him, and there is a moment of perfect oblivion where he is aware of nothing and everything. A kind of peace breaks out behind his eyes. It spreads down from his temples into his chest, to his hands and everywhere. It storms through him — kinetic, sexual, euphoric — like a magnificent hurricane raging at the speed of light. It is the warmest, most tender caress he has ever felt and then, as it recedes, the coldest hand. He misses the feeling even before it's left him and not only does he want more, he needs it.

Meanwhile, a silver-haired, handsome man from home has his arm around him, is stroking his leg and telling him he's going to pack another hit, a bigger one, that they can share. This second time he tries as hard as he can to go slow, but Fitz says he's still drawing too hard, that he'll burn the stem. He barely pulls and again his lungs are full. Again he coughs and again, but bigger this time, there is this blast of feeling and not feeling, awareness of nothing and everything, a furious energy that makes him go still. Fitz takes the stem back and, after it cools, packs his own hit. While Fitz inhales, he motions him to come toward his lips and it's clear that he is offering to exhale smoke into his mouth. And he does, and they start kissing.

Nothing before this has been as thrilling. This raging tempest streaking through his system as he kisses a man — the second or third he's kissed — who is older than his father, whom he's seen in the grocery store and library of his tiny town his whole life. They will make out, get naked, and move the whole project of stems and drugs and kissing into the bedroom. It will be a dizzy blur of smoke and skin, and it will be the only time he ever does this drug where doom does not eclipse bliss, where the two aren't immediately at war. Doom will hit when he leaves a few hours later and realizes it's near midnight and that he is in no shape to see Nell, his girlfriend — the person he has lived with for more than two years despite his growing attraction to men.

Before he leaves Fitz's apartment he goes into the bathroom and carefully washes his hands, which have grown sooty and burnt from the hot stem. He washes his face and fixes his hair so it doesn't look like he's been thrashing around for hours. He checks his clothes, brushes off his blazer, makes sure all his shirt buttons are buttoned, his collar is straight, his fly zipped. Behind the locked door, in the tiny bathroom off the entryway, he runs through all of this — swiftly, mechanically — at least a dozen times. It's as if he's on autopilot, or responding to some primal, animal instinct to transform from one state to another. He pulls up his socks, rubs the spots off his shoe, and wipes his brow once more. As he checks his hair and gargles with the mouthwash he finds in the medicine cabinet, Fitz knocks a few times to make sure everything is okay. *Be right out,* he calls as he takes one last look in the mirror.

He hunts for a cab on Lexington and hopes Nell has gone to sleep. He is startled how time has changed shape, how six hours has felt like a few minutes. He worries he's left something behind. He's not sure what exactly — he has his wallet, his keys, his tie bunched in his blazer pocket — but he's sure something is now missing.

This will be just before or just after the night he meets Noah. Certainly it is before he tells Nell he has to leave her, before he's introducing Noah to his mother, who tells him he must not tell

Kim, or anyone else in the family who might tell her, because the news might cause her to lose the twins she's recently become pregnant with. Before he introduces Noah to his boss, his friends, and the writers he works with. It is before Noah is known to his world, but which came first—the night he met Noah, the night with Fitz—will never be clear. It was a time when everything seemed like a beginning.

Family Reunion

Noah is the first thing I see when I step out of the elevator at the Maritime Hotel. Half crouched, on one knee, bearded and shaky, he appears both on the verge of sprinting and holding up his hands to protect himself from attack. And there's something else — as if he's been caught at something, as if somehow *he* is the guilty party. I haven't seen him since the night at the Carlyle three days ago.

I sprint past him toward the lobby's door. He calls and I don't pause.

From somewhere else I hear: *Billy!*

Billy?

No one calls me Billy — no one but my family, friends from college, and people I grew up with — and I hear the name now as if it's shouted across a dinner table from childhood.

Billy!

It's my little sister, Lisa. I don't see her but know it's her voice. She's twenty-five but already has a voice — smoke-choked and sad-shattered — that should have taken another twenty years to earn. It's the kind of voice that to some sounds like a good time.

I scan the lobby as I move toward the main door, and there they are. My father. Kim. Lisa. My family. My family minus my mother and little brother, Sean. I can't believe they're here. My father would have had to come down from the hills of New Hampshire where he lives alone; my sister, Kim, from her husband and twin boys in Maine; Lisa from Boston.

I slow for a moment to make sure that the little man in the bright blue Windbreaker and gray New Balance running shoes, standing in the chic, dimly lit lobby of the Maritime Hotel, is actually my father. He has never once, in the twelve years I've lived in New York, stood on the island of Manhattan. He has never once seen where I've lived or the offices where I've worked. And, until now, he's never met Noah. I wonder if I am hallucinating.

Willie, c'mon, the man stammers in a tight Boston accent.

It's him. Looking like J. D. Salinger hauled out of rural seclusion and dropped into a big-city setting that could not appear less comfortable.

I can't get out of there fast enough. As I reach the door, Lisa grabs at my jacket. I can smell her perfume and cigarette smoke as I shake her off and run toward Ninth Avenue. She follows fast behind, screaming at me to come back. A cab jerks up to the curb. I get in and yell, *Go!* which, thank God, it does. The sun blazes off the chrome and glass of oncoming traffic and I have to squint to see Lisa run into the street, hail a cab that barely stops as she yanks the door open and jumps in.

As I shout to the driver not to let the cab behind us follow, I cringe in shame at how cartoonishly awful the situation has become. Like so many other moments, this one feels lifted from an after-school special or *Bright Lights, Big City.* The cabdriver plays his part—rolls his eyes, drives on. Through the rear window, I can see my family and Noah scatter onto the street. It is midday in the city and the world rushes on around them. I am struck by how small they are, this is. How swiftly these unseen little urban dramas are done and gone. Doors click shut, motors roar, taxis squeal away, people disperse. Through the window, I watch them recede to dots. Light flashes from everything and I can barely see.

In the Clear

After three years in remission, my mother's breast cancer has returned. The literary agency Kate and I have started has been open for a few months and we finally have phone lines. I am determined to have a 212 area code and, against the advice of several friends, pick ATT as our carrier because it is the only one that won't saddle us with a 646 or, worse, 347 prefix. This matters to me. Many delays and snafus follow, and I come to find out that Verizon controls the equipment in Manhattan, and ATT is their client, so the glitch in our line has to be dealt with through Verizon but mediated by an ATT troubleshooter in Florida. These phone calls take hours each day. At several points during the first weeks of doing business on cell phones, it is made clear that we can easily have phone service if we just give up and go with Verizon. I refuse, again and again, and hold out for the 212 area code. I even instruct the printer to go ahead and print all the stationery before it's clear we'll be able to use those beautiful 212 numbers ATT assigned us months ago.

During this time I sell more books than I had expected to; with Kate's help, staff the agency with assistants and a foreign-rights director; show up for lunches with publishers and authors; and talk to my sister and mother several times a day. My mother is going to a breast cancer clinic in Boston, driving three hours each way from Connecticut to see a doctor who has laid out a course of treatment. After a few weeks it is decided that she will have a double-radical mastectomy and, on the same day, reconstructive surgery. It means she will be in the operating room for eight or nine hours, but she won't have to go back under if all goes well.

I have started seeing a therapist. This one is not the first. The first one was five years before, a balding, wiry man near Gramercy Park named Dr. Dave. Dave is the guy I see when I am twenty-five and still living with Nell, when the once faint, unobtrusive recognition of male beauty begins to bully its way into something more urgent. At that point, my sexual history with men amounts to a urinal skirmish in a train station bathroom in college and a few makeout sessions with an oncology resident who lives near my first apartment in New York. I chalk these up to curiosity and push them from my mind. But toward the end of my relationship with Nell, before meeting Noah, I become preoccupied with men— their bodies, their voices, their smell. I begin trying to remember what it was like kissing Ron, the oncologist, and am only able to recall the thrill of stubble against my face and the smell of his clean, pressed shirts. I call a phone line a few times, advertised in *The Village Voice* for men cruising for sex, and when Nell is away I meet up with a few of them. Nothing will be as exciting as I remember those first moments with Ron, but I am still drawn back to that phone line — listening to what I imagine as lonely, desolate men trawling the night for sex. I think if I go to a shrink and talk it through, I can make that need, that new urgency, go away, or at least recede to a place where I won't need to act on it.

Without going into the reasons, I ask my boss and several friends for names of therapists and psychiatrists. I see five or six, two of them twice, and finally decide on Dr. Dave. He's $175 an hour — down from his usual $250 because I don't make much money — and he wants to see me twice a week. It takes three or four sessions of examining my attraction to men before we get to my boyhood friends — Kenny, Adam, Michael — and whether or not I had sexual feelings for them. I don't think so, and he presses for memories of seeing their penises and whether or not they saw mine. At one point I say, matter-of-factly, that no one would have seen my penis. When Dr. Dave reminds me that I described seeing Michael's several times as we fly-fished on the Housatonic River, I say, again matter-of-factly, that I never peed in the river but instead always went to shore and into the woods.

Why? he asks.

I don't know, I answer.

Were you ashamed or embarrassed by your penis? he continues.

No, I don't think so.

Then, why?

Why? he repeats.

And then. There I am. Eleven or twelve. In the woods, behind some tangle of branches, thrashing and jumping and manhandling my dick as if it's on fire and I'm trying to put it out. And with that one memory, all at once a million memories. I don't believe them at first, but there is some physical sensation, some old bodily recognition, then and after, that keeps me from dismissing them as crossed wires in my mind.

Dr. Dave and I spend a year and a half remembering all of it — the nurse's bathroom, the blood-spotted underwear, my father. We spend a lot of time on him. What he said, how he said it, how it made me feel. All that. And then, after I meet Noah and we move in together six months later, I grow weary of reoccupying my boyhood struggles and stop seeing Dr. Dave. One day I just don't go. He leaves a few messages, but I pay his bill and don't return his call. I don't say anything about what I remembered to anyone, and after a while I begin again to wonder if I had made it all up. Eventually it recedes and, for the most part, fades from my thoughts.

Now, three years later, I'm thirty years old, and I have left the job I've been in for seven years, the only job I've had in New York, to start an agency with a friend. I have met Noah by now—on a night when Nell is out of town and I call one of those phone lines. He walks into the entryway of my apartment and without speaking we kiss. We talk all night. He is manly but silly, too, and warm, and I tell him I am a year younger than I am, that I went to Harvard, and that my father grew up on Marlborough Street in Boston. I correct the first two lies before morning but leave the last one untouched. It will be my father, years later, when they meet for the first and last time, who will tell Noah that he grew up in Dedham, Mass., a middle-class bedroom town just outside Boston.

We tell everyone that we met at a birthday party in Brooklyn for a client of mine who is an old schoolmate of Noah's. This is the first secret we keep together.

I drink too much, and I can't keep from dialing dealers and staying out until all hours. I'm a crack addict, I know this, Noah knows this, but to everyone else I am a dependable, decent guy with a promising new company and a great boyfriend. We live in a beautiful apartment that Noah's grandmother paid cash for, and we've filled it with vintage photographs and furniture and expensive Persian rugs. From a distance, it looks like an enviable life. Up close, it's partly what it looks like: I'm in love with Noah, but beyond the drug-related infidelities, I've had two affairs—one with a man and another with a woman. It is my firm belief that he has been faithful to me throughout the relationship. We're proud of the apartment, the things we've carefully arranged there, but we both call it One Fifth instead of home.

It feels as if each week, there is some lunch or some dinner or some phone call that is going to blow my cover, reveal that I am not nearly as bright or well read or business savvy or connected as I think people imagine me to be. My bank account is always empty, and when I look at the ledgers at the agency, I wonder how we will pay our employees, the rent, the phone bill, without Kate writing another check to float us. Noah is covering my expenses at home, but we are keeping a tally so that I will pay him back once the money from commissions starts coming into the agency. I remember the lines from a Merwin poem I used to read to Nell all the time, *I have been a poor man living in a rich man's house,* and cringe each time. I often wish it all felt the way it looked, that I could actually be living the life everyone thinks they see. But it feels like a rigged show, one loose cable away from collapse.

Noah is making trips to L.A. and Memphis to rustle up producers and cast and money for the film he has been working on for years. When he is away, I call Rico or Happy or go see Julio, a guy I meet through another guy I met at Fitz's place on the second and last time I went there. This guy, a twenty-year-old Hispanic kid with gray teeth, will invite me to Julio's, and I will end up going there for years. People come to Julio's and he lets them do drugs and have sex, as long as they share both. These nights were once few and far between— every two or three months—but now they are every other week, and while they would once end around one, they are now creeping closer and closer toward dawn.

After another rough morning, after Noah has begged me to get help, I agree to see a psychiatrist who specializes in addiction issues. We get a name from a college friend of Noah's and I go. His office is in his very large, very elegant Riverside Drive apartment. It's a short meeting. He asks why I'm there. I tell him about my drug use and how I want to stop but can't seem to and he asks about my drinking. *My drinking?* I ask, as if he's suddenly mentioned the weather in Peru or the price of IBM stock. He says I need to stop drinking before he will agree to see me and I politely excuse myself and leave.

Half a year later, after another string of bad nights, there is another name, another therapist, recommended by some other friend. This one is different, calls himself a Harm Reduction Counselor, which is another way of saying someone who helps you plan your alcohol and drug use, to get it under control. I go to this person once. He is a very attractive man in his early forties with a chic apartment-like office in Chelsea. We make an elaborate plan—this number of drinks a night, that number of times I will smoke crack a month— and I'm excited that my drinking and drug use are now doctor approved. Within a week I exceed the limits we've established and then miss the second appointment because of staying up all night the night before. I never return.

Months later: another rough morning, another name from a friend of Noah's. This time it's Gary, and he's gentle and sweet and his office is a few blocks from the agency. Gary asks why I have come to see him and I tell him. He pokes around about the childhood stuff, we talk about the peeing, the hard father, the frightened mother. How they met when he was a pilot for TWA and she was a young, pretty stewardess. When we get to the part about my father, he asks what my mother said at the dinner table when things got rough. I describe how cruel he was to her, how poor she was growing up in Youngstown, how much younger she is than my father, how her own father died when she was a teenager. He says, *Fine fine fine, but what did she say? Where was she?*

Amazing, the power of three words. These will open up such a can of worms. I will sit there and think about all the sessions with Dr. Dave, when I went through, blow by blow, how my father was during that time—how he sounded, what he said—and realize that we never talked about her. Not once. *She was one of us,* I think, and maybe even say. He was awful to her. Criticized her cooking, her clothes, her intelligence, her interests, her friends. Just as he did with me and with Kim and, to a lesser extent, Lisa and Sean. But I can't remember my mother beyond this shared circumstance. Can't remember her saying anything to me about my problem. Acknowledging it, even. Can't remember a word of comfort or concern about any of it. Broken legs, yes. Mean teachers, you bet.

But this, never. Nor can I even see her at those dinner tables when guests were over, when my father would get tipsy and begin his taunting and threatening. It's as if that whole corridor of my growing up held only me and my father, and while it happened in the same rooms, with everyone else, no one else saw or heard what was going on. I suddenly feel very tired.

About six months later my mother calls to say that her mammogram has come back with bad news, that her cancer has returned and she's going to Boston for more tests. I have called her only rarely over the past months. The sessions with Gary are like removing all the photographs of my mother from the family album and replacing them with someone who resembles her but is clearly someone else, someone I am only now beginning to see. She has been confused and hurt by my spare contact, as we used to speak several times a week. She complains to Kim, and Kim asks me what's going on. I tell her it's been incredibly busy at work.

After the call about the bad mammogram, I am in touch more. It takes a few weeks, but the seriousness of what's going on sinks in. Soon she is scheduled for surgery and the doctors tell us that it's a long shot that they'll be able to remove all of the cancer, and, if they do, an even longer shot that it won't return, even after an aggressive course of chemotherapy.

Kim and I go over our mother's finances. There are piles of credit-card bills, and she's still digging out from the mountain of legal fees that came with divorcing my father a few years before. It has been a long and messy divorce, and at one point she asks me to fly up to New Hampshire, where they are living, to testify in court on her behalf—to uphold a restraining order against my father. I fly up, though before I do, the judge says I don't have to, that he will uphold the restraining order without my testimony. I'm relieved but still feel ashamed as I see my father, briefly and without words, in the lobby of the courthouse.

Insurance is covering most of my mother's treatment, but there are ancillary bills adding up and she hasn't been able to paint any of the murals or portraits she's been commissioned to paint, which is how she supports herself; nor will she be able to for a long time after the surgery. We talk seriously about what our roles will need to be, financially, and I pretend I am not worried and that money has begun to flow into the agency. My family thinks of me as a success, and I don't want to tarnish that image. Kim tells me that our mother has decided I should be executor of her will and that papers to that effect will need to be signed. *She may not make it,* Kim says, and the words just hang there.

This is the spring of 2001. My mother's surgery is in May, and I fly to Boston. Kim has been there all week with my little sister, Lisa, who lives nearby. Sean is now nineteen and sullenly haunts the halls and rooms around the hospital. The surgery is successful and when we're allowed to go in and see her, our mother appears half her usual size and weight—withered and weak and swimming in the hospital gown that falls off her shoulders. I have not seen her for months, and as she speaks, her eyes tear and it seems that her words are too difficult to craft and propel into the world. When I go to the hall and call Noah, I break down and start cying, out of control and awkwardly. Everything—the business, the late nights, the worry about money, the feeling of not being able to live this life I've constructed—seems overwhelming, and now suddenly my mother, whom I haven't spoken to for more than a few minutes at a time over the last six months and who looks like she's dying and I've messed it all up and won't be able to make it right. Through the shaky phone line Noah tells me not to worry, that everything will be okay. I eventually stop sobbing, and as we say good-bye it feels as if he is very far away.

We sit in the hospital room with my mother while she sleeps and whisper as the nurses come in and out and fuss with the tubes and charts around her. Her surgeon, a tall, dark-haired man in his forties with a heavy five-o'clock shadow, comes in and tells us that there were complications with the reconstruction and that they may have to go back in in a few days, but the surgery to remove the cancer and the lymph nodes went very well. I think about the fact that this guy stood over my mother all day and had her life in his hands. My job, the agency, and all my worries shrivel next to this superhero and, not for the first time that day, I feel ashamed.

The day in the hospital ticks by, and at some point, there is a rustle at the door and, miraculously, it's Noah, smiling, holding bags filled with food from Dean & Deluca. After our phone call he booked a flight and came as soon as he could. It feels as if the floor

BILL CLEGG

of the world that had fallen away when I walked into the hospital has suddenly returned. Noah hugs me and I hang on to him for as long as I can.

My mother will move back to her small new house in Connecticut, the one she bought after her divorce, which sits in a field in a small town next to the small town where I grew up. Her many friends will drive her to her chemo and radiation treatments, back and forth to Boston when she needs to see her doctors there, bring her meals round the clock for months, and feed her dog, and slowly, very slowly, she will transform from the pale, bruised waif we saw in the hospital bed back to her cherubic, healthy self. Her hair will return, thinner than before, but when five years pass and she is, as the doctors say, *in the clear,* you will not be able to tell how close she came to death. She and I will see each other and speak often in the first year of her recovery. My mother blameless and wounded is someone I am comfortable with, and the way we are with each other resembles the way we were when I was an adolescent and even after—attentive, sympathetic, encouraging. But as she gets healthier and returns to her life, I will call less and less, limit my visits to Christmas, and, as before, drift away.

Where

Men's Room at the White Plains Metro-North station (rushed hands, crossing from zipper to zipper at the urinal, and then, quickly, into the stall, a rushed mouth on me until it is suddenly, for the first time with a man, over).

Ron's dorm, three blocks away from my first apartment in New York, twice.

On the phone, in the dark. Nell away. All those voices, all that want.

Apartment high above downtown, after a long night of drinking and dancing and pot, with a writer who is represented by my boss, and his boyfriend. Blurry bodies and a hasty retreat before they wake. The snow falling for the first time that winter.

Steam room at the gym on 57th Street. Middle-aged men. Scared, serious, wedding rings foggy and dull on their fingers.

Bathroom on a Metro-North train. A beautiful young man, older than I am but no more than twenty-five, who had been sitting across the aisle and who motions for me to follow as he walks to the end of the car. Kissing. Just kissing and kind hands palming my face and temples. *It will all be okay,* he whispers as he slides the door open and disappears into another car. How did he know I didn't think it would be?

Love

So, out of order, a memory. It's my fourth night at 60 Thompson. My fourth night back in the city after checking in and out of Silver Hill and hiding out in the Courtyard Marriott in Norwalk, Connecticut. I have phoned an escort, let's call him Carlos. Carlos is dark, Brazilian, in his forties, and he's been here before, once, the night I checked in. He is quiet, muscular, and a few inches taller than I am. He costs $400 an hour. I know he has a day job, he's going to night school for a business degree of some kind, and that he's from São Paulo. He's on his way. Happy was just here, so I have plenty of drugs. My phone rings and I can see the number calling in is Noah's. He must be back from Berlin. Without thinking, and overcome by the sudden need to hear his voice, I pick up. His tone is gentle, and I end up telling him where I am and that he can come up, for a little while. I have no idea what will happen, but my need to see him overwhelms my fear of being caught and dragged home. Within minutes he's at the door. I look at him through the peephole but his image is warped and, beyond his clothes, he's unrecognizable. I stand on the other side of the door for a while and watch him before I turn the lock. When I let him in, I notice that his beard is heavier than I've ever seen it and he looks thin. I want to run into his arms, but I feel cautious and hold back. He hesitates, too, and we circle each other warily. I've hidden the drugs, my wallet, and my passport in the bathroom under a pile of towels, in case he tries to take them from me. He starts smoking a cigarette and, even in this space, even now, I make a face and say, *Really?* He ignores me and talks about checking out of the hotel, coming with him, going to rehab. I get angry and tell him I will leave the hotel but not go with him. I'll disappear somewhere else, and the next time I won't pick up the phone when he calls. Twenty or so minutes pass and I'm aware of two things: (1) I haven't taken a hit since just before Noah arrived and I need to, and (2) Carlos will be here at any moment. I tell Noah he has to go and that if he doesn't, I will. He says he won't and I begin going through the exaggerated motions of preparing to leave — putting on my shoes, gathering up my jacket — and he tells me to stop. Time is ticking and whatever high I had before has long since passed and I begin to plummet into a jittery funk. I tell Noah he can stay for a few more minutes but that I need to take a hit. He can stay while I do it or he can leave. He says, *Fine, take a hit.* And so I do. I go to the bathroom, close the door, and pull the pipe and bag from under the towels. I load the hit into the stem before leaving the bathroom, and instead of leaving the drugs behind, I stick them in the front pocket of my jeans. I return to the room, sit on the edge of the bed and ask, *You sure you can handle this?* He says he can. I face Noah directly as I light up and draw as much smoke as I can into my lungs. When I exhale I catch his eye, and though

I see how grim his face appears, I can't tell what he's feeling. The high crashing through my system bullies aside his feelings and any normal response I might have to them. I regard him as someone on a departing train would a stranger on a platform. Curious, faintly connected by met gazes, but essentially indifferent. Noah recedes from view and as he does, I tell him about Carlos. I expect him to explode or yell but he stays calm and says, *Fine. I'll stay. If you won't call him and tell him not to show up, I will stay. Don't worry, I'll be fine.* I hear the words as if from across a vast field or a thick pane of glass and say, because it feels this way, *Fine.*

Carlos arrives. He looks at Noah, turns to me, and asks, *Is he staying?* I say, *Yes, for a while.* They eye each other and Carlos sits down on the bed. I smoke a hit. Noah sits in a chair by the draped window. I smoke another. Noah is silent. Carlos motions for me to come sit on the bed and, with pipe and bag and lighter in hand, I do. I pour another vodka and ask him if he'd like anything. He wants a beer, so I grab one from the minibar, open it, and hand it to him. He takes a long pull and takes off his shirt. He is dark and his skin is flawless, and I watch him remove his watch and begin to unlace his shoes. I pack a hit and by the time I exhale I have nearly forgotten about Noah sitting less than three feet from the bed. Carlos and I kiss. He smells like Old Spice and tobacco, a particular mix of smells I associate with my father. We roll around on the bed, and before long I need another hit and a few big swigs of vodka. I load up my stem again and inhale a large hit and turn around toward Noah as I exhale. I try to read his face and don't find anger or disgust or pain. What I see, or at least I think I do, is compassion. As I step to the bar to pour another drink, I ask him if he's had enough and he says,

No, I'm fine. I want to go to him, be with him, and for the first time resent Carlos for being here. I drink and smoke more before return-ing to the bed and by now my body is alive with desire—roaring, indiscriminate, hungry. Carlos and I are soon completely naked, and when he is on top of me, I turn to Noah and motion to him to come over to the bed. He does and lies down next to me. Carlos and I con-tinue to go at it, and at some point I realize that Noah is holding my hand. I turn to him and his eyes are wet. He caresses my hand and arm and says, *This is okay, you're okay, don't worry, this is okay.* His words, his caressing hand, Carlos on top of me, the drugs and vodka roaring through me—shame, pleasure, care, and approval collide and the worst of the worst no longer seems so bad. One of the most horrible things I can imagine—having sex, high on drugs, in front of Noah—has been reduced to something human, a pain that can be soothed, a monstrous act that can be known and forgiven. *You're okay,* Noah reassures me with his soft voice and gentle strokes, and for a few long moments, I am.

Carlos eventually leaves and Noah and I sit across from each other in chairs by the window. He tells me not to be ashamed of what happened, that I'm not the only one who has messed up in our relationship, that he has, too. He tells me how but I don't believe him. He tells me some of the details but I dismiss them, thinking he's just trying to comfort me.

I tell Noah he has to leave and promise to call him later. He agrees. But I won't call. I'll pack up my things, check out of the hotel, and go to another. I won't remember Noah's visit for a long time. And when I do, every last inch of me will burn with shame. Later still, I will finally be able to look beyond the shame and see how for those few hours, he remained with me, held my hand behind that hotel room door, and told me I was okay. That he loved me. And I will remember how convinced I was that night—as I had been every night with him before—that knowing what he knew, seeing what he'd seen, putting up with what he chose to put up with, he was the only one who ever could. The question I never asked was why.

Blackout

It is the summer of 2003, and through a series of extraordinary mis-
calculations and mishaps by the power company, New York City has
lost electricity. Manhattan is dead and powerless on one of the hottest
days of the year. I am walking down lower Fifth Avenue in a sea of
bewildered office workers, shoppers, and students. My head is heavy
and the late morning sun shines too brightly from the city windows
and the chrome of gridlocked cars. I didn't sleep the night before. I
was up until dawn smoking crack and came home to find all the lights
on in the apartment. Under the mirror, on the bar in the foyer, I find
a note scribbled on the back of an envelope: *3:01am, Can't take this.*
Noah has recently started checking into hotels when I don't come
home. Mostly he ends up at the Sheraton on Park Avenue South.

After a few useless hungover hours at the office, the power quits,
the building goes dark, and I leave for home. As I make my way

into the crowded street, I think this will be the last day like this. No more nights without sleep, no more Noah checking into hotels. All the gritty details from the night before flash through my mind as they always do. Something about crack, for me at least, will always heighten memory instead of erase it. I will never wake the next morning and forget what I did the night before.

I am barely aware of the mounting crisis of the blackout around me—I'm much more concerned with how to appear rested and loving when I see Noah. As the frantic pedestrians shuffle in herds through the middle of Fifth Avenue, I worry how I will persuade him that this day marks the end of the lost nights, of which there have been too many to count. I believe this. Even though the memory of every morning like this over the last three years—and the memory of believing each one was the last—sits like a toad in the path of my new plan, I still believe, again, that this time will be different. That the old tenacious pattern will be broken.

I know that if the power returns before evening, we'll go to the Knickerbocker. I won't drink. Or I will drink, but only wine. Just one. Or probably two. Talk of the power failure and ensuing chaos will distract us from the horror of the night before. I'll threaten to leave when the conversation drifts to *What can we do about this?* or *You've got to get help.* After a few beats of hard silence we'll talk about the waitress with cancer, how brave she is, how hard she works, how cool the clothes she sews and wears to work are. I'll watch her shoulder through the thick bar crowd with heaping trays of steaks and drinks and wonder if ordering a third glass of wine will provoke Noah into more talk of rehab, outpatient services he's researched, AA. I'll be thinking about just exactly how much I can get away with drinking right now without causing a fuss as the waitress brings us our burgers and fries. This will be the only thing on my mind — *one more* — as she describes the chemotherapy and the exhaustion and the sour stomach and hair loss. *You're amazing*, I'll say as I tap the glass and nod for another, avoiding Noah's glare on the other side of the table. And in a flurry of possibility I'll say, *Actually, make it a vodka*. I won't look his way as I jump up for the bathroom, wondering whether or not he'll be there when I return. When I do, he will be — he always is — and in tears. His pleading for me to stop drinking and get treatment, and my threatening to leave — the restaurant, his life — will continue. Silence will eventually follow, the busy restaurant buzzing around us, a TV star in the corner with her husband, someone from publishing in the next room, several regulars leaning into their cups at the bar. These are our nights at the Knickerbocker. So many nights. But this night, the night of the blackout, will not be one of them.

In the sea of people swarming the streets, suddenly: Noah. He's walking up Fifth Avenue and he sees me just as I see him. I am with my assistant and the rights director from the agency, which is a comfort because I don't want to be alone with him. I don't need to look at his face to know that he's furious. He barely says hello to them and to me he says, *Let's go*. His grandmother is in her apartment on the seventeenth floor of the Sherry Netherland and we need to go to her. *Now*.

I tell him I'll see him there later, and right in front of my colleagues he says, *No way, come with me now.* I say, *Relax,* and he says he will once I come with him. I say good-bye to my colleagues, and instead of making a scene I start walking back up Fifth toward the Sherry. I walk ahead of him nearly the entire way uptown, from 14th Street to 58th. The city is a mess, and because of the fresh memory of 9/11, there is a sense of something bigger than a power failure going on. Rumors of terrorists blowing up power plants ricochet through the streets. The air is thick with calamity.

As we near the Sherry we find a gourmet food store. The fancy kind that caters to the people living north of 57th and south of 60th between Fifth and Madison. They sell wine and even have a machine that chills it instantly that, because a generator has been hooked up, still works. The store is dark save for a few candles, and the owner's wife stands near the locked door and is careful about who she lets in. Noah puts a bottle of Sancerre on the counter, and I grab three more. I do this in front of the shopkeeper intentionally so that Noah can't object. He just shakes his head slowly and when he pulls for his wallet, I hand him four twenties. We load up on things like roast chicken, crackers, and cheese and make our way around the corner to the Sherry.

The building is mainly residential but also has hotel rooms. There are porters and bellhops and managers all over the lobby as we enter and explain that we are there to see Noah's grandmother, or as everyone calls her, Neeny. They recognize us, and one of them escorts us to the stairs that they have lit, on the landings, with candles. Before heading up the stairwell I stop at the lobby mirror to make myself presentable, hide the sleeplessness and hangover. I pat my hair into place, wipe the sweat from my face and brow, tuck in my shirt. Luckily I have some Visine, so I squirt both bloodshot eyes with the stuff and hope that in the dim light Neeny won't be able to see them, or any of me, too clearly.

The stairwell is muggy and hot, and the light flickers against the green-and-gold wallpaper. In this shimmery dark it feels as if we are underwater, moving in slow motion, safe. I am exhausted, but the muffled footfalls and muggy air are calming. We are lugging sacks of wine and groceries in a gilded tunnel with light dancing on our skin. The dread from before starts to fade, and when Noah turns on the landing to see if I am still behind him, his eyes are shining with candle flames and are kind again.

We drink and eat with Neeny, touch each other on the arm affectionately as we animate stories of our vacation in Paris, Noah's movie, and my job. I imagine what Neeny would think if she knew that I had been smoking crack in a project on the Lower East Side the night before, in an apartment with four bolts and a steel bar across the door frame. I imagine her face falling as someone tells her. I drink more Sancerre, glass after glass, and let the tide of wine muffle the exhaustion and the creeping shame. I watch Noah amuse Neeny, flatter her, gently walk her through the dark apartment to her bedroom after dinner, stroking her back as they go. I watch them and love this part of him, this tender part that is so devoted to, and comfortable with, his family.

We sleep on couches in the living room and leave the next morning. We walk home, and all that day restaurants and bodegas and grocery stores are closed. The city grinds to a halt. People look distraught as they confront the locked doors and hastily scribbled *We're Closed* signs all over town. Later that afternoon, the power magically comes back on. Everyone forgets, almost instantly, how helpless they were. Life returns and all is as it was.

We have dinner at the Knickerbocker that night, and it plays out like all the others. Pleas, threats, silences, tears. When I get up to go to the bathroom, I remember the night before; how, after we ate, I stood at Neeny's window, dizzy from Sancerre and lack of sleep, and looked out over the southeast corner of Central Park to the Plaza Hotel, which was dark, darker than all the other buildings. I remember how silent the city was—no low hum of air-conditioning, no stray voices from televisions and radios. And how deserted the Plaza looked, huddled below, humbled. The city around it weary, spent, as if it had finally given up on its striving citizens, lost interest in the bother of it all.

Shelter

Where? the cabdriver asks me as we speed south, away from Chelsea, away from the Maritime, away from my family. Lisa's taxi is nowhere to be seen, and in only a few blocks I'm not thinking about her, about them, anymore. I'm thinking about where to go next. I have half a bag in my pocket and a burnt stem. I need to get somewhere to smoke. We sail past the Gansevoort, where I know I can never return. Not after the morning three days ago with Noah and the private investigator. And not after—I think, but I'm not sure, I can't remember exactly—leaving scrapers and ashtrays caked with drug residue in the room, maybe even a stem. I'm usually hypercareful. Usually I wipe everything down meticulously, repeatedly, so that no one who comes into the room to clean will ever know what has gone on. But we left in such a hurry and I was wild with panic from the stories of the police coming to One Fifth looking for me and DEA investigations. I picture the managers at the Gansevoort and the Maritime combing the rooms with police officers and DEA agents — fingerprinting the vodka glasses and television remote controls, collecting flecks of drugs from the carpet to test in a lab, fishing ATM receipts from the trash cans and calling Chase to get all my details. Nowhere seems safe. Whatever anonymity I enjoyed before now feels like it has disappeared. Noah and the private investigator can find me anywhere. I turn my cell phone off. Didn't Brian say something about how they could track me by my cell phone signal? I'll use pay phones to call Happy. I'll tell him my cell is busted.

I finger the tiny plastic bag in my jeans pocket and trace the shapes of the few medium-size rocks it contains. Where can I go? Where? I need to get somewhere safe, and nowhere is. The cabdriver asks me again where I'm going, and I tell him to go east. East of Fifth, somewhere near Houston. East seems like a frontier. An unexplored country worlds away from the West Village and Chelsea where I have been the last few weeks. As we cross down onto Houston and barrel east, I feel like I am crossing out of a ruined country into a fresh new world. I've been here a million times and yet nothing seems familiar. The buildings, signs, restaurants, and even the people seem generic, implausible, somehow unconvincing as New Yorkers, as New York. Like a film shot in Toronto attempting to mimic Manhattan.

I ask the cabdriver to pull over at Houston and Lafayette. I notice the meter has not been turned on. I also notice that the driver's photo has been covered with a strip of cardboard, but even so, I can make out a name, Singh or something like that, something

Indian or Pakistani. The driver is black and definitely not Indian. I start to panic and fish a ten from my jacket and stick it through the small Plexiglas window. The black, non-Indian, meter-neglecting cabdriver laughs as I scramble out the door.

Where am I going? There is only $9,000 and change in my bank account and the end is in sight. I think through the list of hotels I've been in—Gansevoort, 60 Thompson, Washington Square, W, Maritime. I need someplace new and decide to try the Mercer Hotel. It's the closest and I imagine a clean, serene room with extraordinary soaps and a powerful shower that will wash away the gritty ordeals of the last few days. Maybe this will be the last one.

I walk into the chic, quiet lobby and approach the front desk. I ask a young woman if there is a room and she asks me to wait a moment. She returns a minute or two later with a man, someone in his late thirties or early forties, with glasses. He immediately says, *I'm sorry but there is nothing here for you.* I ask him if there is nothing or if there is just nothing for me. He answers, *I think you heard me,* with a hostile expression. The woman looks embarrassed and will not meet my eye. It takes a few beats for me to fully take in what is happening. It must be clear that I am strung out. I realize I haven't looked at myself in a mirror since leaving my room at the Maritime. Are my eyes bloodshot? Do I smell of smoke and alcohol? I can't remember if I showered this morning. My face prickles with shame and I leave without saying a word.

Out on Mercer Street I'm terrified. I have somehow, without seeing it happen, tripped over some boundary, from the place where one can't tell that I'm a crack addict to the place where it is sufficiently obvious to turn me away. I look at my hands to see if they are shaking. Suddenly, for the first time, I feel as if I might look and act and sound in a way that I am not able to see. Like body odor or bad breath that is only detectable to other people, my movements and my whole bearing could be invisible to me. I try to figure out if people are staring. If they are registering disgust as they walk past. My pants feel very loose. It's been over a week since I've had a new hole punched in my belt, and my navy turtleneck hangs stretched and baggy off my frame and must, it just must, reek. Though I have been doing drugs, drinking liters of vodka a day, not sleeping, and running from hotel to hotel for a month, it dawns on me like a great shock that I might actually look like a junkie. I feel that whatever capacity I'd once had to move through the world undetected has vanished, that *CRACK ADDICT* is written on my forehead in ash, and everyone can see.

I am nowhere and belong nowhere. I can now see how it all happens — the gradual slide down, the arrival at each new unthinkable place — the crack den, the rehab, the jail, the street, the homeless shelter, a quick shock and then a new reality that one adjusts to. Am I now in the purgatory between citizen and nobody, between fine young man and bum?

I start walking. It's late morning and the streets are full. They are full, but somehow it seems that a path is being made for me. As if people are stepping aside, avoiding me. Not wanting to brush up against me. Can they ALL see? Is it THAT obvious? Is there blood on my face? I need to get to a mirror. I see a dingy-looking bar somewhere north of Houston. It's open and I head straight for the bathroom. I lock the door and my hands fly to the bag and stem and lighter and furiously pack a hit. I avoid the mirror, because if there is something hideous there I don't want to see it yet, not before taking a blast. I turn the water on to hide the sound of the lighter. I pack nearly half of what's in the bag into the stem and take a giant hit. I pull what feels like a galaxy of smoke into my lungs and hold it there until I choke for air. The room becomes a billowing white cloud, a sauna of crack smoke, and luckily there is a small window above the sink that I immediately open. Next to the sink is a mirror, and as the thick smoke snakes out through the window, I look. My eyes appear green and red, and the turtleneck collar of my sweater has what looks like white paste on it. The sweater and jacket seem three sizes too big, and there is snot dried and packed below my left nostril. Weeks of beard growth have grown in black, with flecks of silver and blond and red. Silver? I see an old man staring back in the mirror: gaunt, shaky, and frightened. Weathered. I take another hard pull of the stem and blow the smoke out the window. I take another. And another. I sit on the toilet and let the drugs dull the horror of the morning, and a low flame of calm begins to rise. Someone finally knocks. I take another quick hit off the stem before I clean off my sweater and face and splash some water on my cheeks. I look in the mirror again and see that I still look pretty rough. But now it seems slightly funny, less dire. The knock comes again and I pack up my stuff, flush the toilet, and head out through the bar to the street without looking left or right.

I see a cab and wave it down. The name of a newish hotel at Park Avenue South and 26th comes to me—the Giraffe—and I tell the cabdriver to go there. *Kinda far,* he says. Or I think he says. *What did you say?* I ask, and he laughs. I repeat the question and he answers, sarcastically, *Glad to take you anywhere you want to go.* The relief of the hits I've just taken fades quickly as we head up Third Avenue. I start wondering if I should get out of the city, but when I think of places like Florida and Boston, I immediately come up against the problem of finding drugs. Also, I can't travel through an airport in the area, certainly not Newark. I imagine photographs of me posted in all of them, and dozens of Penneys swarming the terminals. The cab slows, caught in traffic. As horns sound around us I feel caged and vulnerable. As if the cab could be surrounded at any moment. I throw a twenty into the driver's seat and get out.

The Giraffe is ten blocks away. I begin to monitor my breath and try to impose a sense of ease as I get closer. *Calm,* I repeat to myself. *Calm.* The hotel is empty and smells like ammonia. Everything is very new and much more corporate than I had imagined. It feels wrong. Still, I go up to a guy at the counter and ask for a room. He's cheerful, in his twenties, and says sure. He asks for my I.D. and starts typing away at his keyboard when an older woman joins him behind the desk and says she'll take over. He looks confused and steps aside as she inspects my passport and the screen he had been typing on. *Oh,* she says, *it looks like we're full up.* The young guy begins to say something but stops himself. *Really?* I ask. *Yes,* she says, *we're booked through the rest of the month.* I start to say something but realize there is nothing to say, so I turn around and head through the door, onto the street, where there are two gridlocked corridors of traffic stalled up and down Park Avenue South. If SoHo had seemed a strange landscape, this bustling, steely sliver of the metropolis is utterly other. There is no soft corner, no shadowy sanctuary to hide in. The cold March sun glares everywhere, shines off the cars in traffic, the glass panes showcasing large restaurants with multiple eating levels, the cuff links and briefcase buckles of the perfectly dressed businessmen marching blankly between appointments. I head back to Third Avenue and then south. Again, it seems as if people are clearing a path for me, stepping aside, making way. I remember a dream I had growing up — about a picnic in the woods and an invisible force that magically lifts all the food off the blankets and carries it beyond the tree line. Everyone — my parents, my sister, childhood friends, our neighbors — accepts that the food is gone, but I refuse to let go of a bag of Cheetos. I'm determined not to lose this bag and as I hold on, thrash alone against the unseen hand pulling just as hard to rip it from me, everyone steps away. One by one, they shrink back to the field's perimeter and refuse to come near me. Walking down Third, I shudder at the spooky precision of what the dream forecast. I feel very small and freakishly large at once. Critical and insignificant. At the very center of things and at the farthest edge.

I remember a building, some kind of subsidized housing development on 23rd Street, where I had once seen what I thought were junkies. The memory flashes through me like a strobe of hope. I remember the place was next to a used-furniture store I had gone to, years before, looking for a rug. I pick up my pace and when I hit 23rd Street, head east toward Second. I see the used-furniture shop and then see the building. I can also see—how can I say this?—my kind, everywhere. Shuffling here and there. Leaning against buildings. Arguing into pay phones. They might as well all be dressed in bright orange jumpsuits, they stand out so clearly to me. I exhale and begin to relax. I lean up against the building and let the sun hit my face. The warmth feels wonderful and it's a relief to stop moving. I feel safe for the first time all day.

After a few minutes, I see a guy who apparently has some kind of authority over the scattered flock outside the building. Someone asks for a light, another pats him on the back. He whistles at a middle-aged woman entering the building. By the way she laughs it's clear they know each other. He has a glint of kindness in his eye, but also a toughness. He squats to smoke a cigarette not too far from where I am standing, and I go over to say hi. We talk for a while. He seems to get me. Get what's up without my saying a word. I feel comfortable. Comfortable enough to ask him if there is a place inside where I can hang out. A place I can duck into and crash and be left alone. *It would be worth someone's while,* I add. As I speak, he half smiles, as if he has been expecting every word. After a pause, he says, *I know just the person. And don't worry, no one will bother you.* He says he'll arrange it and quickly disappears into the building. I go to a cash machine at the bodega next door. Twenty or so minutes later he comes out of the building and says, *It's all set, follow me.* I walk in and we go to a desk. They ask to see my passport, and I am given a sign-in sheet where I write my name and the time. My new friend, whose name I don't know, says to the very old man behind the counter that I'm with him and just visiting.

We go up the elevator to a high floor, fifteen or sixteen, and he asks me if all this has been worth his while. I hand him $200 and he smiles and says, *Yes, well, yes, it has.*

We get off the elevator and head down a hall, and for some reason I've not had a jumpy impulse, a nervous second, since entering the building. Even signing in and showing my passport felt perfectly safe. We stop in front of a door and he knocks gently. I can hear a woman's voice on the other side, something thudding to the ground, and a high, squeaky giggle. The door opens and a small black woman stands there, beaming. *Oh, hello, you're the young man Marshall mentioned. C'mon in.* Her accent is tricky—Cajun, southern, something. She tells me her name is Rosie and to sit right down. My new friend, who I now know is named Marshall, excuses himself. The door clicks behind him, and Rosie and I are suddenly all alone in an apartment the size of three refrigerator boxes. I take a seat on a wicker loveseat heaped on either side with boxes and luggage and bags upon bags spilling with string and Styrofoam and towels. There is a familiar smell in the room. Familiar enough that I ask her if she minds if I get high. She says, in that high voice and tricky little accent, *Why, of course I don't mind, so long as you share.*

As we sit down in Rosie's tiny space, I wonder how Marshall knew what she and I had in common. On the surface we couldn't be a less likely pair, but in one way we are the same. We're the Harold and Maude of crack addicts, I think, as she pulls out a green metal box where she stores her stems, scrapers, and lighters. I pull out my bag and off we go, me and Rosie: cleaning our stems, packing hits, getting high.

My bag is soon empty and I ask her if I could have one of my dealers come up, and she says probably not. If I wanted more, I could give her cash and she would just go get some. She makes it sound so easy, so innocent. As if she were just running to get me some aspirin from the corner deli. And so I give her $400 and she shuffles out of the room. By this time the sun has gone down, and aside from the green Christmas lights Rosie has strung up over her stove, I am sitting in the dark. She is gone an hour or more and after I scrape my stem (and hers) and smoke down the last of the residue, I begin, for the first time since I walked up to this building, to worry about something being wrong. The possibilities begin to hatch in the quiet dark of Rosie's den. Has she stolen from me? I wonder, but then I remember I'm in her apartment. Where would she go? She would eventually have to come back here. Or maybe she's been caught scoring and is being dragged back here with a small army of police officers.

I begin to fear that the whole thing is a setup. That Marshall is an undercover cop or a snitch. How else would someone just conveniently have a sweet little old lady crack addict handy to shelter yours truly from the storm?

But Rosie's no snitch. Rosie's been smoking crack under the Christmas lights and showing me her half-finished art projects. At some point I almost leave but the prospect of a big haul of crack on its way is too powerful to abandon. So I close my eyes and wait.

I'm asleep when Rosie unlocks the door. *Ooh, I'm sorry to take so long. It was a little trouble getting so much. But we did and here I am. I think you'll be pleased.* Who is this angel? I think as I wake up. Rosie lights a candle and asks me to hand her my stem. She gives me another new screen and fusses over the stems and the bags like a chemist and finally passes mine back to me with an enormous rock lodged at the end. *Make up for lost time,* she says, and giggles as I draw in a gale of smoke and think, here, here at Rosie's, this is a place I could die.

Rosie talks about New Orleans. She talks about her mother, who was a painter, and all the famous jazz musicians and artists she knew. Her daughters were talented when they were young but they gave it all up. She isn't going to give up, *ever,* and she gestures around us to all the bags of materials she has collected over the years. *You never know what you'll need,* she says, chuckling, *you never know.* Rosie must weigh only eighty pounds. She is no more than five feet tall and her hair, if she has any, is hidden under a faded silver scarf. All her art projects are half to three-quarters finished. *I'll just glue some beads here and it will be just right. All this needs is an old hairnet to fasten around the edges. One of these days I'll paint the unfinished wood on this one.* None of them look like anything, and they are all just one or two little tasks away from being beautiful. Rosie's hands shake violently as she holds each little almost-beautiful nothing up to the light.

After a few hours of smoking and listening (Rosie never asks any questions), I get restless. The room is too small. Rosie never quiets. And I have a little mountain of drugs in my pocket that makes the world seem manageable.

I leave Rosie a few rocks and a hundred dollars, and she pats my forehead as I go and says, *Come back. Don't forget Rosie. Come back.*

I head out through the brightly lit hallway and down the elevator and sign out at the counter. Humming with drugs and shaky from not eating all day, I'm conscious of how ruined I must appear now. Even worse than this morning.

How will I ever be able to check into a hotel in this state, I wonder, as I walk, as slowly and calmly as I can, out onto 23rd Street. It's late in the evening now. People are out, rushing home from dinner, heading to their softly lit apartments, and feeding their cats or dogs or paying their babysitters. Buses squeal down 23rd Street, and guys from karate practice walk together with their uniforms still on and their workout bags slung over their shoulders. My heart pounds hard behind my chest and blood streaks through my veins like electricity. I feel as light as a wafer and my pants won't stay up. I can't use my phone because I'm afraid I'll be tracked down again. There is just over $8,000 left in my account, and I can't fly anywhere, stay anywhere, appear anywhere I am known. I can't just walk into any hotel, because two have already refused me and that was earlier in the day, several bags of crack ago, when I was more presentable. On the corner of 23rd Street and Second Avenue, I am frozen. Where do I go? Every direction is wrong. *Where?*

Just Here

Noah and I are heading out the door for a few weeks of vacation in Cambridge, Mass. I call my friend Robert, whose lymphoma has recently gone into remission, to check in, see how he's doing. He sounds great. His voice is a cross between Truman Capote's and Charles Nelson Reilly's. He is one of the first editors in publishing who called me when I was a young agent and asked me to lunch. He's in his forties, clearly gay, very smart, and wickedly funny. After that lunch we spoke a few times a week about work, authors we had in common, publishing gossip. Robert's references — professional and literary — often went over my head and I would pretend to understand. If he knew, which I'm sure he did, he never let on.

Robert tells me on the phone that he has to head back into the hospital for something having to do with his lungs. *No big deal,* he says, *not to worry.* I startle for a moment and when I ask him again, he reassures me that it's nothing, that it's routine.

We go up to Cambridge. Noah and I read, go to movies at the Brattle, drink lots of coffee, and walk around and look at Harvard and the great houses spread out on all sides of the campus. What we always do. And then one morning one of Robert's colleagues calls to say that he is dead, that he went into the hospital and it turned out he had pneumonia.

I've known Robert for four or five years, see him every two or three months, and we speak on the phone regularly, but I can't say we are close. He is a part of my work life, and a consistently bright part. His battle with lymphoma has gone on, as far as I know, for a few years. He has been, with me anyway, always vague about the details. His treatment had gotten rough for a while, he left work for several months, but the remission seemed strong. He flew to Europe to go to the opera and dove back into publishing. He was back to normal.

I hang up the phone and after a few stunned, still moments, I start sobbing. I cry for days and can't stop. At dinner, during walks around Cambridge, in the shower, at the gym. I cry uncontrollably. The last time I can remember crying was at the hospital with my mother three or four months before. Eventually the tears stop, but the hard fact of never seeing or hearing Robert again plunks down somewhere in my chest and does not leave.

We come back to New York over Labor Day weekend. There is a memorial service for Robert scheduled on September 10 at the University Club. A writer I represent flies to New York from Chicago on the ninth. Robert edited and adored his novel, which is just about to be published. We go to the memorial service and listen to the writers Robert edited tell stories of how brilliantly he edited their work. How well he took care of them. How much fun he was. Their words make me feel alone, lonely. We go to L'acajou and I start drinking right away. Glass after glass, I drink it like water, and my face prickles with the heat of too much alcohol in my blood. I excuse myself to go to the bathroom and call Julio and tell him to call his dealer, that I'm coming over, with cash. Later, after paying the bill, I say my good-byes, get in a cab, run into Julio's building, and pace the elevator as it crawls to his floor.

That night will go by in a flash. I make it home sometime before eight, but after Noah has left for the day. There is no note on the bar. I have a vague memory of a foreign publisher—German? Dutch? I don't remember—who is scheduled to come into the office. I shower and dress and walk up Fifth Avenue to the office, and my head pounds from all the vodka the night before, and the sky is the most extraordinary cloudless blue I have ever seen. North of 14th Street, I see a young editor I know run across Fifth Avenue in a bright white shirt. I wonder why he's running so fast.

When I walk into the agency, everyone is there. A friend calls just then and says that the Twin Towers have been attacked. Almost immediately the office, the people from the other offices on our floor, people calling, are hysterical, and there is an image on CNN .com of one of the towers billowing with smoke. Rumors escalate and the atmosphere is chaotic and frightened. Noah calls. He is crying. He asks if I am okay, does not mention the night before, and says that he is watching the towers from his office window in SoHo. We arrange to meet at the apartment later.

I suddenly remember that the appointment I have is to get my hair cut by Seth. I call to see if he is open. He says to come over. My hair is shaggy, and with my bloodshot eyes and pasty skin, I think it's more obvious than usual that I've been out all night. Getting my hair shampooed and cut can't hurt, I think, as I grab my wallet and head out the door. My assistant asks me where I am going, and when I tell her, *To get my hair cut,* she stares at me, speechless.

As I walk west across 25th Street, a jet flies low enough that the buildings all around me rumble and I crouch on the sidewalk and cover my head with my arms. It will be the only moment of that day that won't feel numb. The rest will be surreal and far away, as if I am watching them on a screen or through a thick lens.

Both towers are still standing when I reach Sixth Avenue. I linger there for a second or two before heading across 22nd Street to Seth's. Everywhere people are quiet. Everywhere people move gently, slowly. They are careful with one another.

Seth's place is empty and we listen to the radio as he washes my hair and slowly cuts it. I wonder if he can tell how polluted I am, how strung out from the night before. Unlike when we engage in our usual chatter of gossip, we barely talk and are silent as the report of the first tower falling comes over the radio. Seth's phone rings but he lets it go on and on until the machine picks up. It takes over an hour for him to cut my hair, and I think it is because he doesn't want to be alone. I am grateful to be here, in this seat, safe.

I leave Seth's and walk back to Sixth Avenue, where a throng of people on the corner are all looking south. Something feels off balance and I have a brief flash of vertigo as I follow their gazes downtown to the now bland tumble of buildings there. The towers have fallen. An hour ago they stood there, on fire, billowing with smoke, and now they are gone. *They were just here,* someone says as I try to locate where exactly in the skyline they used to rise from. But in the cloud of soot and smoke that hangs above the blur of buildings that could be any city now, I can't remember where they once were, what it all looked like. I have already forgotten.

Where

When Noah is away: Home.

When Noah is home: Mark's or Julio's or any satellite thereof. Hotels.

If between home and elsewhere: Back of cabs; bathroom in the lobby of One Fifth; stairwell landing between fifth and sixth floors of One Fifth; video booth at porn store on 14th between Sixth and Seventh and the one at 44th and Eighth, near Orso; bathroom at L'acajou; bathroom at LensCrafters on Fifth Avenue; bathroom at McDonald's on Seventh below 14th Street; desk at my office; bathroom at my office; stairwell of office building; in Central Park behind trees and in bathroom stall by Delacorte Theatre;

Westside Highway under shrubs; in basements of buildings under construction, behind Dumpsters, in Dumpsters, anywhere.

In London: Charlotte Street Hotel, back of hired cars (not black cabs), behind hedges at the top of Highbury Fields.

In Paris: On bench in the Place des Vosges, on bed in brothel; in back of a cab driven by guy who gives you a free bag of hash; in stairwell of apartment building; café bathrooms.

BEAR IN MIND

In transit, let stem cool before shoving it in pocket or it will burn through your pants.

The Jesus Year

This is the year of the most nights out. The most notes left on the bar, the most shattered mornings, the most broken promises to drink only two vodkas at dinner, the most abandoned resolutions to stop calling Rico and Happy and Mark and Julio and anyone else who can lead me to getting high, the most calls to my assistant to say I am sick, the most lies.

It's more than three years after my mother's surgery, a year after she stops chemo, and the year Noah makes his movie in Memphis. The agency is doing well. We're turning a profit, and a number of books that I am selling are not only the subject of heated bidding wars among book publishers but go on to be excerpted in places like *The New Yorker* and reviewed well everywhere, and in one case on the cover of the *New York Times Book Review*. And there will be one, a cherished one, that appears like a winking miracle of enchanted audacity which becomes a finalist for the National Book Award.

Before the nomination, before the publication, there will be a lunch given at La Grenouille, a French restaurant in the East 50s. I ask an acquaintance, an almost-friend, Jean, to come. Jean who never goes to lunch. Jean whom I met in the lobby of the Frankfurter Hof hotel when I was twenty-five and who, for years after, invited me to book parties and other gatherings at her terraced penthouse overlooking the East River. Jean's parties always have a funny mix of staggering accomplishment, fame, wealth, political passion, and genuine strangeness. Sometimes there are small dinners and sometimes seats at benefit tables. But as years pass, there is always a seat at the table. And every time feels like the last. The one where I will say the thing that will correct whatever mistaken illusion she has of me and reveal the fraudulent imbecile that I am.

So I invite Jean to the lunch at La Grenouille. I invite her because the book she wrote about the gritty-fabulous rise and fall of a Wasp princess is a favorite of the author of the Winking Miracle. I invite her because of her literary glamour, because she matters to the author, and because she is also a friend of the author's Legendary Editor. For all these reasons, and because she has invited me to so much, and because when she is around I feel, strange and unlikely as it seems, loved, I ask her to come. Impossibly, she agrees, and I am excited for the rare energy she will bring to the event, the likes of which are organized purely to generate energy to launch whatever new literary rocket into orbit. Months go into getting this lunch together. There is a generous friend of the author's who has agreed to sponsor it, and because of the elegance of the restaurant and the influence of the author's Legendary Editor, and the hustling on everyone's part, there is an unusually august group of literary lights scheduled to attend.

Why do certain things shimmer on the horizon with fairy dust and others not? This lunch, on the calendar for months, sparkles in blue ink every time I open that page to pencil something else in on either side. I flush with excitement when anything associated with it crosses my mind or my desk — the book, Jean, La Grenouille, the Legendary Editor — all of it, folded together into a shiny promise of something blessed.

I need a suit, and in a burst of recklessness I go to Saks and pick out a slim black/navy lightly striped Gucci suit that costs over $3,000. The most money I've ever spent on any one piece of clothing. In it, in the dressing room, I look for a moment like someone I don't recognize. Someone who has dozens of suits, dozens of pairs of shoes to go with them, and money to afford them all. Not recognizing yourself in the mirror is like seeing a photo that someone takes of you at a party and having your jealous eye drawn to the unfettered, attractive, someone-who-belongs-everywhere person gazing through the photograph over an impassable distance between their world and yours; you see that lucky bastard who you imagine has never had an uncomfortable, insecure, unadored moment in his life and you despise his ease instantly. And then you find out it's you. It can't be, you're sure it's not you. But when you see that he has your clothes on and, yes, Jesus, yes, he has the same large ear that sticks out and the other, smaller one that lies flat to his head; when you see that it's you, you think for a second: Is it possible that someone might make the same mistaken assumptions about the you who is not you? It shakes you for a moment and you decide that in some essential way, the person staring back through the photograph is actually someone else. Or rather, he doesn't exist. The angle of the photograph and the lie it achieves are like the suit. So if you're standing in a dressing room, looking in the mirror, and see someone who looks like the person in that photograph, you buy the suit, because if that person can't actually exist, it might as well look as if he does.

Two nights before the lunch, I'm at a dinner. I can't remember which one or with whom but a few things can be counted on. I'm at l'acajou. I drink vodka. The waiters and waitresses top off my glass through the night. A gentle calm spreads into my chest with each glass and, gradually, the symphony of usual worries dies down. As those instruments still, and after the brief patch of ease begins to ebb, other sounds rise up from the pit. Agitated strings. Bullying horns. The pesky, restless want that feels like need. As I talk and listen and eat and laugh, I am waving my conducting wand, commanding the instruments to quiet. But as I wave more, I drink more, and as I drink, the sounds rise, become more insistent, and I excuse myself and go to the bathroom and call a number. This time it's Mark's and I arrange to go to his place after dinner. I worry a moment that the lunch for the author of the Winking Miracle is two days away and I need to be in top shape for that. But it's two whole days, I reason. Even if I stay up most of the night, I'll still have a full twenty-four hours to regain my footing.

I go to Mark's and there is a blur of smoke and flesh and other people, and in the morning, this time, I don't want it to end. The lunch is the next day, but still, somehow, it feels far away. A whole day and night and morning between now and then. It will work out. It always does. But this is the first night that wants to be two. Why this one and not the others? I look at the calendar from that time and it is graffitied with ink. Scribbled notes about lunch meetings, coffee dates, phone dates, drinks dates, trips to London, L.A., Frankfurt. Weddings, birthdays, benefits, plays, operas, book parties, screenings. So much to show up for, so much to camouflage for, to worry over. There is no busier period than that year when I am thirty-two and thirty-three. The sunstruck runup to the Jesus year. Someone—was it Marie?—always joked about thirty-three being the Jesus year—how it marked the end of one life and the beginning of another, the end of youth and the beginning of the undebatable status of adulthood. But I was twenty-four when she turned thirty-three, and adulthood seemed a world away.

Why was that the night that became three? Why did all the things that to anyone else, even to me, looked lucky, enviable, feel like burdens? It was the year I got tired, the year I began to give up. It was when the conducting wand broke and the sounds from the pit overwhelmed the conductor and drowned the hall.

I leave Mark's by midday and check into a small hotel around the corner from the agency. It's a cheap tourist hotel, one step up from a hostel, and I go there because Mark's place is too sloppy, too smoke-charred, too exposed. The jittery paranoia I have seen in most of the crack smokers I have known has, during the last three or four times getting high, started to afflict me. This time it's the most nagging, most persistent, and when I am at Mark's, I find myself at the window, seeing what I think are unmarked police cars parked in front of his building. By morning I need to get out of there. I have Rico's number, and I am pretty sure I can get him to deliver more in the afternoon. And so he does, and I stay up all night, alone and with reruns of the dingy and dated cable-access *Robin Byrd Show,* where rough-around-the-edges go-go boys and girls strip and let Robin perform oral sex on them. When this is over, I leave the station on all night. It runs low-tech ads for 1-900 numbers, with naked and half-naked men and women wooing the camera with talk of raunchy phone sex. The hotel room looks out onto an alley, and I lean out and look up at the panels of light reflected from other hotel rooms. Occasionally there will be a silhouette of a man or woman flickering across the brick, and I imagine a million scenarios. Sometimes a sound—a low crack, a muffled scraping, a window slamming shut—will echo through the alley, and a few times I call out, *Hello.*

Morning comes on fast, and by ten o'clock I realize I need to get home to fetch my suit for the lunch at La Grenouille. Noah has left dozens of messages, and beyond one phone call two nights before, saying I was alive and fine and not to worry, I have not called him. I still have a large bag from the night before and it gives me some comfort as I begin to face the day ahead. I reserve the hotel room again and take a cab to One Fifth to get my suit. Thankfully, Noah is not there, so I grab the suit, black shoes, and socks and haul out of the apartment, back into a cab and to the hotel room. It is noon by now and the lunch is at one. I can't believe I've disappeared for two nights and a full day. Noah must be out of his mind with worry. But as much as I know this, I don't call him, don't track him down to let him know I am okay. I left a message on the voice mail for my assistant at eight a.m. to say that I would be going straight to the lunch, so that base is, for now, covered. But the lunch! Oh, Jesus, how can I go in this shape? I sit on the bed, pack the burnt, oily stem from the night before with a large rock, and inhale. My terror over the lunch, Noah, my office, and everything else vanishes like a flame suddenly cut off from oxygen. I roll up in the bedspread and let the flash of warm lightning race through my system. I lie on the bed for what seems like only a few minutes, but when I sit up again, it is five after one. The lunch. The glittering happy event that has sung its siren call for months has already begun, and I am strung out, unshowered, unshaven, and skinny from not eating. I take another hit and rush into the shower. It is almost two by the time I get out of the hotel and into a cab. After a shave and shower and the suit, I look in the mirror and, God help me, I convince myself that I look good. A little gaunt and shaky, but the suit, not to mention the bag and pipe and lighter I have in the breast pocket, gives me a shred of hope that I will be able to wing my way through the next few hours.

I get there and go straight to the bar and down a huge vodka. The lunch is on the second floor in a private dining room outside of which is a small bathroom. I duck into the gilded little toilet stall and scramble to pack the stem. My hands are shaking, as it's been over twenty minutes since I took my last hit at the hotel and I can barely keep the flame steady. I inhale and hold it until my lungs sting and cough out the smoke. I wash my hands and rinse my mouth with soap to hide the smell and blow on the stem to cool it before wrapping it in toilet paper and putting it in my suit pocket.

The room has a long table, with flowers and bound galleys of the book arranged beautifully. People apparently have just sat down. There has been a sort of mingling with cocktails before the lunch, so luckily I haven't been as obviously absent as I would have been if they had sat down at one o'clock. Jean stands as I walk in the door. *I just got here! I'm so sorry I was late!* she coos. So Jean doesn't even know that I'm late. Another miracle. Somehow I talk to the author, her Legendary Editor, and a few others and sit down at the table, next to Jean, and the event glides on without my help and with no apparent controversy over my lateness. I tell everyone I have the flu and am not feeling well. I make up a story for Jean about some trouble in my family that I had to attend to, and she shivers with genuine concern. I excuse myself twice during the lunch to slam glasses of vodka at the bar downstairs and duck into the toilet to smoke. I say good-bye to everyone around three thirty, wander out onto Fifth Avenue, and when I see a man in his thirties handing out flyers for some discount men's store, I recognize something in him and ask him if he parties. When he says yes, I ask, *With rock?* He flashes a smile and laughs more than says, *Oh boy.*

I won't remember this guy's name, but we become fast friends. We hunt for a cab together to get back to the hotel on 24th Street but can't find one. A van pulls up next to me as it stops for a light, and I ask the guy driving if we can hitch a ride and, amazingly, he says yes. My new pal—who has ditched his flyers in a trash can—giggles in the back of the van and for a moment he's Kenny in the woods with a bottle of Scotch, Max in the cooler setting up lines of coke, Ian wielding a fire extinguisher. I giggle, too, exhilarated to be on the other side of the lunch, on the other side of the line that separates me and my new friend from the rest of the world. The van rattles down Fifth. Drugs in pocket, partner in crime at my side, hotel key in hand, a whole night ahead.

The afternoon and night play out. We don't have sex, though I want to. Rico comes at ten with more, and it is all gone by four in the morning. My pal gets restless and disappears. He asks for $50 for a cab up to Harlem and I give him $40. Alone, I smoke down the few crumbs I'd hidden. Alone, I scrape the broken stem for the last resin and burn the pipe black as charcoal trying to suck the last drop of venom out of it. Alone, I look at the window and wonder if I am high enough up to die if I crawl through and jump into the air shaft. Fourth floor. Not even close.

And then, because there is no other thought or action or crack crumb left to get in the way, I think one thought: Noah. I can't bear it and I pick up the last burnt stem from the ashtray to make sure there is nothing left. I scan the floor to see if there is one last dropped chunk of drug kicked to the carpet's edge, waiting for me to rescue it so that it can rescue me. But there is nothing. Not a thing left but me and the knowledge that I have not called Noah in three days. It's seven in the morning and I'm alone in a hotel room on the other end of a three-day crack binge. I'm in unfamiliar territory, terrified. I feel as if I have been picked up by a tornado and spit out in pieces. Why did I drink so much at L'acajou three nights ago? WHY, oh, Jesus Christ, WHY? I've asked myself the question hundreds of times in the harsh light of hundreds of mornings and, as always, there's no answer. I pick up the mess, gather my few belongings, and walk down Fifth Avenue in the dark, silent morning, toward what I hope is still home.

Noah is not at the apartment when I come in. I call and leave a message to say that I am at the apartment, in bed, and safe. That I am sorry and that this is the last time. That I love him. I crash asleep for what seems like a few minutes but is actually three or four hours. Noah wakes me sometime after morning. He has tears in his eyes and speaks in kinder tones than I could possibly have hoped for. He hugs me as I lie in the bed and pats my back like a child who needs consoling. He looks worried and I know something is not quite right. *There are some people here to see you,* he says, and I know right away that, after all this time, all these nights and mornings, the jig is finally up. *Who?* I ask, and he tells me that my sister Kim, David, and Kate are in the living room. The world stands still. Time stops. I can't believe they know. That they're here. Noah holds my hand and I am grateful for his tenderness. That he is not leaving me. But the horror of what is happening thunders down on me, and I am numb with shock. *Let's go,* he prods. And with his help I put on my bathrobe and shuffle toward the door from the bedroom into the living room. Noah has his hand on my shoulder as I open the door and see them sitting around the coffee table in the sun-flooded living room, looking up, seeing me for the first time.

I don't struggle, not yet. I am quiet and cooperative as each of them, in turn—Kim, Kate, Noah, David—tells me they will support my getting sober but won't support me, won't have anything to do with me, if I continue to use. There are many tears and I feel that I'm underwater and their words seem as if they have to swim a great distance to reach me. There is a car downstairs, tickets purchased to fly to a rehab in Oregon, bags packed, and a bed waiting. The ex-cop or ex–Army Green Beret or ex-gym teacher who stands alongside them with muscles and crossed arms and barks at me in stern tones is someone I instinctively know to erase. I do not look at or speak to or interact with him in any way and I agree to go to the airport as long as he does not come with us. And so we go. Noah, Kate, and I get in the car and go to La Guardia. It is early afternoon, and when we get to the terminal, I say I need food and order a plate of eggs and a bottle of white wine and drink it all and barely touch the food. I drink vodka on the flight to Oregon while Noah and Kate look on silently or sleep.

The place is an hour away from Portland and looks like a small elementary school nestled in the middle of rolling wine country. It does not rain once when I am there, and the sky is a dark, unsullied blue that turns pink toward the end of the day and scarlet at sunset. My roommate is a pill-addicted brain surgeon from Los

Angeles whose gorgeous Swedish girlfriend comes up several
times and takes us on car rides to Portland and to the coast. There
are other guys, too — the retired ambulance driver from Washington State who drank himself into a stupor every night and
who would go weeks without a word to another human being; the
mouthy rich kid from New York who wore gold Adidas track suits
and talked like a mobster; the spooked meth addict from the San
Fernando Valley who lined his basement with aluminum foil to
outsmart the Feds and cops who he just knew were tracking his
every movement. I relate to them all. On the second or third day,
after dozens of pleading phone calls to Noah and Kate and my
sister, each one a failed attempt to get back to New York, I finally
accept the fact that I am in rehab, that I am stuck. Once I stop trying to get home, I am amazed how at ease with these guys I feel,
how much the same, and how exhilarating it is to be honest, about
everything, for the first time. Each night I walk alone in a gentle
field and watch the sky darken and streak with pinks and reds. I
walk in that field and feel scared about returning to New York,
worry what people will think, but after a few weeks begin to feel
hopeful.

I volunteer to stay for an extra week — partly because I want to
demonstrate to Noah and Kate that I have taken this seriously,
but mostly because by the fourth week I am deeply enmeshed in
the community of patients and counselors. I am not in a hurry
to leave this process of letting go of the many secrets that I had
spent a lifetime squirreling away, hanging on to, buckling under
the weight of.

In a group discussion one morning I talk, for the first time since the sessions with Dr. Dave, about my struggle with peeing. After the group, another guy, a banker from San Francisco with four kids, tells me that he wrestled with the same problem as a boy. Two days before I go home, he will sneak off the rehab property, relapse on tequila in a strip club down the road, and be asked to leave.

When I return to New York, my mother calls and wants to see me. I put off getting together for nearly a month and eventually agree to have lunch. On that day she is an hour and a half late. She finally shows up and as we order food, she describes the generations of alcoholism and drug addiction in her family and my father's, and tells me I'm one in a long line. Despite my initial agitation with her for being late, I am surprisingly relaxed with her and feel a little of our old ease return. I ask if I can bring up something from childhood, something that I hadn't talked to anyone in the family about but that I've remembered only recently. She says yes and before I get the word *peeing* out of my mouth, she holds her hand up above the table and shakes her head. I say a few more words, but she is now crying, asking me if I've agreed to have lunch only to tell her what a terrible mother she is. Stunned by her sudden outburst, I say that I only need her to tell me if she remembers anything, to confirm that it happened, because all I have are a pile of chaotic memories shaken to life by a shrink. Through tears she says something that sounds like *I'm not going to talk about that, your father was the one*... The last thing I remember is her asking me if I knew how hard it was for her then, what a nightmare those years were for her. I say yes, that she's been very good at letting us know how hard it was for her, and she leaves the restaurant. I follow her out to the street as she disappears into a cab without a word. I return to the restaurant, settle the bill, and by the time I make my way three blocks north to my office, I lose my wallet, my keys, and my sunglasses.

I start an outpatient program that I never finish, follow the suggestions to stay sober that I was given at rehab and then don't, talk on the phone a few times to my roommate and some of the other guys—the ones who just weeks before felt like family—and then, within the first month at home, lose touch with them all.

I think I have it licked. I throw myself into my job, the agency, the writers I represent, and the storm of work seems like something that I can hide in, that will protect me from temptation. I watch people drink at dinners and parties and, at first, am relieved I don't have to anymore. As months pass, though, I grow resentful. Little fantasies of getting high will start to appear like thought bubbles in cartoons, when I am alone, mainly, and at the end of long workdays, days when I have had little sleep the night before or missed lunch and am light-headed with hunger. In October I find an old crack pipe stuffed in the pocket of a blazer hanging in our bedroom closet. I hide it in various places and circle the thing like a hawk for weeks until I finally scrape it clean of its old residue and take a hit. I feel only the faintest gust of a high, which quickly dies with the panic that I've relapsed. It's over just as it starts, and Noah walks in right after it happens and agrees to tell no one. I hide the stem, bring it to my office, and somehow misplace it. I worry for weeks

that someone there—my assistant, Kate, the cleaning woman—
has found it and is waiting to confront me. No one ever does.

And then, seven months later, just before going to Park City,
Utah, for the Sundance Film Festival, I have a plan to meet Noah
for a sushi dinner at Japonica. On the morning of the day before
that dinner, the thought of getting high bubbles up, but instead of
flicking it away as I usually do, this time I don't and it lingers. And
it lingers long enough for me to ask: Why not? Noah is leaving
tomorrow and I'll have almost two full days in the city alone. I've
been working hard, everything is going well, no one will suspect
a thing. Within seconds I'm on my cell phone, calling Stephen for
the first time in almost a year. We'd stopped using him to bartend
our parties, but despite being advised at rehab to erase all drug-
related numbers from my cell phone, I still have his. He picks up
on the first ring and we make a plan to meet later, on the corner
outside my office building. At six I go downstairs and see him
leaning against the building. He's skinnier than I remembered,
older. I barely say hello, though he seems eager to hang out. I give
him $400 to score and $200 for doing the dirty work and agree
to meet him the next day. As much as I don't want to reconnect
with Stephen, scoring through him somehow feels less wrong. As
long as I don't start up with the dealers again, I reason, if I don't
remember their numbers, this tiny treat will be just a one-time-
only thing, an anomaly, a harmless but needed vacation.

I meet Stephen on the same corner the next day, tingling with
anticipation. This time he's all business. He hands me a small

brown paper bag filled with drugs and stems. I thank him and hurry away, back to my office.

I plan to smoke the bags the next night, after Noah leaves, a day and a half before I join him in Utah for the premiere of his movie. This can work, I think, this will be just a little release, a little nothing, a harmless blowing off of steam. In the swarm of faulty reasoning I still know this will end badly, that it always does, and that I'm loading a gun and pointing it at my temple. But that voice, instead of being a deterrent, becomes part of the persuasion. On the other side of this bag is either a groggy day and a no-harm-done return to life or some kind of apocalypse. Lose nothing or lose everything. And losing everything sounds like a relief.

I return to the office and make some phone calls, say good-bye to my colleagues as they leave, and see that I have two hours before I'm to meet Noah for dinner. Two hours. Just one hit now would wear off before then. Why not? I get up from my desk and lock the office door. I find a lighter in my assistant's desk drawer, sit down at my desk, take the drugs from my jacket pocket, and hold the two little baggies in my hand. I pull out the clean, clear stem — so much lighter than I remembered. It feels like a dream as I split off a little creamy chunk of crack and load it into the end of the stem. It doesn't seem as if it's actually happening when I spark the lighter and move the flame toward the pipe. It doesn't feel the least bit wrong in those first seconds after exhaling the familiar smoke, no more than a reunion with an old friend, a returning to the most incredible conversation I've ever had, one that got interrupted seven months ago and, now that it's started up again, hasn't skipped a beat. But it's more than just a conversation, it's the best sex, the most delicious meal, the most engrossing book—it's like returning to all of these at once, coming home, and the primary feeling I have as I collapse back into my desk chair and watch the smoke roll through my office is: *Why on earth did I ever leave?*

I sit at my desk for three hours, smoking down one of the bags, and finally race out, suddenly panicked, to Japonica, to Noah, whom I was supposed to meet an hour ago. I run into the restaurant and see him sitting at a table, his back to the wall, clearly worried, and when he sees me, he goes white and begins weeping. I remember his weeping. I lie to him and say I got caught on a phone call at work, that I didn't hear him ringing my cell or the landline at the office, and that it's all okay, don't worry, stop crying. He sleeps on the couch that night and leaves quietly in the morning, asking only one thing: Will I make it to Sundance? And I say, yes, yes, of course. I promise.

And I do make it. But I stay only one night, the night of his premiere and the party after with his friends and producers and family. I smile and nod and engage and play the part of a supportive boyfriend. But I'm fixated on the little zip-lock bag wrapped in tissue nestled in the pocket of my navy blazer hanging in the bedroom closet at One Fifth. I imagine the clear glass stem resting next to that bag, and the lighter on the dresser nearby. I picture these things every second I'm in Utah. From the moment I get there I need to leave. From the second I leave New York I need to return, to get back to that conversation, the one that just started up again; and now that it has, nothing but death can keep me from it.

Last Door

I need a new sweater. I need to clean up before I try to check into another hotel. It is evening but some stores may still be open. I get in a cab and ask the driver to go to SoHo. He hums as he drives and I can't bear looking to see if his license photo is obscured by cardboard or paper or just not there, like all the others. *Here okay?* he asks, as he pulls to the corner of Houston and Wooster. I shove $10 in the money slot and don't bother looking at the fare.

The stores south of Houston look like Christmas. Extraordinary displays—animated, art-directed, intelligently lit—beckon and intimidate from the windows along Wooster. I remember, as a kid, coming into the city with my fourth- or fifth-grade class to see the Radio City Music Hall Christmas show. The streets in midtown were jammed with tourists and city people, and they were lined up by the hundreds to see the decorated windows of Saks Fifth

Avenue and Lord & Taylor. I remember being confused about why the windows were important to see but also excited that I was involved in something famous, something big. It was the same feeling when we got to Radio City Music Hall. My mother told me it was the best theater in the whole world and that the Rockettes were the most beautiful, most talented performers anywhere, whom people came from around the world to see. When my class finally made its way through the crowds into Radio City I could barely breathe. We were here, in this place that people traveled from everywhere to be, where the Rockettes performed (what exactly they did I still had no idea). The gold fixtures and red carpeting exaggerated the dizzy Christmas-in-NY adrenaline pumping through me, and I remember literally shaking with excitement. At the top of the first set of stairs, there was a bank of pay phones. I made a beeline for the nearest one and dialed zero. I told the operater I wanted to call home, collect. The phone rang and no one answered. This was before answering machines. Before voice mail. So I hung up. But I was bursting and had to tell someone, had to put the excitement somewhere. So I picked up the phone and dialed the operator again—a different one answered this time—and immediately started gushing to her about where I was, what I could see, what I had already seen on this, one of my first trips into the city. I don't remember anything about the performance that night but I always remember that call, the friendly operator, her kind voice, and how she told me to go find my teacher, to be careful not to get lost.

I wander past the bright, contrived windows along Wooster and try to remember what time of year it is. It looks like Christmas but I'm sure it's not. It takes longer than a few beats to remember that it's March. I make my way into a wide, light, serene store, with low tables and discreet racks hanging with what look to be carefully curated garments. I ask a dark-haired saleswoman with eyes like opals—blue with flashing gold and red—if they have any men's turtleneck sweaters. I tell her I'm visiting and have run the one I'm wearing into the ground. She looks down my torso at what I am wearing, and her frown and wrinkled brow seem to agree. She directs me down a flight of steps to the lower level. Near the bottom of the stairs is a small basket of folded cashmere turtlenecks, and I pick the smallest one they have, in burgundy, with a cable knit pattern, and find a changing room. The moment the door clicks shut, I pack a thick hit, cough loudly to mask the sound of the lighter, and hungrily draw from the stem. I blow the smoke wide and close my eyes for a few minutes. I have no idea where I will go next and I lean against the back of the changing room wall and let the warm glow of the drug shield me from caring. This little changing room, nothing more than a cube of light and mirror and white paint, is safe, and for a moment I am calm.

I slump further down the wall and let every tense, clenched muscle loosen. It feels as if each limb, every digit, could fall off. The contraption of my body feels barely assembled, on the verge of collapse. Out of nowhere comes a memory of Noah weeping at Japonica. Shaking his head and sobbing. Telling me not to explain, not to say another word, that he knew I was high, could see it on every inch of me.

I pack a hit as big and as fast as I possibly can. It takes a few deep draws for the vision of Noah to dim, and after a few more hits the exorcism is complete. The tiny changing room is thick with smoke, and I know I need to leave. After another big hit, I suddenly remember the SoHo Grand Hotel, which can't be far and where, thankfully, I have no history.

I sit up and shimmer with the promise of a clean, new hotel room as more smoke curls around the ceiling of the changing cubicle. Energized now with a plan, finally a place I can go, I cool off the lighter and stem and head back into the store. As I walk, I notice that my jeans won't stay up anymore. My old blue cashmere sweater is tucked in all around my waist, but the soiled, worn-thin Levis are still slipping off me. I need to get a new hole punched in my belt before going to the hotel.

The downstairs of the store is brighter now than I remembered, and smaller. I worry they've been listening to me get high and that they can smell the smoke pouring from the now open door of the changing room. Without trying on the sweater, I race upstairs to the opal-eyed woman and tell her I'd like to buy it. She runs my debit card through and as she pulls out the bag that has the words *Christopher Fischer* scrawled across its meridian, I look around the store. Where once it had a sleek impenetrable chic, it now has a slapped-together, flimsy quality. The bag looks odd, too thick, too bright, too big, as if it were a prop bag for some off-Broadway play that involved shopping. The opal-eyed woman folds the sweater in a confection of tissue, places it in the phony bag, and hands me my receipt as she tells me to have a nice evening. I can feel my grip on reality loosen as I take the bag. Is this some setup? But how would they know I'd come here? I rush out of the store and onto Wooster Street.

A few beats later I hear my name being called in a high-pitched, nervous, southern accent. *Bill, oh, hello, Bill.* I freeze. *ROSIE?!* Old art-project, crack-smoking, 23rd Street Rosie? What's she doing here? Jesus, is she in on this? I look around and can't see anyone I know. My heart pounds and my neck chokes with a sudden rush of blood to my head. And there she is: Barbara. A lovely middle-aged, impeccably dressed woman who acts as an adviser to foreign publishing houses, what people in publishing call a scout. I've known her, not well, for years. She eyes me with worry, but kindly, and quickly I say hello and move on before a conversation can take root. Seeing her jolts me into thinking about book publishing, the agency, Kate, our employees, my writers—Jesus, all those writers. And with them the names and faces and voices of all the publishers, editors, agents, scouts, publicists, and assistants roar to life, one by one, like a great, animated mural—scolding and disgusted. And then, again, memories of rehab and Noah flood back in. With my fake shopping bag in one hand and debit card in the other, I start hustling west toward the SoHo Grand.

I see—oh, dear God, thank you—a leather shop and immediately go in, take off my belt, and ask to have a few new holes punched. This is the third time I have done this in the last five weeks. At one point, in some hotel room, I have taken a knife and stabbed out a new, albeit rougher, hole. The old guy behind the stack of bags and wallets eyes the weathered belt and me cautiously and says, *You're going to need more than just a few.* He makes three and when I put the belt on it links, easily, to the last one. I consider having him make another, but judging by how quickly he makes the holes and rings up the price, it seems he wants me gone. I walk for a few blocks toward the hotel, but before I get there I know I need to change out of my mangy blue sweater. I've been wearing it for over a month. It's stretched out of shape and the unidentifiable residue that crusts and streaks along the neck and chest is, I'm worried but not exactly sure, beginning to smell.

A few blocks away, I see a small Chinese restaurant. It's the kind with only three or four tables that is mostly for takeout. There are no other customers in the store when I enter. I step up to the counter and ask if I can use the bathroom, and the boy there, no more than sixteen, says that it's for customer use only. A woman I assume is his mother joins him and repeats that it's not for public use.

I am desperate to change and also getting antsy for a hit, so I order three dishes and some egg rolls for takeout and ask, a little impatiently, if I can use the bathroom *now.* The woman says, yes, if I pay first. So I do. I walk past the counter to the back of the kitchen, where there is a tiny bathroom. Luckily it has a window and a mirror. I run the water and flush the toilet to mask the sounds of the clicking lighter and the popping sound the drug makes when it's lit. I pack the stem and light up. I load it again, since I'm feeling far from relieved after the first hit. The rock pops at the end of the stem when I pull, and the glass at the very end cracks apart. This sometimes happens when you put a big cold chunk of crack in a still-hot stem and light up too quickly. I scramble as quietly as I can to clean up the small bits of glass, find the thank-God-still-intact rock of crack, and reload the broken stem. My agitation is high, so I pack in even more. The hit is big and I blow the smoke out the window and, thankfully, begin to feel a wash of relief as I exhale. I wriggle out of my sweater and see my torso in the little mirror. Ribs and bones jut everywhere, and the color of my skin is light gray. Little scrapes and burn marks and scabs speckle my arms, chest, and stomach. I feel, for the first time, beyond the desire for sex, as if I have passed into another state of being high, where sex no longer matters. I am relieved, because the body in the mirror is not one I would want anyone to see. I look more closely at the worst burn marks and cuts, the ones on my hands and forearms, and I shudder. I look in the mirror again and see how little skin I have, how my frame seems covered by the thinnest sheet, pulled tight. I look like I crawled out of a fire, starving. I have never seen my pelvic bones winging from my abdomen in the way they do now and I'm relieved, as I pull the sweater over my head, that this glorious, thick miracle of costly fabric covers all of it. I wash my face and hands, wipe away various stains on my jeans, and pick lint and hair and detritus from the rim of my trusty cap. I find Visine in my jacket and drown my eyes in it. I wash my mouth out with soap and rub it under my armpits to cover up whatever odor may be coming from there. I fire up another blast, blow on the stem, wrap it up, put the old sweater in the bag, and open the door that leads to the kitchen and the front of the shop. There are two men—heavy-jacketed, dull-panted, gray-shoed

Penneys—and they are looking directly at me as I step toward
the counter. The food is in bags, ready, and I grab them, thank
the woman and the boy, and leave. As I walk west, I turn back
and see the two Penneys exit the restaurant and begin walking
my way. I change directions several times, and after twenty or so
minutes I think I've lost them. I throw the Chinese food and the
shopping bag with my old sweater into a garbage can. My heart is
racing and I'm worried that I'll be too panicky to make it through
the check-in process at the front desk of the SoHo Grand. I'm too
jumpy to stop at a bar and get a drink, so I decide to just go for it.
Just get to the room. Once there, I will be okay. Once there, I can
order room service, call Happy, drink bottles of vodka to take the
sharp edges off. I am focused on the short-term relief of the hotel
room, but under everything is a creeping knowledge that with not
much money left, not much more weight to lose, and not many
more places to hide, this is it. An end of some kind is near.

I stop by a deli around the corner from the hotel and get ten lighters, six boxes of sleeping pills, and a six-pack of beer so that I have
something to drink the second I get to the room. I wish I could
take a hit before going into the hotel, but I know it's now or never.
I head into the new brick-and-glass building, and as I march, as
slowly and calmly as I can, up the steps, I think of the clean sheets,
the gushing shower, the room service, the immaculate surfaces,
the safety. The place is crawling with guys who look like production assistants on movies—all hats and jeans and scruff. Thank
God. Thank God I don't stick out. Instantly I imagine I am in
town from L.A. on a shoot and that anyone noticing my weight,
the rings under my bloodshot eyes, the greasy hair poking out

from my cap, will just chalk it up to a tight production schedule and late nights in the editing room going over the dailies. So with this fantasy flickering behind my movements, I go to the front desk and ask for a room. *How many nights?* the woman asks, and I make a quick calculation of the $500 room rate and the amount of crack I plan on buying from Happy. I tell her four nights and that I need to check in under an alias as well as needing a smoking room. She doesn't skip a beat. She says, *Fine,* runs my debit card, looks at my passport, hands me a plastic room card, and off I go. I practically giggle from excitement and relief in the elevator as I'm heading up to what is the third floor from the top of the building. I clock that it's high enough for a jump to matter. If all else fails, there is that.

The room is small, on the southwest corner, and dimly lit. The lights of SoHo, Tribeca, and Wall Street dance and blink on the other side of the large windows, and it feels, when I first step into the room, like being on the inside of a snow globe suspended in midair, high above the city. I stand at the window and call Happy for the last time.

He arrives around one. I'd smoked down what I had left from the bag at Rosie's an hour ago, and my stem is now less than two inches long, caked with burnt, unsmokable residue. When I called hours earlier I asked for $2,000 worth. More than I've ever ordered. I can only give him $1,500 in cash—what was left of my limit when I went to the ATM before midnight and a new grand after. I ask him, this one time, to sport me the difference. He pauses,

briefly, and starts counting out the bags and new stems. *Nice hotel,*
he says, commenting for the first time ever on where I'm staying.
Nice room. And he leaves. Looking at the forty bags of crack on
my bedspread, the most I have ever seen in one place, makes me
feel safer than I have felt all day. The bags look fuller, more jam-
packed than usual, and the abundance, the dancing light outside
the window, and the awareness that I will never leave this room
sends a high through my system before I even light up. I lie down
on the bed and drop the bags on my chest and face, one by one,
and then all at once. It feels like an arrival. The end of a journey. Not just the panicked one of days and nights and weeks after
relapsing, but the long one, the whole useless struggle. The lines
from that novel rise up again, but this time with new meaning. *It
would be now.*

I pull the curtains shut and pack a hit with one of the new stems
and, more than ever before, let the crumbs scatter about. It won't
matter. I won't see the end of this pile. There is no way I can survive
this. I pack another hit. Another. And another. Happy has given
me eight stems, and I load two more so I don't have to wait for one
to cool before I start the next. I inhale smoke nonstop for nearly an
hour, naked and breathing more smoke than air. I am filled with
smoke — warm, electric, big. I feel weightless in this dim room. I
am almost nothing. I am, finally, about to be nothing.

I order bottles and bottles of vodka from room service, no
food. I smoke and drink all night, and by morning I have gone
through a third of what I bought from Happy and panic that I

won't have enough. By midnight, I decide to get $1,000 from the ATM and call Rico and ask him to float me a grand's worth until the next day. I've never asked Rico for an advance but he doesn't hesitate. When he comes around two in the morning— heavyset, cranky, and in a bulky red sweatshirt—he throws in a couple hundred extra, in addition to the thousand on credit. *On the house. Eat something, man,* he says, and for a moment he looks worried. But only for a moment and then he's gone. I gather all the little bags together. A bigger pile than the night before and now, with only $4,000 in my account and a hotel bill ticking up, I worry, again, if I will have enough. Death and an empty bank account are racing neck and neck, and it's the former I am pinning everything on.

I take all the sleeping pills out of their boxes and pop each one free from the thick sheets of safety packaging. I put the pills in a clear water glass from the bathroom and empty all the crack into another. My hands shake as I move the pills and the crack, and my whole body rocks in time with my heartbeat. I am drinking vodka like water and nervous each time I have to order another couple bottles that the room-service boys will report to the desk that there is something funny going on in my room.

The second morning comes on and the room seems smaller. I open the curtains and the day outside is gray, still. I am looking out the window at neighborhoods I've eaten and shopped and walked in for years, and yet I feel as if I'm seeing a city I've never been to. Nothing appears familiar and it seems less like a place I could go down the elevator and visit, and more like a photograph or a mural I can only regard.

I continue to smoke and am grateful for a ventilation system that draws the billowing clouds away as soon as I exhale. I have kept a window cracked to allow fresh air in, and for once I don't worry about the smell seeping down the hall to alert other guests or hotel employees.

I stand at the window, towel around my waist, and notice across the lot behind the hotel a string of black SUVs and several dark sedans lined up in a row. There must be nine of them, and I think but am not sure I see two people sitting in the front seat of each. I stop breathing. One of them seems to be holding a pair of binoculars. My heart begins to slam in my chest. It looks as if they all have binoculars. Eighteen pairs of them, trained directly on this window, this room, me. My towel slips off and I drop to my knees and kneel up to the window. One of them is waving. It's hard to tell but I'm sure he's waving from behind the glass. There's a reflection, but yes, yes, his arm is waving. Fuck, they're all waving. Waving with one hand and holding binoculars in the other. I feel like I've been electrocuted. My arms and neck ache, and I think I'm having a heart attack. Fuck, fuck, fuck, fuck, FUCK! I shout to myself as I pace the room and pour a full glass of vodka, downing it in one gulp. FUCK. I immediately grab a new stem and jam it full. SHIT! I scream as I stop myself from lighting up. I can't smoke it with the curtains open. Not with them all watching. But I can't close them, they'll storm the room. Oh, my God, they are going to storm the room. I run to the bathroom and turn on the shower to hide the sound of the lighter and the loud popping sound of the flame scorching the too-large chunk of crack at the end of the stem. It takes three long pulls to smoke the stem down, and I grab a towel and lay it across the base of the door to the room. Suddenly I notice that the ventilation system in the bathroom isn't very good. The smoke hangs heavy and slow in the air at the top of the ceiling. I open the door and return to the room. Without looking out the window, I close the curtains, sit down on the bed, load up the stem, and smoke. And again. And again. I am low on vodka and without it I will shake out of control. After a few moments pass, I do it again. I'm terrified now of calling downstairs for more, but I do. I grab shampoo and streak the walls around the bathroom door and the vents of the air system, hoping to create a fresh smell. I drink the last of the vodka, load up more hits, and look at my watch and see that it's after one o'clock. I have one more night left in the hotel and I know there is not enough money in my account for another. The vodka comes, and the boy who delivers it is not a boy but a man and too smooth, I think, too in control, and too, well, manly to be a room-service waiter. Fuck, I think. Undercover. I thank him, sign the bill, and when he asks if there's anything else, I think, GET THE FUCK OUT! but gently say, *No thanks,* and keep my shaking hands behind my back. He leaves and I think I hear something above me. Is there another room above me or the roof? I can't remember. I pace the room, light a hit, and decide whether to open the curtains and look up. It takes forty-five minutes and nearly half a bottle of vodka for me to pull back the curtains, lean out, look up, and notice that there is an open roof above this room and not another room. The building steps back at the top, and my floor is the last before it narrows. I look out across the lot to the line of black SUVs and sedans and think I see the flash of a lighter go off in one. And another. Are they trying to drive me insane? Why are they watching me? Why don't they just arrest me? WHO THE FUCK ARE THEY? I suddenly feel light, flimsy. Defenseless. I try to stand but stay bent with dread, like a half-closed jackknife. I close the curtains and crouch on tiptoes back to the bed. The noises above—footfalls? Something dragging? Are they planning on scaling down from the roof and coming in through the windows? I realize how small this room is and wonder if they've rigged it this way solely for me—is it usually part of a larger suite, but when they saw me coming, they created a wired, camera equipped, roof-accessible space to corner me into a bust? A radio sounds from somewhere—in the hall? The roof? I jump off the bed toward the dresser. My towel comes off again, and I see in the mirror a rickety skeleton—elbows and knees and knuckles bulging like bolted wooden joints strung with thread. I am the marionette I have seen hundreds of times before but never thought was me. I am only sticks and strings and spasms. Money gone. Love gone. Career gone. Reputation gone. Friends gone. Hope gone. Compassion gone. Usefulness gone. Second chances gone. And if there had been any hesitation about dying, that's gone now, too. I take a huge hit. There must be almost $2,000 worth of crack left in the glass cup. I have almost two full bottles of vodka, a water glass full of sleeping pills, two clean and three rough-but-usable stems left. I need to get it all down as fast as possible, to wallop my system hard enough before anyone breaks into the room. I've slept only a handful of hours over the last six weeks. I cannot remember eating. I'm sure my racked body won't survive if I overwhelm it with what I have. The team of binocular-holding, lighter-flashing, hand-waving SUV drivers outside, who now seem to be on the roof, are, at any second, it seems, about to explode through the door and windows.

As fast as I can, I put on my boxer shorts. It is suddenly, urgently, important to have boxers on and for everything to be clean. If the room gets stormed, I don't want it streaked with residue and mess and I don't want to be naked. I wipe down the surfaces of the bathroom and the bedroom and gather the glasses with the pills and the crack next to the bed. I set up the bottles of vodka on the floor and bring an empty one to pee into. At some point during the cleaning and gathering I decide that once I lie down on the bed I will not leave it. I sit at its edge and pack a hit. I smoke hit after hit, but it seems I can't make a dent in the pile of drugs in the glass. I begin to take the pills. One after another, with big mouthfuls of vodka. I hear footsteps on the roof. The sound of ropes, of heavy boots, of cables. Boxes piled with guns scraping the concrete. Surveillance equipment being hauled. More footsteps. More hits. More pills and larger gulps of vodka. This goes on and on in the half-lit room, the late morning sun seeping through the closed curtains. The surfaces that had once seemed to shimmer with the most inviting urban glamour now look cheap and cold and ordinary. I hear a helicopter and imagine the men above fastening the roof with cables lowered from a large, powerful chopper that will—any second now—lift the little cube of a room into the air, away from the city, and behind the walls of a federal prison. The bed feels as if it is rocking, and I cannot tell if it is me, the bed, or the entire room. I down more pills. I smoke more. Drink more. Find a piece of paper and, as Noah wrote so many times on the back of envelopes and left on the bar in our foyer, write *Can't take it,* and leave it next to the bed. I can barely move my arms, and my legs begin to ache. My heart feels like it is a rocket taking off from inside my chest, but at the same time a low, dull wave of drowsy energy begins to roll at the back of my neck and head.

The pills are nearly gone. I wonder, for the first time, if I really want to go through with this. There still might be a chance to crawl up and out of this deep well. Do I really want to die? I stop and the sounds on the roof stop, too. Everything is silent but for the roaring of blood behind my eyes and ears and chest. All I can hear is life slamming through my tired, aching body. Do I want to do this? Now? The sound of something snapping comes from the roof and I startle.

Yes, I think as I lean over to pick up the glass with the pills and slide the last ten or so into my mouth. *Yes,* I say out loud to the men on the roof and the ones in the vans who must be listening. *YES,* I shout, before I chug the dregs of vodka from the bottle. *Yes,* I whisper angrily, packing the only clean stem until it bulges. Yes and Yes and Yes as I finish it all and my limbs slow and the great drowsy, long-awaited wave rises, crests and, at last, crashes down. Yes.

For a long time, the next thing I remembered was being in the lobby of One Fifth, holding on to the front desk, telling Luis that I needed the new key. But over time I remember standing on the northeast corner of Fifth Avenue and Washington Square Park. Did a cab leave me here? Did I walk from the hotel? I had no idea then and have no idea now. But I remember standing at the corner, not knowing what to do. Whether to go home or not. I have no money. Nothing. And I can barely stay awake. I can lie down on the sidewalk and sleep so easily. If I can just find a spot, out of the way, where I won't get arrested or harassed. Sleep is on me like the heaviest blanket, and I can't stand still without stumbling. I start walking north up Fifth, toward home.

And so Luis—thirty-something, extremely polite, Hispanic, the same doorman I have waved hello to coming in and out of the lobby for years—is telling me that Noah is not at home and that I'm not allowed in the building. He says it nicely, but he says it. I ask him to just please give me the new key. I tell him it will be fine, Noah won't mind. He tells me he's been instructed not to give it to me, and I tell him if I don't lie down somewhere I will die. I can now barely stand up. He calls John, the building manager. John comes down and asks me to follow him. We go to the second floor, where he has a small office, and he suggests I wait with him until Noah gets back. I tell him he has to call Noah. My cell phone is dead. He dials the number and hands me the phone. Noah's voice mail picks up, and I tell him I'm home and they won't let me in. At some point during the message I fall down. My legs give out and I'm on the floor in front of John's desk. He helps me up, but there is nowhere to sit. I hang on to the door frame behind me. I am awake and asleep, alive and dead, and I don't know how I got here. John is talking, and I'm no longer hearing his words. His phone rings and he puts it to my ear. It's Noah. *Hi*, I say. *I'm home. Help. Please.* I give the phone to John and more sounds happen and then John is walking me downstairs, to Luis's desk. Give him the key, John says, and Luis opens the cabinet to get it. There is some confusion about old and new keys, but eventually a key ends up in my hand and I start heading for the elevator. When I get in, I can't remember what floor we lived on. Three? I hit three and know it's not right. Five? Six? Six. Six. Six W. So I hit six. The doors open and close on three, and for a moment I forget it's not my floor and move toward the door. I remember, but when I stop, my body buckles again and I'm on the floor. The doors shut and I manage to stand up as the doors open on six. The apartment is to the right of the elevator, the last door on the left. I start toward the door and hang on to the wall the whole way. I finally get there and see the shiny new steel lock where the old copper-colored one had been. I don't know what I've done with the key and as I search my pockets I realize it's still in my right hand. Now I just need to open the door. But I can't seem to guide the key into the lock. It must be the wrong one. Maybe we live on the seventh floor. Maybe the fourth. I keep poking at the lock, but my hand is shaking and I can't make it go in. Now that I've stopped walking, the drowsiness hits like a tidal wave. I'm leaning against the wall next to the door, but I can't stay up. I'm going down and hold on to the knob to keep from falling backwards. I sway in place for a while, and as it all begins to go dark, there are hands at my back, along my arms, taking the key, pulling me up. I see them on my wrists, and they are the most beautiful things I've ever seen. Made of light, not flesh, winging around me with good purpose and grace. Noah. He pulls me against him — he smells like dry cleaning and cigarettes — helps me stay up with one hand and unlocks the door with the other. He is speaking but the words are too far away. He tries to hold me up as the door opens but I'm already down. The light from the apartment streaks toward us. I fall in.

White Plains

An ambulance will wait by the service entrance at One Fifth to take me to Lenox Hill Hospital. Unlike the ride to the hospital when I am twelve, this one won't be remembered—there will be no surfacing between awake and unawake, no comforting voices. I won't remember the emergency room, won't remember the elevator to the psych ward, won't remember anything beyond falling through the apartment door, Noah behind me, the light.

I wake in a room, alone, strapped to a bed, with no idea where I am. It takes several minutes to register that I am alive, and when it does, I am furious. Nurses come. A doctor. People—my family, Noah—are outside the door, but I tell the nurses not to let anyone in. I stay frozen, in the room, with only one thought: What now?

Julia, a friend from Los Angeles, keeps calling. Nurses come in many times a day to say she is either waiting on the pay phone line or has left another message that I should call her. She does this for days and finally, before I speak to or see anyone else, I go to the phone. I leave the bed and room for the first time and wander toward the pay phone by the nurses' station. *Hi,* I say, and she fills my ears with her words. For a while, hers are the only words I can hear and she will say them over and over and keep saying them for weeks, then months.

I am given another room. It is small, with two beds, and looks out onto a church on 77th Street. When I get to the room it is empty and there is no sign of a roommate. An enormous white orchid is sitting on the dresser. It has two tall bamboo stakes with sharp, pointy ends to support the plant. It's from Jean and there is a note that asks me to be on the board of her literary magazine — *I keep meaning to ask you,* it says as if nothing has gone on, and it closes with *So much love.* I stare at the orchid, her scrawled handwriting, the thick, creamy stationery, and wonder who it was she thought she knew, who she thought she loved. I take one of the bamboo stakes, snap it in half, and go into the bright blue-tiled bathroom and start jamming it into my wrist. I keep jamming, harder and harder, until the skin breaks and blood comes, and I look down at my fist pumping the little weapon into my arm, see how dreadful what I am doing is, and register, in that instant, that I don't want to die. Suddenly and for the first time, dying seems like the last thing I want. I stop, grateful not to have caused more damage, put my arm under cold water, rinse the wound, wrap it in paper towels, and sit on the small bed facing the window. I sit there for a long time. I look at the church steeple and wait.

Before I see anyone, most of my family return to their lives in New England. My mother stays in a friend's apartment on the Upper West Side, but I ask not to see her. Noah comes a few times and looks more handsome than I have ever seen him. He sits across a cafeteria table from me and I am both shamed and dazzled by him. I weigh just over 130 pounds, almost 40 pounds less than my usual weight, swimming in pajama bottoms and a sweatshirt, and he glows in an elegant agnès b. shirt, collared English sweater, and chic gray city coat. I remember his buying each of these things. It is never said, but it is clear that it is over, that our lives, bound together for so long, will now be lived apart. Everything that we were, the whole magical, horrible opera, is now over. We are only a table apart but we're in different worlds. He seems less like a person and more like a figment from a dream I once had, some nocturnal wonder I cannot revive after sleep, only remember.

And then Katherine appears. After waking from a nightmare where she sees me wandering in city traffic, careening between cabs and buses, she calls her father, who has just heard from someone in our small town that there is trouble. Katherine hangs up the phone, drives to the airport in Lubbock, Texas, where she is living, catches the next plane to New York, and arrives the day before I stumble home, before the ambulance comes. She sits through two weeks of visiting hours, in the hall, mostly alone, always with a book. When people come to see me, she returns to the hall, and when they leave and I am on my own, she comes back.

One afternoon, she tells me the story of a plane we planned to steal the summer between our graduating from grammar school and entering high school. It was called *The Alaskan Express,* she reminds me, and describes how we had hatched an exhaustive plan — with maps and diagrams and budgets — to fly it to a deserted island in the Caribbean. Our friend Michael, who knew how to fly from his father, who was a pilot, was part of the scheme, too. She reminds me all about it — how we planned to pack seeds to plant elaborate gardens and find equipment to convert salt water to fresh; how the three of us had figured out a way to not have to leave one another, not have to move on. I had forgotten about the plane, the whole story, how possible it all seemed then. I listen to her and feel as I did when I was ten — awed by what she knows and grateful for her attention. But mostly we don't talk. She holds my hand and we sit, in a hospital again, just as we were at the beginning, together and without words.

Two weeks later, Noah, Katherine, and I meet with the psychiatrist I've been assigned and discuss rehabs. We pick one. Katherine goes to One Fifth and packs up some of my clothes and a few books. She helps me to the street with my bags, hugs me goodbye, and returns to Texas. We will drift apart again, she will go to Belize and for months I won't hear anything, but she will resurface — a phone call, an e-mail — and the fabric will mend again, for a little while.

David, whom I haven't seen since our breakfast at Marquet, is waiting outside Lenox Hill, on the corner of 77th and Park Avenue, with his Jeep. He is both warm and cautious, and we drive, mostly in silence, to White Plains, N.Y., to the grounds of an old asylum turned into a psychiatric hospital, with a small rehab center tucked in the back. We stop at a large drugstore near the rehab, and I look at the people wandering the aisles and wonder how they live their lives, how anyone does. He walks me through the store like a father taking his son to camp, asks me if I want toothpaste, candy, notebooks. He buys me two notebooks. I will fill them.

During those first nights in White Plains, I wonder about the boy who is assigned to the room across the hall — and his worried mother, setting his things down, eyeing him as if he will take flight or disappear in a flash if she turns her back. She reminds me of Noah. And when the boy looks at me, briefly, with eyes that are two black marbles, drained of hope and color and life, I see myself.

In the evenings, I walk in a gentle, sloping field, much like the one in Oregon, and wonder what will happen next. There is one late afternoon, a few days before I return to New York, when anxiety and despair overwhelm me and I get on my knees at the top of the field. It's wet from rain earlier in the day and the sky is lightless and gray with fog. I lie down in the damp and muddy grass and whisper into the soil for help. I do this for a long time and at some point stand up, pants soaked at the knees and thighs, hands and elbows caked with mud. When I stand, I see a small break in the wall of cloud and through it a faint streak of light. It is pale and pink and the most beautiful thing I have ever seen. The cloud opens wider, the light grows, and as it does, I feel an easing. I know, if only for that moment, that my worry will change nothing and that everything is as it's supposed to be. That I will be okay.

I walk down the field as night falls. When I reach the bottom, the large maple tree anchoring the corner of the field erupts with a racket of birds. The entire tree is covered with them, and they scream and caw and flap as loudly as a roaring stadium. I stand and watch them for a long time, mesmerized by the great movement and sound. Then, all at once, the tree rushes with wings and the flock takes off, sailing out over the field, banking left, then right, and off behind the church, gone. When I return to my room, the phone is ringing. It's Julia, who asks me to be the godfather of her first child, Kate, who will be born just after I return to New York.

At night I hear the wind scream between the buildings and rattle the windows. I hear shouting down the hall and wonder whether my door will burst open, as it did on the first night, when a dark-haired girl dropped to her knees in the doorway and asked if I was God. I watch the space under my door and see light happen from the other side. Sometimes it is faint, other times bright, then nothing.

In that room, I sit in a chair and feel lighter than I have ever felt—relieved, an impossible weight lifted—until faces begin to appear like fireworks. They keep coming, one after the other—they belonged to my life once, I think—and I feel, sharply, the anger and grief and disappointment and scorn I imagine they hold. I feel heavy again in that chair and sometimes I sit there for hours. I pace my room and leave messages on cell phones and voice mails. Some call back, some never do. I crouch on my knees and pray. For help. For a way through this. For forgiveness. I think of one of my favorite poems and see the predictions it held. I remember my life, how it all mattered so much once, and then not at all. I remember the last lines of a book I believed I understood. *When it feels like the end of the world, it never is.* I knead these words like a rosary and write them in letters and speak them over the phone and into the wind in that field. I lose faith in them, but pray they are true. They are.

I remember all the cabdrivers and hotel employees, dealers, and addicts. The ones who prickled with disgust, fear, or ecstasy, and the ones who said in the same gentle tone that everything would work out, that it would all be okay. I wonder who they thought they were talking to, who it was they saw, who they were. There are things that will always puzzle me—the conversations, the great ballet of taxis and cars, government agents and cops, the JCPenneys—that I will never be able to see clearly enough to distinguish truth from delusion. With these things, these memories, I am only able to remember what they looked like, how they sounded, how it felt. I remember looking out from the balcony of the Gansevoort Hotel that morning. All those people strolling, impossibly, at five a.m.; the Town Cars and the words written on cards that I will always wonder about and often think I should look up to find some meaning in but never do. I remember the seagulls wheeling in great arcs above the river. There were so many.

There is a time, much later, when I imagine what it was like for everyone else, those who were by blood, accident, or inclination involved. Those who were wounded, who wounded. The former came first and fiercest: the employees at the agency who lost their jobs; the writers I represented who depended on me and had to scramble to find new agents; family; friends; Kate. Noah. At first I'm consumed with shame and guilt and regret, but slowly, with the help of kindred spirits, these feelings evolve, are still evolving, into something less self-concerned. The landscape of the latter, with the daily help of those same kindred spirits, is journeyed into. Much remains a frontier.

I wonder what it was like for my father. How the hours I remember from my childhood were for him. What worry he knew. How that drive back from the doctor in Boston went for him. And after. What did he think after the car doors slammed shut and I'd disappeared into the house? Where did he go? To his den to pour himself a Scotch? Around the side of the house to pee in the pachysandra? Or did he stay in the garage and listen to the cooling engine tick down, the tread of footfalls above him in the kitchen. How long might he have stayed there? Did he worry that he'd taken the wrong tack? Been too tough? Too harsh? How would his father have handled it? How much of that man could he even remember? Nineteen years old, when his father died, was a long time ago. He was in college then, planning to join the navy and fly. Fly away from Boston. Jets, cargo planes, it didn't matter — just take flight. How far away did nineteen feel to him that day? How far six? Six years old. What did he know about six-year-old boys? How frightened was he? What didn't he do that day in order to drive his boy to Boston from Fairfield County, Connecticut? What bills didn't get paid? What lawn didn't get mowed? What small plane didn't get fixed or flown in order to do what he thought might help this boy, this boy of his who danced like someone had set him on fire every time he peed? This same boy the doctor said had nothing wrong with him. What the hell was he supposed to do? Wasn't he supposed to be firm? Isn't that how children learned? Wasn't that how men were with their boys?

I wonder if he worried like this. Or did he simply believe that whatever was broken could be fixed by force, that something bent could be hammered straight.

I return to New York and find a small, bright studio with a terrace, and from every corner of the place, I'm able to see the Empire State Building. I kiss someone on the Fourth of July, a friend who becomes more, and he loans me money to afford that place. I sell a photograph I had purchased years before, and with that money and the borrowed money, I am able to live in New York, not work for the first time since I was a teenager, and find, with help, a way to get through the days and nights without escaping them. Gradually, mornings become merely mornings, not panic-stricken hours managing the consequences of not coming home before daybreak, and evenings aren't spent imagining excuses and schemes to get through the next day. Days are just days, not stages where I'm choreographing some complicated piece of theater—the lights, the lines, the costumes—in order to control the outcome, protect myself, get what I think I need.

Returning to publishing doesn't seem possible. It feels like a scorched field that can no longer hold life. But I am wrong. A woman I met once at a party, years before, calls and asks me to lunch, and at that lunch she offers me a job. She talks about courage and no new damage and we eat and drink coffee and it feels like home. The first days back are terrifying, but not in the same way as before. I don't worry about being a fraud or being found out, as I had for all those years. I show up at that office representing one writer—Jean, who, when I told her I was going back to work, wrote her very established agent to say she was switching her representation. Walking through the shiny doors of the agency that day, I somehow trust that if it turns out to be my last one, and she my last client, I will be fine—that the sky won't fall, that it's just not meant to be. It turned out that day was not my last. I'm still in that same office, and have other clients to keep Jean company.

For a long time, I will hear Noah's despairing voice pleading with me, so many times—from behind closed doors, across tables, through phone lines. I will remember every night at the Knickerbocker, every extra drink I snuck when he went to the bathroom. I will remember his coming out to Oregon for family week, standing in the parking lot in his gray snap-front jacket and beard, looking so clean and honest and faithful and loving. I will remember how grateful I was that he never left me. I will remember how his beautiful hands pulled me up that last time and how I fell away from them — finally, because I had to — and moved through the doorway, alone.

In the year before I go back to work, I call my father at least a few times a week, often in the morning as I walk along the Hudson River in a lush park I had, before, not even known was there. We talk, for the first time in many years, and each time, I'm amazed. The very first time we speak is when I'm still in White Plains. The phone rings in my room, I answer, and he is on the line. *Willie,* he says, after a while, *I'm sorry.* He tells me everything he remembers and I listen, quiet, and grateful that I hadn't made it all up. I tell him that my being in rehab is not his fault, that my boyhood struggles did not cause what happened, merely shaped it. Time stops during that phone call; I want it to be over and also never to end.

That October, he asks me to fly in his Cessna from Connecticut to Maine. The small airport is just down the road from where we lived, a few minutes from my high school. I had forgotten how loud small planes are, how light, and how confident my father is in them. His hands glide with easy purpose over the same gadgets and knobs and lights and flaps he handled when I was a boy, and all of it is just as mysterious, just as unknowable. We take off in a field that is also a runway. We shudder along in the way little airplanes do and then, in the split second that always feels as if fairy dust has been sprinkled, we leave the earth, lift quickly, higher and higher, above the towns and schools and the colorful rot of autumn. The roar of the engine and wind make talk impossible. A pile of maps rests in my lap. Side by side, tossing in air, above the fields and hills and roads where everything happened, we are silent.

The Hollow

He's almost two. Walking now. Chubby and cheerful, eats everything put in front of him and always wants more. He disappears
into daydreams and collapses into fits of uncontrollable laughter.
His sister is skinny and fair, his father is dark and smells of smoke,
and his mother is every color in between, every shape, every smell.
She has the bluest eyes. She plants flowers, plants them everywhere—in rock gardens that rise from the lawn into the woods,
along walkways, in pots that sit on windowsills, on steps.

She is planting flowers now, and he is nearby, on a blanket littered
with toys. They are on the lawn behind the house, just at its edge,
where it rises and descends into what they call the hollow, a low,
damp bowl of lawn spotted with outcroppings of granite ledge.
Along the ridge and down along the hollow, there are thickets of
blueberry bushes and, behind those, the woods.

His mother calls to him in her singsong way from behind an enormous straw hat. The two cats sit at the edge of the blanket and watch him. He can hear them purring and he wants to hold them and somehow bring their softness and their sounds closer, into him. He reaches for them and they meow, slink patiently away, and settle in the just-far-enough-away grass.

Past the cats the dark green lawn stretches toward the woods. These things, these places, the whole world beyond the immediate perimeter of his blanket and his mother, have only lately begun to occur to him. Each new miracle hatches alive, new and beguiling. A bee, a plane flying overhead, an anthill at the edge of the blanket, a great wind roaring in the trees. He wants to see it all at once and right away.

This is the first summer he can walk. The first summer he can move himself closer to what he wants. Away from what he does not want. He is still in diapers but those will be gone soon. He looks up past the little ridge, beyond the hollow, and sees a great shimmering of branches and leaves rising from an army of tree trunks. A gust of wind sends the leaves into hysterics, and he hears the sound, like water thundering from the faucet when his mother draws him a bath. But this new sound is greater, wilder, more thrilling than anything he's ever heard.

His mother, in her flowers, hums a song, swats flies from her face. He stands up from the blanket and rocks on his dimpled legs. A blast of wind in the trees stirs up another momentary chaos. His heart races, and he tilts toward the tree line on the other side of the hollow and begins to move. The swooping birds, the cresting green lawn, the buzzing insects, the tufts of seed and summer flotsam drifting in slow motion through the air, the blueberry bushes at the edge of the wood—all of it dazzles before him. Every gorgeous new inch of it beckons as he walks faster, more deliberately, faster still, until walking isn't fast enough and he begins to run. He's running now, to the top of the lawn, toward the creaking branches, the flashing leaves, the avalanche of sound.

He clears the ridge and, all at once, the slope on the other side is steeper than he expects. His legs whirl beneath him and he struggles not to fall. He's running faster than he has ever run before, and for a second he feels a distance between himself and his body—as if one has departed from the other and is a witness to its new speed and not its cause. The lawn, his legs, his body all blur below him, and he begins to let go, to allow the momentum to carry him.

A great wind pounds through the hollow and he feels on the verge of flight, that the earth will release him and he will surge beyond the lawn, over the vegetable garden and swing set, to the treetops. His mother calls out from somewhere. She is shouting his name, but her voice is small and known and behind him now. Everything that once held his attention, every little and large thing he has remembered, disappears as he races ahead, legs pumping under him, air rushing at his face, terror and wonder bursting from his small heart.

As he careens down the slope, another first, another new magic: calm, like peaceful lightning, flashing through his rioting limbs, stilling every streaking inch of him, caressing him in the half seconds before he stumbles, before he scrapes his elbows and knees and face on the outcropping of granite ledge. Before he wails with shock and his mother descends on him in a flap of hat and tears. Before she gathers him into her and he forgets his fright because he is held in familiar arms that smell of potting soil and flowers. Before all this, a God-kissed, God-cursed calm, debuting at the zenith of his velocity, the peak of his want—a moment that's over before it's even a moment, the one he will scrape his skin hundreds of times to recapture. Before, despite, and because of all the things he senses await him, he leans, then leaps, into the wind, away.

Acknowledgements

Great Force Who Came: Jennifer Rudolph Walsh; Perfect Editor: Pat Strachan; Brilliant Publishers: Michael Pietsch, David Young; Wise Comrade: Robin Robertson; Right Hand: Matt Hudson; Beloved Team: Jonathan Galassi, Nick Flynn, John Bowe, Jill Bialosky, Christopher Potter; Care and Counsel: Adam McLaughlin, David Gilbert, Lili Taylor, Cy O'Neal, Julia Eisenman, James Lecesne, Chris Pomeroy, Laura Gersh, Courtney Hodell, Eliza Griswold, Lee Brackstone, Lisa Story, Roger Manix, Susannah Meadows, Ally Watson, Monica Martin; Love: Jean Stein; Hero: Kim Nichols; My Enduring Family: Mom, Dad, Kim, Lisa, Sean, Matt, Ben, Brian.

NINETY DAYS

For Polly, Annie, Jack & Asa
and Everyone Counting Days

As snow fills the places
where you must have walked,
you start back to where you began, that place you again prepare to leave,
alone and warm, again intact, starting out.

DANIEL HALPERN, FROM 'WHITE FIELD'

Forget yourself.

HENRY MILLER

Borrow Mine

It looks like Oz. This is what I think as Manhattan comes into view through the windshield of Dave's jeep. The crowded towers poke the sky with their metal and glass and in the midday haze look far-away, mythic, more idea than place. We're driving in thick traffic that moves swiftly and in unison. A month ago I hadn't noticed the city receding behind us as we drove from Lenox Hill Hospital to the rehab in White Plains. We didn't talk much then and we're not talking much now.

Dave is playing music I don't recognize. A charcoal-voiced girl is crying with as much earnestness as irony alongside an acoustic guitar. He tells me her name and it sounds more like a department store than a person. He compares her to another singer I don't know, and I feel as if I've lost fluency in a language that once was second nature. Between Lenox Hill and rehab I've been in treatment for six weeks, but it seems

like years, and I imagine during that time new bands coming and going, movies capturing the attention of the masses and being forgotten,
books sparking controversy or indifference, and the roar of it all fading
to make way for new entries in the cultural lottery. Dave tells me about
a play he and Susie have just seen and I feel myself shrinking in the
seat, becoming kid-sized. Up ahead, Oz juts higher above the horizon.

It's early April, a Monday. We're driving to Dave's writing studio
on Charles Street in the West Village. He's offered me the place for
a few weeks while I find somewhere to live. I've just finished four
weeks in a small drug and alcohol rehab on the grounds of an old
mental asylum. Dave drove me there after I was released from the
psych ward at Lenox Hill Hospital, where I wound up after a two-
month bender that ended in a fistful of sleeping pills, a bottle of vodka, a crack pipe stuffed to bursting, and an ambulance. The small
literary agency I co-owned and ran for four years is gone, all my
clients have found new agents, our employees have scattered to new
jobs or left New York, and whatever money I once had has been
wiped out, leaving in its place a rising debt of legal, hospital, and
rehab bills. The eight-year relationship with my boyfriend, Noah,
is over, and the apartment at One Fifth Avenue his grandmother
bought him, where we lived for six years, is no longer my home. I
can sleep at Dave's office, but I have to be out between ten and five
so he can work.

The song changes—the girl is talking more than singing, the guitar
is now a cello—and I wonder what I'll do all day, how I'll fill up the
hours, where I'll go.

Sure you want to do this? Dave asks cautiously. *Sure you should be coming back here?* He turns the music down and keeps his eyes on the road while he voices my own doubts. I'm not sure of anything. I'm thirty-four years old. Unemployed. Unemployable in a field I worked in for twelve years. I have a mountain of terrifying paper waiting for me: the settlement agreement with my ex-business partner, Kate, dismantling the agency; bills from my lawyers; hospital bills and insurance forms; e-mails and letters—angry, loving, and everything in between—from friends, former colleagues, and family. The balance of the rehab bill is at least forty thousand dollars and likely much more. My sister Kim, who lives in Maine, in the midst of picking up and dropping off her twin boys from school, play dates, and baseball practice, has taken over the bills, the accounts, the lawyer, and our plan is to go over every last difficult bit of it once I'm settled in at Dave's.

I've arranged to see my sponsor, Jack, at an evening meeting in the West Village—*a beginner's meeting* is how he describes it. I first met Jack on the third or fourth day in the hospital. After a rough, shame-shocked start there when I refused to see or speak to anyone, I eventually agreed to meet him—a friend of a friend, my age, curly haired, boyish, gay— and he offered to be my sponsor, a sort of coach/big brother/guide, in a fellowship for people with alcoholism and drug addiction. I learned later, in rehab, that there are many fellowships—some free, some not, most with organized meetings—where people go for help with addictions like mine. The one Jack belongs to is the one I join.

Dave pulls up in front of an old ivy-covered apartment building on Charles Street between Bleecker and West 4th. I step onto the sidewalk and wait while he makes a phone call from the front seat. It's quiet. The air is humid and the streets are speckled with afternoon light. A young, high-cheekboned couple walk by, speaking what sounds like Russian into their cell phones. A fire engine wails. A trim young man with a Great Dane on a leash bends with a plastic bag in hand to scoop up a pile of the elegant dog's poop. *New York*, I think. *I'm back in New York*. I see a middle-aged man walking alone with an earpiece connected to a wire that disappears into his tan windbreak-er. He looks at me a beat too long and a little too seriously and an old familiar panic flashes in my chest. Dave comes around to the side of the jeep and grabs two bags from the back and barks, *C'mon, I have to meet Susie*. I rush to help, and when I turn to look for the tan-jacketed man, he's gone.

I follow Dave up three flights of exceedingly creaky stairs as he tells me how the old woman on the second floor, just below his studio, is highly sensitive, extremely cranky, and will call him day or night if she feels anything is awry. I wonder if this is his way of discouraging any funny business. A little barricade against what he and everyone else in my life fear will happen now that I've returned to New York: relapse.

The apartment is a bright studio with a fireplace, high ceilings, and a small, dangling crystal chandelier. It looks like the study in a much larger, very nice old house. Dave's books line the mantel and shelves, and there are old rugs scattered about. The small brown couch un-folds into a bed that I'll sleep on for the next few weeks. Dave rat-a-tat-tats a tour of the basics—towels, locks, a pile of blankets, tricky windows, cutlery, cups, coffee machine, keys—and then he's gone. I had imagined having coffee with him at a nearby café and a brotherly speech about how it's all going to work out—that I have to be brave, that I can count on him, et cetera—but what he offers instead is help with the bags, another warning about the downstairs neighbor, a worried look, and a hurried good-bye.

The apartment looks onto a garden behind a town house. It's a minimalist oasis: boxwood, teak, reflecting pool. The town house has large clear panes of glass that frame exquisite mid-century modern furniture on the second floor, and a clean geometry of stainless steel, marble, and what looks like suede in the kitchen below. Order and wealth hum from the place and I can barely look. I close my eyes and only then do I hear the bright racket of songbirds. They sound exactly like the birds that covered the trees near the field where I walked on the grounds in rehab. I imagine a flock flying just above Dave's jeep the whole way down from White Plains, descending now upon the branches outside to chirp and coo their encouragement.

Hi guys, I say and am startled by the sound of my voice. *Thanks for the welcome home party*, I whisper, and though I'm embarrassed by the fantasy of the birds escorting me back to New York, I'm still glad for any kindness—made up, even—coming from the greenery outside. I lie down on the couch and listen.

The birds carry on. Voices drift in from outside. The refrigerator hums in the little kitchen. And all at once it hits me: I'm alone. No one besides Dave knows exactly where I am. I could be doing anything. I've been an in-patient for weeks, under the thumb of nurses and doctors and counselors the entire time. No more morning gatherings, group meals, and in-bed-by-ten room checks. I'm alone and unaccountable. And then, like a dead ember blown to life, I think about my old dealers, Rico and Happy. I remember how I owe each of them a thousand dollars and wonder—despite all that's been lost, everyone hurt, despite everything—how I'm going to get two grand to pay these guys off so I can buy more. I start to puzzle through credit cards and PIN codes for cash advances. Suddenly a few thousand dollars seems within reach and I can feel that old burn, that hibernating want, come awake. I imagine the relief that first hit will deliver and I'm suddenly up off the couch and pacing. *No no no*, I chant. *No fucking way*. That craving, once it begins, is almost impossible to reverse. What my addict mind imagines, my addict body chases. It's like Bruce Banner as he's turning into the Incredible Hulk. Once his muscles begin to strain against his clothes and his skin goes green, he has no choice but to let the monster spring from him and unleash its inevitable damage.

I step on a creaky floorboard and remember the old lady below. I think of Dave and how he's spent most of his day driving to White Plains and back; how he's trusting me with his place, and how worried he looked when he left. I look at my watch. It's 3:50 and I remember Jack had suggested I go to a four o'clock meeting around the corner if I returned to the city in time. *I can make it,* I think desperately, meaning both the meeting and in general. I grab the set of keys from the mantel and, as gently as I can, descend the three flights of noisy stairs and hurry out to the street.

By the time I get to the meeting it's packed and I have to wedge myself through the crowd to grab what looks like the last seat. I sit down against a wall painted robin's egg blue and as I do, I see Jack. He's sitting in the seat directly across from mine with a big glad-you-could-make-it smile. We're not supposed to meet until later, but he's surprised me by showing up at my first meeting back in the city. *Welcome home*, he whispers seriously as the lights go down and the meeting begins.

I have met Jack only three times—twice at Lenox Hill and once during the last week at rehab when we went for a long walk and sat in a white gazebo and listened to the head counselor say he believed I was someone who would make it, someone he didn't see relapsing. Jack is a music critic and lives in the city with his boyfriend. He wasn't a crack addict, but his history with drugs and alcohol reminds me of my own, and every time I think I've told him something too embarrassing or too shameful, he's quick with a story that reminds me we've sunk to the same depths. I keep needing to remind myself that Jack is a drug addict. He's so put together, so clear-eyed and wholesome. It surprises me when he describes doing things when he was high that I'm convinced no one else but me has done. Like hitting on taxicab drivers. He tells me this the first time we meet at Lenox Hill, when I'm still paranoid about being followed by undercover DEA agents. My first response is *How did you know?* To which he responds, *What do you mean? I was there!* And after a beat I understand that he was there when *he* had done it, not when I had.

The meeting ends and we go for coffee. I tell him about the craving I had an hour ago in Dave's apartment. He tells me if it happens again—*and it will*—I need to immediately call him or someone else who is sober. If I get his voice mail I should leave messages describing what's going on, even if it's to say I plan on getting drugs or that I'm about to drink. Just speak it through and then once I've done that, if I can, try to imagine every beat of what will follow. Paying the dealer. Scoring the drugs. Getting high until the drugs are gone and then calling the dealer for more. And more. Running out of money. Getting paranoid. Not picking up the phone when worried friends call. The next day. The horror of morning. The empty bank account. The need to get more. Do more. And on and on.

Back at Dave's a few hours ago, I hadn't imagined anything beyond getting high. Just the high. As we now sit in a crowded coffee shop on Jane Street and talk through where it would lead, I can feel the once-hot little ember of craving cool down. As we talk I wish I could go home with Jack. Move in with him and his boyfriend, at least until I have ninety days clean, which is just a month away. Ninety days is a milestone that many fellowships and organizations dealing with alcohol and substance abuse use to mark a strong foothold in sobriety. Many suggest what I've heard Jack refer to a few times as a *ninety-in-ninety*, which means going to ninety meetings in ninety days. Jack has recommended, since I'm not working and have little else to do, that I go to two meetings a day. At least. The meetings are excruciating sometimes. I have a hard time keeping focused, keeping my mind off how I'm going to figure out and fix my living situation, my finances, and nearly every relationship I have. I can't imagine how I'll make it through two meetings a day for ninety days. *One meeting at a time, one day at a time,* Jack chants when I tell him my worry and it shuts me up. Reaching ninety days has become an important focus of our talks, and though I can't imagine sitting through all those meetings, listening to all those drunks and addicts, can't imagine a future or how I'll sort out the huge mess that is my life, I can sometimes see ahead to ninety days. Jack has even suggested that until I have ninety days I should resist reconnecting with too many people in the city, avoid engaging too much in sorting through the business and financial wreckage. The simplicity of reaching ninety days is calming, and when my head swarms with everything that's happened and everything that might, I think, *Ninety days, ninety days*. Eventually it's all I can see, the only thing before me that needs to be done.

When I'm speaking with Jack I often don't feel the now-usual panic about not having money, a job, or any idea about what I will do with my life. He metabolizes what I imagine are insurmountable obstacles into simple phrases like *One day at a time* and *Take it easy*, which I find at once baffling, patronizing, and comforting. He tells me to have faith that everything has happened just as it's supposed to and that if I just stay sober it will all turn out OK, that before I know it I'll be helping someone else get and stay sober. Help someone else? *Not likely*, I tell him. How can I? I have absolutely nothing to offer. And faith? I don't have any. Certainly not in myself or in any grand design that makes what has happened and what I've done over the last few months and the years leading up to them acceptable. When I tell him I don't have much faith, he says simply, *Borrow mine*.

After coffee, Jack takes me to another meeting of the same organization, a few blocks away, in the basement of a beautiful old brick church. It's the meeting, he says, where he got sober. The one he goes to still.

As we head back through the courtyard toward the meeting, we bump into a few people who nod hello to Jack, sometimes giving him a gentle hug and moving on. He smiles and waves to several others and as he leads me toward the front row I feel proud to be with him. It strikes me then, as it has before, that I barely know him. I don't know his boyfriend's name, most of his friends, or where he lives in the city, but I imagine him a sober superhero, a kind of Clark Kent by day and Super Sponsor by night. I look around the room at the dozens and dozens of people sitting in folding chairs—sipping coffee, talking, waiting for the meeting to begin—and no one seems as attractive and confident and kind as Jack does. I'm overwhelmed with gratitude that he stepped into my life when he did. We've spoken on the phone at least once a day since Lenox Hill, and he's talked me through a whole universe of panics. *What a miracle this guy is*, I think, and as I do he tells me I need to raise my hand during the meeting and let the whole room know that I just got out of rehab and that this is my first day back in town.

There are over fifty people in the room. There were only four other patients in rehab, so the group meetings were never this large or remotely this intimidating. I shake my head no and Jack leans in and says, *You don't have a choice. We had a deal: As long as you follow my suggestions, I'm your sponsor. If you don't, I'm not.* And so, a few minutes later, when the guy running the meeting asks if there is anyone in the room under ninety days, I raise my hand and do what I'm told.

The meeting ends and many people, mostly men and gay at that, linger in the courtyard afterwards. Within a minute, a group of guys—young, skinny, with exquisite hair and many, I notice, wearing white belts—come over to say hi. They welcome me and ask if I would like to join them for dinner. *Thanks*, I say graciously, *but I'm having dinner with my sponsor*. But when the last word is out of my mouth I hear Jack behind me saying, *No you're not*. I turn to look at him and see the stern face of a parent ditching his kid at sleep-away camp. Before I can say another word he gives me a hug and tells me to leave him a message on his voice mail when I get home. As I watch him go I consider sneaking back to Charles Street, but too many people are introducing themselves, handing me their phone numbers scrawled on little scraps of paper, for me to be able to disappear unnoticed.

So I go to dinner. The group consists of fifteen guys at least. All gay. Most young. Some cute. Most not. All loud. As we walk toward Chelsea I try to lag behind so it doesn't appear that I'm with them, but each time I do someone drops back to chat with me. *How much time do you have?* is the usual question and I answer, *Fifty-nine days*. I'm embarrassed to tell them my story so I just allude to a rough patch. They seem to get it and don't press.

Eventually we end up at the New Venus diner in Chelsea, where the waiters shove a bunch of tables together to form one long one at the front of the restaurant. In the scuffle of who-sits-where, I wind up toward the end, near the door. As I take my seat, I see a tall, pale guy with red hair and a white Izod shirt sit down directly across from me. He looks Scottish, but too exotic to be Scottish. Maybe Scandinavian, I think, but then wonder if there are red-haired Scandinavians. He's very fit, very pale, loaded with freckles, and his clothes seem to glow they are so clean. *Hi*, he says. *I'm Asa*.

Asa is a few years younger than I am, in graduate school for urban
planning, and has been sober three years from a heroin addiction
that wiped out his savings and forced him to drop out of school.
When I ask him about the red hair he tells me it's a mystery, no one
in his family has it, just as no one in his family is an alcoholic or
addict. He was raised in what he describes as an eccentric Presbyterian household in Baltimore, but unless there is a meeting being
held in one, he no longer goes to church. He seems too well educated and serious for this gaggle of former club kids, but he couldn't
appear more comfortable in their company. I tell him my story and
he listens and nods and asks the occasional question. I worry that
he thinks I'm making up the parts about the agency, Noah, the life
I once had, and the two months in hotel rooms that ended it. But
at the same time I don't want him to think that I'm trying to impress or shock him. I want to tell him I wasn't always this pathetic,
this broken, that it took a long time to get here and no one saw it
happening. No one, that is, except Noah. When I hear myself say
I used to go to London a lot, I realize I *am* trying to impress him
and shut up.

Dinner ends and we talk on the corner of 22nd Street and Eighth
Avenue as one by one the sweet, noisy boys I'm embarrassed to be
seen with disappear into the night. *Call me,* most say, but I've already
thrown out their numbers in the bathroom at the diner. Asa, I've decided, is the one I can relate to. He has the same cautious, easy-does-
it tone that Jack has but he's less distant, softer. He tells me about
a meeting I should try. Everyone calls it The Library because it's
located in some kind of research library and, it turns out, it's a few
blocks from One Fifth, where I lived with Noah until two months

ago. He describes the people there as a mix of gay and straight, educated and not, all very serious about sobriety. He gives me the address—which I write down on the slip of paper where I've written Dave's Charles Street address—and tells me to meet him there tomorrow, ten minutes before the 12:30 meeting.

It's late. Midnight or after. We walk a few blocks and I say good-bye to Asa on the corner of 17th Street and Eighth Avenue. *I'll see you at the meeting*, he says and reminds me again where it is and when. *Absolutely*, I say, pathetically grateful I have somewhere to go tomorrow, someone to meet. I realize that beyond this and dinner with my friend Jean later in the week, I have no plans. No lunches, dinner parties, movie dates, plays, concerts, conference calls, business trips, breakfast meetings. Nothing. Asa gives me a hug and walks east down 17th Street. I watch him go, watch his white shirt and red hair bob through the dark until they disappear.

I get lost on my way back to Dave's writing studio on Charles Street. I'm not familiar with the West Village even though I've lived four blocks east of here for six years and a few blocks north for three. The streets jumble together, and after going this way and that, each time I'm convinced I've finally figured out where I am, I stumble—again and then again—onto Seventh Avenue. It's as if a spell has been cast and I'm doomed to end up there no matter what route I take. I'm exhausted and consider hailing a cab but I'm too broke and too embarrassed to ask for a ride that may be only one block. I feel as if I'm twenty-one again and have just moved to New York from Connecticut. I'm lost, have no apartment, no job, no family, no spouse. No one is expecting me. Every lit window taunts with the smug glow of an enviable life. Through heavy drapes and tasseled blinds I see the edges of beautiful living rooms shining with lamps and polished wood, perfectly littered with framed but not yet hung art and piles of books. Couples scurry home, leaning into each other, whispering stories and stressing opinions. *Do they know how lucky they are?* I think as they rush toward what I imagine are paid-for, mortgage-less, rent-free apartments and town houses. I watch them and wonder what Noah is doing. My chest tightens as I picture him winding down the evening with someone else, the two of them returning home together as we had countless times. I imagine him telling the story of his awful addict ex-boyfriend for the first time to astonished, sympathetic ears.

I finally end up back on Charles Street. All the buildings look the same, so I double-check the scrap of paper to make sure I have the right address. It's now almost one o'clock and every light in the building is off. I fiddle with the lock, turn the key, and, as softly as I can, enter the vestibule. I take my shoes off—gently, quietly—and toe the first step. The wood beneath the carpet croaks like the loudest frog. How can I ascend these stairs without making a racket? How do I get back to the safe, chandeliered little apartment without waking the whole building? I climb the second and third steps and they're even louder than the first. I'm sure the woman on the second floor is already calling Dave. Telling him that the hooligan staying in his apartment is thrashing in the stairwell, waking everyone. I can almost hear Dave cursing to Susie, swearing to her that this is the last straw, that he can no longer help me and I will need to find some-where else to crash while I get back on my feet.

I go slowly. I stop and start dozens of times on the stairs and rest even longer on the first- and second-floor landings. I'm almost to the third floor, nearly at the top of the last flight, when I lose my grip on one of the shoes and—*oh God no*—it falls and bangs loudly down the entire flight of stairs. When it finally smacks against the landing below I freeze and listen for footfalls, creaking floorboards, any signs of suddenly awake tenants. A few minutes pass and with my breath held I reach up and place the remaining shoe at the top of the stairs so I don't drop it. I inch back down until I reach the landing. The steps creak and belch the whole way and my progress—with numerous stops and starts—is excruciatingly slow. I pick up the renegade shoe and squeeze and twist and shake the thing viciously to punish it for causing so much trouble.

I turn back and look up the narrow flight of stairs to the third-floor landing. Nothing has ever seemed so far away. I consider going to sleep right where I stand. I can't bear the sound of another plank of wood screaming under my feet. How did I end up here? Homeless, broke, alone, and frozen with panic on the second-floor landing of someone else's building? How will I ever put my life back together? I stand very still.

Shaking off the drowsiness that's tugging my eyes closed and making my body sag against the wall, I try to be hopeful. The apartment is only one more flight. If I'm quiet enough no one will hear me. If I'm careful enough no one will be angry. The air is damp in the stairwell and my shirt is soaked through with sweat. I imagine everyone in the city safely tucked away in their beds. I wonder again if Noah is alone or with someone. I think of the thirty-one days I have to go until I reach ninety and decide, ominously, that it's easier to count days in psych wards and rehab, not so easy in the city.

Up ahead, the other shoe is sitting at the top of the stairs, exactly where I left it. It's inches from Dave's door, steps from the pullout bed I can collapse into and the pile of blankets I can hide beneath. Eventually, I move toward the bottom step. The wood moans under my feet. My damp back itches but I don't dare scratch it. A toilet flushes on a higher floor and a door slams somewhere below. I wait for what seems like forever before taking the next step. There is a long way to go.

Home

Sixty days. It's my first thought before opening my eyes after a restless night on Dave's pullout. And then: *Thirty to go.* I look at my watch and it's a few minutes past nine. I jump from the creaky pullout, hurry through my shower, get dressed, fold the mattress back into the couch, rearrange the cushions, and tidy up the place. I want to be up and out by the time Dave arrives. I don't want to be underfoot and, more than that, I don't want—not right now—to see him. I can't bear that look of worry on his face. Though we've been friends for years, the look belongs to someone more warden than friend. It says without saying a word, *Get sober and then we'll talk*, and I don't blame him. So I tiptoe down those wretched steps and leave for the day.

It's almost ten by the time I'm out of the building. I buy a cup of coffee from the closest bodega and wander around the neighborhood to get my bearings. None of it seems familiar. I've lived in New York for twelve years and I feel like I've never been here before. It's quiet and leafy and appears unimaginably expensive. Every shop is one I haven't seen before, every restaurant a place I can't afford. I eventually make my way toward the meeting to see Asa, as planned, and as I'm approaching 10th Street and Fifth Avenue I remember a deal I struck with Jack: never to step within a two-block radius of One Fifth. This rules out Washington Square Park, all of University Place and Sixth Avenue between 8th and 10th Streets, and Fifth Avenue south of 10th Street. I'm also not to go within a two-block radius of Sixth Avenue and Houston, where my old drug buddy Mark's apartment is and where much of my last drug use happened. The area around the now shut literary agency I co-owned, just north of Madison Square Park, is also off-limits. These places are what Jack calls triggers and I am to avoid them at all costs. For a moment I worry that the meeting where I'm joining Asa is off-limits, but then realize it sits on the 10th Street border, half a block east of Fifth. If it were one door south of 10th Street, I wouldn't be able to go.

I reach Fifth Avenue—the first time since coming home—and as the old familiar Art Deco tower that is One Fifth comes into view I feel like a ghost haunting my old life. How many times did I rush down this street toward home, worrying that Noah had changed the locks? How many times did I walk up Fifth toward the agency with a blistering hangover, gutted from being up the night before? Standing on the same pavement where I once walked with such agony I can't help but wonder: *How was I that person? How did it go on for so long?* I walk toward the meeting and begin to think I should never have come back, that I should have accepted my sister Kim's offer to live with her in Maine. How did I think it was possible to

be here? Every inch of this neighborhood carries a memory of my
life before. I look south, toward Washington Square Park, and I can
see, just a few blocks away, the two oversized green awnings of One
Fifth jutting out over the sidewalk. As clear as day I can see the corner windows of the apartment where Noah and I lived for six years,
where Noah still lives. The last six weeks have passed in hospital
rooms, rehab, and, last night, an unfamiliar apartment. Everything
that has happened—breaking up with Noah, everyone knowing I'm
a crack addict, the end of my career, the company gone, all the anger
and disappointment—these things have all registered, yes, but collectively and in the abstract. This moment, however, is as concrete as
the sidewalk I am standing on. This place before me—with shining
windows and green awnings flapping in the breeze—was home and
now is not. I no longer belong here. From some far memory comes
the doomy voice of my childhood piano teacher, who predicted, after
too many hours spent attempting to teach my distracted, unpracticed
self, that I would one day grow up to become a crack addict, just as
the most notorious girl in my hometown had. *You'll have your come-
uppance*, she forecast on more than one occasion, without a hint of
doubt in her Irish brogue. *One day you'll have a rude awakening, and
when you do it will take your breath away.* And so it has.

I turn onto the street where the meeting is and see a blond woman
pushing a stroller toward me. It's Jane, an old friend of Noah's from
Yale and the wife of a former client whom I haven't spoken to in
many months. Jane's also a bestselling and highly respected author,
and as she approaches I think, *Of all the people in the world who I could
run into, why her?* As she looks up it occurs to me that she might not
say a word, that she may just pass me by and pretend I'm not there.

Of course she will. I'm a pariah now. That's what people do when they encounter a pariah. They don't see them.

Jane slows down, kick-locks the stroller, and steps toward me. Without a word, she gently grabs my arms, pulls me in, and kisses me on the cheek. Quick, without ceremony, over-before-it's-happened. She pats my shoulders, looks at me tenderly, and steps away. *Jane*, is all I manage to stammer before she's unlocked the stroller and is off again down the street.

It's 12:25 and I'm already late to meet Asa. I sprint toward the meeting, still bewildered by Jane's kindness. I see the research library where the meeting is held and go in. The security guard asks me to sign a sheet and tells me the meeting is on the fifth floor. *How does he know I'm going to the meeting?* I think, worried that I look as unbuckled as I feel. I scribble my name and the time, and hurry up the stairs. On the fifth floor there is a reading room with beautifully carved bookshelves and wide panes of glass that look out onto the planted terraces and curtained windows adorning the backs of town houses and apartment buildings on 11th Street. Something about the room feels familiar, tugs at an old memory, like a room from a house I knew in childhood, but I know I've never been here before. Midday light streams in from the windows. Before I look around for Asa I sit down, rest my chin against my chest, close my eyes, and exhale. The shaky alienation I felt on the street just minutes ago calms with each breath. I feel small but safe, and at the edge of tears. I look up and Asa is in the seat next to me. Perfect khakis, black Izod, pink belt, freckled everywhere. *Hi*, he says, smiling. *I wondered if you'd show.*

His red hair, in the gushing light, glows like a halo. It's preposterous, I know this, but it really does. He puts his hand on my shoulder, this person I've known for less than twenty-four hours but who feels like my best friend in the world. He puts his hand on my shoulder, leans forward, and gives me a powerful hug. *You're a mess,* he says. *You're a mess and you're going to be just fine.*

Speck in Streetscape

I'm lost in the West Village again. I've been at Dave's for almost a week and the streets west of Seventh Avenue are still hexed in some way that makes me always end up in front of the small park at the top of Horatio Street, or anywhere on Seventh Avenue south of 14th. It's raining. I'm on Jane Street. I know there's a coffee shop nearby, the one Jack and I went to between meetings on my first day back. I head what I think is west and recognize a little green banner at the end of the block. I'm splattered with rain but still basically dry by the time I get there. There is an advertisement for a pottery studio above the coffee shop sign but there is no pottery, not a trace of it, in the place. The owner is one of the most beautiful men in New York (Jack and I had decided this last week) and also one of the meanest.

The small, low-ceilinged room is packed. Scruffy twenty-year-olds who look like they star in their own reality shows huddle into their laptops writing—what? screenplays? short stories? Are these the people who used to send me their manuscripts with letters that began with plot summaries? Why are they all so relentlessly attractive? No one moves from their seat and I realize I don't have any cash on me. There's no cash machine in the shop and the rain is pelting outside. *Can I help you?* the mean beauty snaps from behind jars overflowing with complicated cookies. His eyes, I notice, are green and gold and flash my way with nothing but contempt and impatience. *I'm waiting for someone,* I stutter, and as if he's been expecting this exact response he says, *Well, how about ordering something while you do that.*

Is this actually happening? Do I now have some scent or sign that lets people know that I'm down, I'm broke, banished, have few defenses, and can be kicked?

Maybe is all I come up with as I turn my back to him and pretend to make a phone call. Who can I call? I can't call Jack again. I've left three messages between last night and this morning already. I'm seeing Asa at a meeting in a church uptown later and, as I have with Jack, I've left too many voice mails to leave another. I can feel the barista's eyes flashing anger at my back. I dial fake random numbers and say *hey* in the most casual, I-have-dozens-of-friends-happy-to-hear-from-me kind of way. I perform one half of an intimate conversation and worry that at any second this guy is going to escort me out the door and into the rain. I fib a quick *See you later,* flip the phone shut, turn around, and sure enough, the pretty prick is leaning against the counter, arms crossed, with a look on his face that can only be described as disgust.

I can't take another second so I leave. The rain is coming down in sheets and the streets are empty. I walk to the end of the block and head what I think is east. It's 3:30, I've already been to my gym (the year's membership has luckily been paid) and two meetings, but have two hours to kill before I can go back to Dave's place before meeting Asa later. I stumble onto Hudson and realize I've gone west. Barnes & Noble in Union Square is the only place I can think of going where I can disappear for a few hours without it being obvious that I have nowhere else to go. It's at least a twenty-minute walk, but I turn around anyway and head back toward Jane. The rain is colder than it was before, pushier. I find a broken umbrella sticking out of a Dumpster and for a few blocks agree to a fiction that it's actually keeping me dry. There is a moment—water sloshing from my shoes, T-shirt plastered to my chest, rain dripping from the brim of my NYC Parks Department cap—when I stop and look around. I have no idea where I am. Not one building or business looks familiar. I've gone east past Jane and what I thought was north. I don't see any street signs. Am I anywhere? I wonder. Do I even exist anymore? I've lost all sense of direction and feel as if the rain is about to blast me into a billion microscopic particles. I've never felt so small. I start calling people—Dave, Jack, Kim, Jean, Asa—and reach only outgoing voice mail messages. I have nothing to say so I hang up each time and dial the next number. I imagine them all safe in their warm, dry offices and apartments, surrounded by colleagues, pets, ringing phones, and freshly brewed coffee. I think of the agency, now gone, and the night only months ago when I showed up and the locks had been changed. How on the other side of that locked door sat furniture that Kate and I had picked out and carried from a store on Park Avenue South. After that night, I would never see that office again. I stop dialing the phone, which is now slick with rainwater and very likely to be broken soon.

I've been back for five days, have sixty-four days sober, and with ninety days almost in sight I don't know how, on the other side of it, I'll be able to hold things together, how I'll stay in the city. Jack's slogans and Asa's assurances aren't helping. There is no money coming in, it's all going out, the bills are mounting, and I have to find an apartment in the next week before Dave throws me out. I feel like one of the street urchins Dickens describes in his books. Like little Jo in *Bleak House*, who dies of something bronchial and grim like consumption once his use to the world has expired. Mine has too. Like this ridiculous umbrella, whatever fantasy I had of being OK, of making my way back in a city of overachieving winners, is now quite obviously a figment, a pathetic shield against an overwhelming truth. It's over. I'm a Dickensian speck in a city that no longer has use for me. I had my time here and in that time got lucky, played my cards well for a while, and then very badly.

I put the umbrella down, let the rain drench any remaining patches of dry clothing and skin, put my face to the sky and think, and then say, *OK*. The city disappears around me and there are only the elements. Wind and water, freezing and clean. *OK*, I say again, not really understanding what it is I am agreeing to, what it is precisely I am accepting. But I am accepting something. The truth of my circumstances?

The reality I have until now avoided? It's much worse than I imagined and also somehow better. Is this the bottom I hear people refer to in meetings? The grim despair that makes change possible?

I walk without any sense of direction. At this point I don't care where I go. I'll walk until five, get soaked until Dave has left the studio. There is no one on the sidewalks, no cars on the streets. The maze of the West Village is empty. Thunderclaps and wild sheets of rain slap against the asphalt. Had I ever heard thunder in New York? Was it like everything else that I took for granted—these streets, the cost of things, love—and can only now recognize?

Up ahead an awning sticks out over a dry patch of sidewalk and I quickly walk toward it and duck under. It's a small real estate agency and in the window there are photographs of apartments. I remember when Noah and I would stand in front of windows like this one and gawk at the high-ceilinged, new-kitchened beauties. Looking at these shiny, meticulous spaces now only reminds me that I don't have my own and the one I'll end up in—should I end up in one at all—will not be like these.

The wind starts blowing the rain horizontally and the awning no longer provides protection. A sudden squall of rain explodes against the window, the awning, the drenched length of me, and in a panic I jump inside the real estate agency. Dripping wet, I close the door, and as I do four people sitting at desks look up and say hello in unison. I tell them I'm looking for an apartment to rent, which is true, though I have no plan to go through an agency and pay the outrageous broker's fee that is usually at least two months' rent. Still, the little place is warm and dry and I have time to kill. I tell them that I'm taking a sabbatical from work and looking for a cheaper place to rent. Computers flutter to life, images of apartments with rental statistics shine from screens, and one of the agents, a middle-aged bald man, says he knows of a great studio with a terrace that's about to come on the market. Turns out it's just a few blocks from here and he could get me in tomorrow at noon before anyone else sees it. *Sure,* I say, with no intention at all of showing up. We exchange numbers, he gives me the address where I am to meet him the next day, and after a round of good-byes I'm back on the street.

I keep the little slip of paper in my pocket through the meeting that night and miraculously it finds its way into my pants the next day. I pull it from my front pocket around 11:30 that morning and think of the bald guy showing up at the building and me nowhere to be found. It seems like something I might have done before and felt guilty about. Something I would have cringed over later as I downed vodka after vodka until I forgot it altogether. So I go meet the guy in front of the building at 15th Street and Seventh Avenue. When I get there I realize this is the block where I lived when I first met Noah. The block where the apartment I owned when I was twenty-five is and where my girlfriend Nell and I lived for almost three years. I always felt more comfortable on this street than I did at One Fifth, and as I look down the block I see that it hasn't changed much. It's still a mix of rent-controlled mid-century apartment buildings, older tenements, hair salons, and renovated brownstones. I can't remember the last time I was here. I sold the apartment—the second floor of a carriage house at the back of a courtyard—years ago so I'd have money once we started the literary agency, but after that I don't think I ever came back.

I meet the bald guy in the small lobby and we go up to the seventeenth floor. As he unlocks the door to the apartment, I have a strong feeling of déjà vu, not unlike the feeling I had that first day at the Library meeting. We walk into the short hallway and before we've reached the one and only room, before I've seen the small terrace that looks out over the city, to the Empire State Building and beyond, before I see the little kitchen with space enough for a desk, and the simple black-and-white-tiled bathroom, and before I worry where I'll find the money for the first and last months' rent, the deposit, and the broker's fee, before any of this, words come out of my mouth, and as I say them I know they're true: *This is it. I'm home.*

Re-entry

Seventy-four days. Sixteen to go. First morning waking up in the apartment on 15th Street. I stay up until midnight the night before and, from my bed, watch the lights of the Empire State Building click off. I can almost hear the old skyscraper sigh as it goes dark, as if exhausted from the long day. I haven't unpacked or set the place up yet, but I've moved my things in from One Fifth. Noah and I agree I should move out without him around, so three days before I move out of Dave's (and with permission from Jack to cross into the trigger zone), I go. I ask my friend Cy if she'll come with me and she agrees. I ask her for several reasons. One, she's been up to White Plains a few times and has been supportive. Two, she's worked as a counselor for people diagnosed with HIV, AIDS, and other fatal illnesses since the eighties and very little makes her blink. Three, she's dropdead gorgeous, unusually chic, and, well, the woman can enter a building. It comforts me somewhat that she will be at my side, like a glamorous force field, as I re-enter for the first time the building I left on a stretcher. She meets me in front of One Fifth, looking like she always does, thank God, hooks her arm in mine, and says, *OK, kid, let's get this over with.* I practically hide behind her as we enter. Even though Noah arranges for keys to be left at the front desk, and even with Cy at my side, I'm afraid they won't let me in. It's been two months since I collapsed through these same doors, unable to stand up, begging for a key. Two months since the ambulance drove me away to Lenox Hill.

José, one of the doormen, is at the desk and the moment he sees me says, with exaggerated kindness and what I can't help but suspect is sarcasm, *Noah has left you keys.* How many times did José buzz up one of my dealers or watch me come in the door with shady characters I'd picked up in Washington Square Park when Noah was away? He can be sarcastic all he wants, I think, and suddenly wonder how many other people in the building carried on the way I had. Anyone? Many? In rehab and in the meetings I've heard dozens of stories like mine—on-the-surface successful people carrying on what look like respectable lives in buildings like this one, who at night turned into drug-addled zombies, buzzing up drug-dealing-and-using vampires from their lobbies. Maybe I wasn't the only one at One Fifth living such a messy life. Maybe I wasn't anything out of the ordinary. As much as I want to believe this, the wary and pitying look in José's eyes suggests otherwise.

Cy and I get in the elevator and get off on the sixth floor. The hallway is just as it was, just a hallway. Indifferent, a little stuffy with its green-and-gold-striped walls and beige corporate carpeting. The new locks in the door are still shiny, and as we enter the apartment, Benny is right away at our feet—meowing and purring and then, unlike her, immediately slinking away, out of sight. She disappears into the den and only later creeps to the edge of the bedroom while I'm packing my clothes into duffel bags. *Join the club*, I say to her as she eyes me doubtfully from across the room and keeps her distance.

It will take two and a half days to get all my stuff, including the cat, out of Noah's and over to 15th Street. Cy doesn't come back the next days but it's OK. I race through the place taking clothes from drawers, jackets and shoes from closets, and pulling books off the shelves Noah and I had built when we first moved in. The ones we found the design for in a book called *Living with Books*. We bought a pile of similar books and over dinner one night at L'Acajou pored over the glossy pages until we found a simple design that fit the place. Did I get drunk that night? I wonder painfully. Pulling my books from the shelves and shoving them into cardboard boxes, I cringe with regret and wish that I could go back in time and do it all differently. But even if I could, would I be able to keep from drinking? Keep from sneaking into the bathroom and calling a dealer? Even within spitting distance of ninety days I'm not so sure.

I snoop for signs of a new love. I'm queasy with jealousy, even though I ended our relationship at the strong recommendation of my counselor in rehab, my sister, and several close friends who all urged me to get sober on my own, away from what each described in one way or another as a codependent dynamic of addict and enabler that Noah and I had, it seems, perfected. My desperation and need of their support were and are so great that I didn't question them and agreed. Noah is angry with me at first, but a counselor from the rehab calls and explains and asks him to give me the space I need to get healthy. I have not seen him for over two months, and our only contact has been crisp and spare and specific to the details of my moving out. Rarely does an hour go by when I don't question the decision to break up, doubt that it's the right choice. But something more than the advice of others keeps me from changing my mind, something beyond logic or want that keeps me from calling Noah and running back into his arms.

In between packing boxes and duffel bags, I check the caller ID box for unfamiliar and frequently appearing phone numbers (too many to form any conclusions); sift through the bedside table drawers for evidence of sex—lubricant, condoms—and find nothing; frisk Noah's gray Helmut Lang blazer and the pockets of his gray snap-front jacket and, again, nothing. Just lighters and cigarettes, which it's clear he's now taken up again, openly. I'd been a tyrant about smoking when we were together, which now seems just as ironic and hypocritical as it was.

On the last day, once everything is packed and ready to go, I sit in the corner window of the living room and finger the beige and brown animal print fabric on the window seat. There is a small square pillow made with the same fabric leaning against the window and I wonder if I should take it with me. The fabric came from a store in Islington, in London, where we spent four or five weekends in an apartment I split the rent on in my twenties. Buying that fabric, having that window seat cushion and pillow made, seemed, at twenty-seven, like the most adult, most worldly thing one could do. I laugh out loud at my younger, now faraway self and am amused for a brief flash before the tight fist of grief returns. I watch the early evening lights blink on up lower Fifth Avenue and the white headlights rush toward me. How many times had I sat here? And in what states—furious, ashamed, worried, high, hopeful, hating, drunk, arrogant, panicked, exhausted, in love? I sit for a few more minutes and remember as much as I can before I go. I leave the pillow behind.

Several nights later, Dave organizes tickets to go to the opera. I think but am not sure we see *Aida* that night. I remember it was long and one of the older Zeffirelli productions at the Met. We eat dinner in the overpriced, still glamorous restaurant on the Grand Tier level of the building. Starters and main course during the first intermission and dessert and coffee during the second. Dave's seats at the opera are good ones—center Grand Tier, which is the second balcony, second row, in the middle—and the people seated around us all look like longtime operagoers, dressed nicely, not extravagantly like the tourists in the orchestra section. I can't help but think everyone here has been sitting in these seats since they were teenagers, have seen these operas hundreds of times, and are quite alert to the polluting presence of anyone who has not. Having spent the day at the 12:30 and two o'clock Library meetings, and the afternoon sitting in Union Square with Asa, telling him about some of the grittier details of the double life I lived as an addict, I find that this refined evening-scape does not feel comfortable.

Over dinner, Dave keeps talk within the firm boundaries of opera, his family, and popular culture. Only once does he ask how things are going and I am careful not to sound too positive or too discouraged. I don't actually say, *One day at a time*, but I might as well. I am like a careful apprentice with a benevolent but stern mentor. Aware at every second that I am lucky to be given any time at all in light of his many kindnesses—the pickup and drop-off at rehab, the use of the writing studio on Charles Street, all the phone calls and e-mails he's had to field from concerned and angry people who became aware that he was in contact with me after I disappeared months ago. I tread carefully and wonder if we'll ever be at ease with each other again.

Once the opera is over we take a cab downtown. I'm grateful he directs the driver to my address first and then his own, as I know my days of paying for cab rides are over. We say our good-byes and I head into my building for what will be my second night there. I get into the elevator, which—despite the fact that the apartment is relatively cheap and the building is all rentals—has an elevator man. The one on duty now is not one I've seen before, so I tell him to go to seventeen. He says, *OK, boss*, in an accent that I think must be either Croatian or Georgian. I get to my apartment and notice two large paper shopping bags hanging from the doorknob. When I see the quiche boxes from Eli's bakery jutting out from one of the bags, I know they're from Jean. There is a card taped to a handle and on it my name is scrawled in Jean's inimitably looping and jagged cursive. Inside it reads, *Welcome to your new home and your new life. With so much love, Jean.* I open the door and unpack the bags, which are filled with quiches and salads and roasted meats. Some of the food is from Eli's bakery, some from Zabar's, and some made by Jean's chef, Paul.

There are even delicate Austrian chocolates from the Neue Gallerie. After I put the food away, I stand in front of the now full refrigerator and shout, *THANK YOU, JEAN!* I realize, with relief and a little gust of confidence, that I don't have to buy food for at least a week.

I go out to the terrace. It's a crisp spring night and the lights of the city are dancing. It's after midnight, so I can make out only the ghosty outline of the now dark Empire State Building. I'm relieved to be away from Dave, away from what I imagine to be his nervous scrutiny. I think about his writing studio on Charles Street—the creaky steps, the downstairs neighbor poised to pounce at the slightest hint of nefarious activity. I think of the entire precarious time there and remember how during the first afternoon, within minutes of Dave's leaving, I'd been consumed with the desire to get high. How lucky I didn't, I think. What a miracle the craving passed. The city blinks its light, police sirens sound, faint music from another apartment comes and goes with the breeze. And then, just as it had that afternoon, the old craving returns. How do I describe it? It's like skin that feels perfectly fine one moment and then is ablaze with an itch the next. It looks the same: skin—harmless, unfettered skin. But all at once it's screaming to be ravaged with fingernails and rubbed raw.

I look back into the apartment through the small square window in the door and think, *There is nothing and no one to stop me.* I can get high in this apartment, which is mine alone, and no one is coming home or arriving in the morning. I then look down at the scattered traffic on Seventh Avenue and think, *If all else fails there are seventeen floors and a hard sidewalk.* I know I should call Jack. Or Asa. Or one of the dozen numbers that are now in my phone from people at The Library and other meetings. *CALL SOMEONE!* I say out loud, but even as I say the words I know it's too late. My mind whizzes with ways to get drugs. Since Jack made me get a new cell phone, I don't have Happy's or Rico's numbers. And I can't remember them. Then it occurs to me: Mark's place on Houston and Sixth. He's always using and always up. It's midweek and before 1:00 a.m. If he doesn't already have drugs in the apartment he can easily get some. Better to go there than to call Happy or Rico anyway, since I owe them each a thousand dollars.

I go. Out the door, down the elevator, and onto Seventh Avenue, where I quickly duck into a bodega and head to the cash machine. I have less than two hundred dollars in my checking account, but I also have three credit cards with separate limits for cash advances. I dimly remember being asked to set a PIN code for at least one. I am practically dancing as I scour my wallet for credit cards. I try one and use the PIN for my regular cash card and it doesn't work. I try another and get the same result. I try the third, and again no luck. So I go back to the first and play around with a few combinations of the PIN code for my cash card.

I replace the last two numbers with zeros and BINGO!!!—it works. I advance four hundred dollars and am electric with the anticipation of getting high. It's been so long. I rush out onto Seventh Avenue and a cab immediately pulls up. I step in and realize that at some point, either on the terrace or just after, I have left the world I had been living in and entered another—or rather re-entered the one that had been waiting.

I tell the cabdriver the address and I think I hear him say, *Didn't take long*. Right away, I ask him what he just said and he responds calmly, in a Jamaican accent, *Nothing my friend, nothing*. We're at Mark's in a few minutes and to my surprise the meter registers a fare, which he is clearly waiting for. I pay and he mumbles something which I hear as *Be God*, but figure he means *Be good*.

I'm at the door. The same door I've stood at dozens and dozens of times. Looking at the same buzzer and hoping the same hope: that Mark is home and that Mark has drugs. Whatever hesitation struggled against desire on the terrace less than an hour before is now gone. I am giddy and antsy and shuffling before the door as if something wonderful is waiting on the other side. Nothing of the past months, nothing of the ruin and upset my using has caused, figures into this moment. Or if it does, it's a dim unpleasantness that, along with every other worry, is being escaped. The world and its woe exist on this side of the door, where I am now; the place to hide from it all is on the other, where I'm going. I press the button and in seconds hear Mark's voice, metallic and loud through the intercom. *Who is it?* he squawks, and before I say my name the door is buzzing open.

One Day

It's early afternoon, two days after showing up at Mark's apartment, when I return home. Benny hasn't been fed for almost three days, and when I open the door she is meowing desperately. I immediately open a fresh can of cat food, put water in her bone-dry dish, and try to pet her, but she bites at my hands and skitters away. I plug in my cell phone, which is dead and I know will be full of messages— from Jack, Asa, Kim, Jean, Dave. I'm starving and I take one of the quiches from the refrigerator and eat the entire thing. I've purchased Tylenol PM from the bodega downstairs and take a handful to cushion the crash. I wish I had vodka or beer or some kind of alcohol, but even after forty-eight hours of crack and vodka at Mark's the idea of bringing booze into this apartment seems out of bounds. So the Tylenol PM will have to do. Once the phone is charged I listen to the messages: three from Kim—each more worried than the one before—two from Dave, whom Kim has called because she has not heard from me, none from Jack, two from Asa, and one from Polly.

Polly is a few years younger than I am, lives with her twin sister, Heather, who is the bartender at an Irish tavern in the West Village that serves burgers and steaks and chicken pot pies. Heather and Polly are coke addicts. Polly is trying to get sober, Heather is not.

Polly has six or seven days clean. I met her at that first meeting at The Library with Asa. When I raised my hand that day, as Jack had insisted I do, and said I had sixty days, Polly waved to me from across the room and smiled while everyone else clapped. Later, Polly raised her hand and shared that she was afraid Heather would overdose and that it had been difficult to put together more than a few days clean when their dealer was still coming in and out of the apartment at all hours.

One of the most frightening things Polly said that day was that she once had six years sober. She and Heather got sober after college and then, four years ago, after graduate school and a few broken hearts between them, they moved in together. Three years later, they both relapsed. Neither had gone more than a week since without getting high.

Polly lost her job as a schoolteacher six months ago and walks dogs to pay the few hundred dollars that is her portion of the rent-controlled apartment they share on St. Mark's Place. Polly is my height, very thin, and is often wearing sweatpants and T-shirts that don't look washed. Her hair is shoulder length, dirty blond, and greasy, and she reeks of cigarette smoke. She has a dog named Essie—a fat, midsized gray-and-white mutt she walks up and down the side streets of the East Village while she chain-smokes. Her clothes are usually covered in dog hair.

My first response to Polly when she smiled at me at The Library was *Fuck, I hope she doesn't want to talk after the meeting;* but when she described—plainly, clearly—how desperate she was not to use again but feared she would, there was a moment when I confused the words she was saying with the words I was thinking, believed momentarily that they were coming from inside my head and not from across the room. I looked again at this skeletal, disheveled, unwashed mess, and as she spoke I got very still because everything she was relating was something I had felt before and in precisely the same way. When the meeting ended, I was the one to chase after her, down the stairs and into the street, to ask for her phone number.

Polly's voice mail message is short and sweet: *Hey, I didn't see you in the meeting yesterday or today. What's up? Call me.* I do. She picks up on the first ring and says in a playful, school-teacher tone, *Billy boy, did you relapse?* I mumble in response some kind of yes. She laughs. She actually laughs, and says, *Get to a meeting, don't sit on the pity pot, just get to a meeting. Don't make a big deal out of it, just get back on the beam. And call your sponsor.* I listen to Polly like I'm listening to someone telling me how to defuse a bomb strapped to my ankle. *OK, OK,* I say and agree to call her later that night.

It's Thursday evening and I've already missed two meetings at The Library. I sit on my bed and look out the window toward the building that used to be Barneys but is now, vaguely and in ways that don't make sense to me, a museum for Tibetan culture. Things change, things stay the same, but I remain an addict. I think about one of the writers I represented whose book is now on the bestseller list and being smothered in acclaim. She has kept in touch, came to rehab once for a walk, and gave me the first signed copy of the book, but she is gone now and my professional relationship to her work a thing of the past. As with Kate and Noah, and even friends like Dave and Jean, I can only envision her happiness and success and my lack of both. I don't imagine that within any of their lives there is strife or fear or regret or sadness. When I have tried to explain this to Jack, he interrupts me and says, *ENOUGH SELF-PITY!* which of course I find humiliating. I also find it strange that with all the people who have left me messages on my cell phone, Jack is not one of them. I'm sure Kim called him—she's had his number since I was in the hospital.

As the Tylenol PM begins to kick in, I start thinking about Jack's patronizing phrases, his dismissive accusations of self-pity, and how he never just listens to what I'm feeling, what I'm going through. If not him, then who? He's my sponsor, isn't he? I think about going back to Mark's, but I know there won't be any more drugs there until evening when he can call Happy or Rico. Mark agreed not to tell Happy that I was in the bedroom when he came with the drugs two nights ago, because of the money I owe him. I wonder if Mark kept his word or instead tipped him off that I'm back in town. Worry about Happy mingles with my rising resentment toward Jack, and in a burst of frustration I pick up the lamp next to my bed and throw it against a wall. The light bulb shatters but the small wooden base remains intact. Next to the wall where I've thrown the lamp I see a meeting book. Reluctantly, I pick it up to see if there is a mid-afternoon meeting nearby. I can't bear to call anyone else back and have no idea what I will say when I eventually do. I flip through the meeting book and see one starting in ten minutes a few blocks away at the gay and lesbian center. I go.

The meeting is small, gloomy, and filled with mostly middle-aged gay men who look sick. I'm on the end of two days smoking crack and guzzling vodka with no food or sleep, so I don't look so hot either. The meeting is a round robin format where everyone is expected to talk once the speaker has qualified, which means he describes, in ten to thirty minutes, what it was like when he used, how he got sober, and what it's like now. I make it through the first ten minutes of the speaker's qualification and I can't bear the idea of talking, of having to admit I've just relapsed; and I don't want these guys crowding me after the meeting with their numbers and their understanding faces. I want to leave, so I do.

I call Polly from the street and she picks up right away. *Did you go to a meeting and say that you've relapsed?* she snaps without salutation and I lie and say yes. *Which one?* she asks doubtfully and I tell her. *Did you call your sponsor?* I lie again and say yes. *So what are you going to do now?* she asks, and the truth is I have no idea. I tell her so and she says, *Well, let's talk.* I don't remember everything we talked about that night, but I do remember her telling me a story of getting drunk on a flight to Dallas, where, once she landed, she blew off the rehearsal dinner for a wedding she was supposed to be a bridesmaid in to go looking for an ex-boyfriend. She hit a bar on the way and ended up

walking in traffic on a freeway outside the city and getting arrested. I tell her how I was—just three months earlier—thrown off a
flight to Berlin because I was convinced the plane was crawling with
DEA agents and said something bizarre to the flight attendant. We
talk and trade war stories, and I walk west on 15th Street, north on
Eighth Avenue, east on 16th Street, south on Seventh Avenue, west
on 15th, completing the loop around the block again and again and
again. Polly keeps me on the phone a long time, and I remember several times thinking that the dealers will be back in business soon and
maybe I should get off the phone and go over to Mark's. But I stay on
the phone, walk in circles until I'm exhausted, and, finally, go home.

I call Kim that night. Dave and Jean and Asa, too. The call with Dave
lasts less than ten seconds and he says, *Good luck, call Kim.* It's clear
he's had it and that I am not his problem anymore. Kim is similarly
short with me. I leave a message for Jean on her answering machine
that I'm OK and will speak with her in the morning. Asa and I talk.
As with Polly, we stay on for a long time. Long enough for me to fall
asleep, because I wake up at four or five in the morning with all the
lights on and my cell phone pressed between my ear and the pillow. I
get up to turn off the lights and find Benny asleep next to the door. I
want to pet her, tell her how sorry I am for leaving her alone without
food for over two days, but I'm afraid she'll bite me again, so I leave
her alone and go back to bed.

It's after one o'clock when I wake up the next day. It's Friday and
I've missed the 12:30 meeting at The Library, but I make coffee, eat
a bowl of granola, shower, dress, and get out the door to make the

two o'clock. Polly and Asa are both there when I walk in but I don't recognize anyone else. *C'mere, Crackhead,* Polly says and pats the seat next to her. She is wearing what looks like pajama bottoms. Asa, freckled and immaculate in his usual uniform of tight Izod, jeans, and colored belt, sits on my other side. I've never been so happy to see anyone as I am these two.

The meeting begins. There are two speakers—one with just over a year sober and the other with decades—who talk about early sobriety and the first ninety days. Of all days I should be listening, but I can't stop thinking about the four-hundred-dollar cash advance I put on my credit card to buy drugs. I start thinking about how much money I have left on that card and the others. I tally up ten grand or so and begin to imagine how I could put together a war chest of drugs for one last bender and then make use of the seventeenth-floor balcony off my apartment. No pills this time, no chance of failing again. Polly rubs the back of my neck and I can smell the cigarette smoke coming off her clothes. The speakers go on speaking, a hat gets passed and fills up with dollars, people raise their hands and announce their day counts—twenty-four, eighty-eight, thirty. People clap. Polly raises her hand and says nine or ten or something in that range. More clapping. She pinches my leg, I raise my hand. *One day,* I say, and the place explodes.

The meeting ends and as it breaks up six or seven people approach me, give me their numbers, and tell me to call anytime. I notice a short, thin, dark-haired girl wearing overalls and a striped cardigan whom I think I know from somewhere. I'm pretty sure it's the on-again, off-again girlfriend of Noah's screenwriting partner, but I can't think of her name. She disappears through the door and up the stairs before I can remember.

I go with Polly to the dog run in Union Square Park and watch Essie get humped by the smallest dog I've ever seen. She wanders slowly around the narrow dirt yard, but her suitor keeps pace, bouncing from behind on brittle twig-thin legs. Polly and I drink coffee and the afternoon slips by. She tells me about having been a competitive swimmer in college and, years later, getting drunk on beer in the morning before going to work teaching elementary school kids. *Here we are, Crackhead*, she says, gesturing with her right hand toward the dog run, and then, like a wise sober owl, says, *Exactly where we're supposed to be*.

Three days later I don't see Polly at the 12:30 or two o'clock meetings at The Library. She doesn't show up to the Tuesday meeting either. She doesn't return my calls, and the few people we have in common haven't seen or heard from her since last Friday. Despite Jack's warnings that I should keep my distance and not chase after her, I hang out in front of the building where she and Heather live. She never appears. Finally, on Wednesday, she shows up at the two o'clock meeting, late, and sits toward the back. I try to catch her eye but she stares into her lap. She looks even more unkempt and ragged than usual and after the speaker finishes qualifying, she raises the same hand she used six days before to gesture grandly toward the dog run, Union Square, our lives. *I'm Polly*, she mutters. *I have one day*.

The Rooms

I have eight days now and Polly has three. The last few days we've met at the 12:30, stayed for the two o'clock, and each time ended up at the dog run. I'm getting used to the dog run smells of piss and shit and am no longer worried that someone I know will see me. The same people are usually there. A few old ladies, several professional dog walkers like Polly, who come with dozens of cool-tempered, strangely obedient dogs on leashes. And then there are the young guys in tracksuits, expensive ones like my friend Lotto's. We met in the rehab Noah and Kate sent me to in Oregon last year after they organized an intervention with Dave and Kim. Lotto's a rich kid from New York and at the age of twenty-two has been to ten or eleven rehabs and two therapeutic boarding schools, something I didn't know existed before meeting him. He wears tracksuits—either Adidas brand or the shiny plush kind with fancy zippers and logos, the ones that look like they were purchased at expensive resorts. According to the last text he sent me, Lotto's at the Betty Ford Center in California, already having relapsed two or three times since returning to New York from Oregon. These guys in the dog park remind me of him, just older, twenty-seven, twenty-eight, maybe thirty. I imagine they do coke all night and stumble out in the afternoons to let their dogs go to the bathroom. With bloodshot eyes and jumbo coffee containers from Dean & Deluca and Starbucks, they text and call from their cell phones and I imagine them scoring bags of drugs for the coming night. I wonder who lives like this—expensive dogs, good haircuts, new running shoes, worked-out bodies, fancy phones, tracksuits. Who other than people like me and Polly who've wiped out and are getting sober can dawdle in a dog run at three o'clock on a weekday afternoon? Dealers? None of my dealers were ever white. But that doesn't mean that these guys aren't dealing. Maybe they're slightly older Lottos with families who've cut them off, so they deal drugs to keep using. The lifespan of this kind of dealer/user/aging rich kid must be short, I think, as I watch them retreat to the far benches of the dog run and grumble into their phones. I try to remember war stories from the meetings, or what Polly and Asa and lately I refer to as *the rooms*, to align with this profile but come up with nothing.

My mind dances through these possibilities but I don't share them with Polly for fear the speculation about dealers and using will trigger her. We talk a lot about Heather, how she's starting to shoot coke with needles, is missing work and being warned. *She's going to lose her job, get arrested, or die*, Polly says as she exhales a giant plume of cigarette smoke. *And every time I turn around there's a dealer in the living room and a bag of coke on the coffee table.* I offer, careful not to be too pushy, to help Polly look for a rehab or move her to a new apartment—at least until she has ninety days—but Polly's not ready. She says she'll take me up on either offer if it ever seems necessary or gets too bad at home.

We don't usually stay in the dog run longer than forty-five minutes, so on most days I'm back in my apartment for at least the last half of *The Oprah Winfrey Show*. In the last few episodes there has been little in the way of redemption stories. Instead, there is lots of shopping and *THINGS I LOVE*, like pies and perfumes, and accessories. Still, I'm transfixed by the show, which, up until now, I'd never really watched. I'm tempted to, but don't, rush Polly out of the dog run so I can catch as much of the show as possible. Somehow the four o'clock airing feels like an occasion, has the fizzy energy of watching the Academy Awards or the Grammys. There is a sense that the rest of the world is tuning in, and even though the show is taped, it feels live, as if Oprah is revealing something terribly important each day that her audience, which seems like everyone, absolutely must know. Even something as trivial as the best brownie in New England gets the royal treatment, or the doughnut that is *OUT OF THIS WORLD*, which she'll shout about loudly and with mannish glee. Whatever it is she's shouting about, I'm there. And I'm sorry it's over when it is. There are more commercials in the second half hour, so my glimpses of the show are skimpy and I'm cranky it doesn't start later. The first time I get back to the apartment by four o'clock, I can't believe how long the show goes on without a commercial break at the beginning.

Later that year, in the fall, Oprah picks a book about drug addiction for her book club. The book came out a few years before and, at the time, I started to read it but stopped. I'm not sure exactly why I stopped—probably because I had too much reading and editing to do for work—but I didn't make it past the first twenty or so pages, which I barely remember. I do remember thinking it had a macho arrogance but that the writing—vivid, swift, fresh—was very good. That's all. This was during a period when I was struggling—and not successfully—to control my drug use and my drinking. No one but Noah knew I smoked crack. But this guy, this author, said he smoked crack, too, and I was fascinated that he was able to get sober. I read many of the interviews with him when the book was first published, pored over the articles where he talked about rehab, what they tried to teach him there, the tools for recovery they suggested he use—the Twelve Steps, the support of other alcoholics and addicts—and how he rejected it all and relied on his own willpower to quit. Over the years, Noah had begged me to go to rehab, but like this guy I didn't think I needed what they had. In all of his interviews and later, on *Oprah*, he described confidently, persuasively, how he realized he could quit on his own and he didn't, and still doesn't, need a program of recovery. It was all very appealing, what he described, and the willpower he cited appeared to be incredibly strong. He simply chose to stop drinking and drugging because, he said, he knew if he didn't he would die. Back when the book first came out, when I first heard what he had to say about recovery, it sounded perfectly logical, and I strongly identified with the belief that the usual routes of rehab, Twelve Steps groups, and other fellowships of recovery were not for everyone. Not for this guy. Not for me. I just hadn't made the choice yet, I reasoned then, and figured that when I finally did decide to stop, I would, like this guy, be able to.

Now, after losing most everything, going to rehab twice, and only eight days from my last relapse, I cannot identify with him at all.

What he describes seems superhuman. Why is it so easy for some people? I wonder. It must be that I'm made of lesser matter, I decide, and continue to believe that, later, when I see Oprah heap praise on him for being so strong. When I see the show featuring the author that fall, I am still going to three meetings a day, have no job or other obligations, and watch people in the same situation relapsing as I did again and again and again. And this guy, well, he just chose to stop using. By his own account, he doesn't go to meetings, certainly not three a day. He's like those people who don't have to work out to have perfect bodies. I'd give anything to be one of those people. Pizza, ice cream, bowls and bowls of granola, and six-pack abs. No meetings, no sponsor, no fellowship and—poof!—long-term sobriety. But it's still April and that author won't appear on the *Oprah* show until September. The book is already a big success before Oprah picks it for her book club, and from time to time over that spring and summer I hear people who don't want to go to meetings or work with a sponsor use the book as an example of how it's possible to stay clean on one's own, without help, through sheer willpower.

Eight days sober and finishing my fourth bowl of granola as the *Oprah* show ends, my willpower isn't feeling so formidable. I think about skipping the six o'clock at the Meeting House—a Library-like evening meeting I go to at the end of most weekdays—and begin to think about going down to Mark's to get high. It's less than a moment between fleeting thought and full-blown fantasy, barely a second before becoming a fully articulated obsessive vision of getting to Mark's, calling a dealer, loading a pipe, and inhaling that first hit. My phone starts ringing—it's my father—and as I hear the phone ring a few more times and let the call go to voice mail, the spell is broken long enough for me to bolt out the door toward the Meeting House a few blocks away. The meeting doesn't start for an hour, so I make phone calls to Kim, Polly, and Jack until the doors are unlocked. I cannot understand why I still want to use. Cannot understand why I have so little defense against picking up once the idea pops into my head. I know the consequences, know it will devolve into paranoid desperation almost as soon as it begins, but smoking crack still seems like a good idea. *It's insane*, I think, and not for the first time. I'm insane. Am I one of those people in the rooms whom I hear others talk about, who quite literally cannot get sober—one of those cases who are incapable of being honest with themselves? And what does honesty with oneself have to do with anything?

The doors are still locked and I cross the street so I don't seem as desperate as I am. *What am I doing wrong?* I think. I'm getting sober the way Jack has told me to: I go to as many meetings as I can, call him every day, do what he says, and when in doubt or I can't reach him, I call other addicts and alcoholics in recovery. Which is what I'm doing right now. BUT NOBODY IS PICKING UP THEIR FUCKING PHONE! I lean against a building across from the Meeting House, try to calm down, and think back over the last few weeks. In a short time my days have become predictable: wake up, feed Benny, gym; 12:30 Library meeting, which I arrive at early because it's much more crowded than the one at two o'clock; a short break to get a coffee and rush back to the same seat for the two o'clock meeting. The 12:30 meeting—filled with well-dressed nine-to-five types wedging a lunch hour meeting into their workday—has a much higher wattage than the two o'clock, which is smaller and attended by a mix of out-of-work and newly sober day counters, artists,

actors, writers, evening-shift waiters, and others with flexible schedules. Some of the most articulate, charismatic, persuasive people I
have ever encountered are in the 12:30 meeting. The only speaking
I do there is to share my day count. The same people tend to be
encouraging afterward: Rafe, one of the most visible, is one. He's
super-sober, super-visible, and super-gay. *Good to see you, Bill, keep
coming back,* he'll say in his particular intonation, with a knowing
emphasis on the word *Bill*. There is also Madge, an ex–Max's Kansas
City intellectual rock chick with an eye patch, a Jane-Fonda-in-*Klute*
shag haircut, and a sandpaper and gravel voice shaped as much by
Upper East Side, Martha's Vineyard privilege as it is by drugs and
thousands of hours logged in the smoky urban underground of New
York. Madge is the unofficial matriarch of The Library, and when
she raises her hand—like a rebel leader about to brief her loyal fight-
ers on the blueprint of their next attack—she always gets called on.
She has a dozen sponsees, a lightning-strike clarity, and an aura of
cool that is as welcoming as it is daunting. Madge doesn't so much
ever speak to me as she does grin, nod her head in my direction, and
wink her non-patched eye to signal that she's watching and on my
side. One generation older than Madge is Pam, who worked in fashion in the seventies and spent as much time at Studio 54 as Madge did
at Max's. Though her era was the seventies and eighties, Pam has a
gentle sixties-style vibe to her. Many of her sentences begin with *Oh,
honey*. Her addictions were booze and pills, and what got her sober
were her two kids, who were one or two benders away from being
removed from her care by Social Services. Pam and Rafe and Madge
are all sober for many years, but because of their schedules—Rafe is
a nutritionist and singing coach, Madge is a counselor of some kind,
and Pam does freelance fashion publicity—all come to the 12:30 and/
or the two o'clock each day. I think of them as the Big Kids of the

meeting and I'm both intimidated and comforted by them. I usually see Asa at the 12:30 and make sure we sit together. His class schedule allows him to go to meetings in the middle of the day, and sometimes he'll meet me here or at the Meeting House in the evening, after which we'll usually hang out at a coffeehouse on Greenwich Avenue or the diner on Seventh Avenue and 15th Street near my apartment.

When I look at Asa and Madge, it amazes me that such successful, happy, long-sober people still bother going to so many meetings. They seem as if they have it licked. I think back on my life when I was working and can't fathom how I'd have been able to fit as much recovery into my schedule as they do. Were there any sober people in book publishing? I can't remember any. That world seems forever closed to me now, but even if it wasn't, I think perhaps it's not a business one can stay sober in. I couldn't. When I came back from rehab in Oregon the year before, I went to one meeting a week, somehow couldn't manage that, and eventually went to none. I had a sponsor, but that guy wanted to meet every week and for me to call every day—just as Jack does now. I was busy and believed that the people who needed all these meetings and phone calls were either lonely or underemployed. I never shared or raised my hand in meetings then, never met one other person besides that sponsor whom my rehab arranged for me to meet when I returned to the city. When I tell Jack about trying to get sober a year ago, he says, *It sounds like ME versus THEM and never WE, and the only way to get and stay sober is when it becomes WE.* He also tells me that getting and staying sober—even after ninety days—needs to remain forever my first priority; that whatever I put in front of it I will eventually lose. *Career, family, boyfriend—all of it—you'll lose it. Lose again, in your case.* He tells me these things for the first time when he visits me in White Plains, and even though the words he is saying are as simple and basic as a child's box of crayons, I have no idea what he is talking about.

As I pace and fret in front of the Meeting House and watch crisp-suited, shiny-watched Chelsea residents scurry home from their day, it strikes me again, as it has more than once over the last few weeks, that I'm qualified to do absolutely nothing. I don't even have restaurant experience, save for the four days I waited tables in Connecticut after I was thrown out of school for spraying fire extinguishers in a drunken rampage with my housemates. I was fired on the fourth day of the job for lack of focus and dropping too many dishes. I think of all the pot I smoked back then—from morning until night—and I wonder how I was ever able to crawl out of that haze into any job, to go or get anywhere.

I have no retail experience, no bankable talents. I remember how a colleague at my first job in New York took copywriting courses at the Learning Annex, left publishing, and became a successful advertising executive. But this guy was brilliant, exceptionally brilliant, and that world would require, I imagine, schmoozing with potential clients, wooing new business over dinners and drinks, and without booze to get me through, it does not seem possible. Graduate school of any kind would be a decent way to delay the oncoming future, but with what money? How could I incur student loans on top of the already formidable and growing debt I've amassed from rehab, legal bills, and credit cards? Never mind that my third-tier college transcript is a speckled mess of mediocre grades and summer courses at the University of Connecticut to make up for the semester I lost when I was expelled. What graduate school would have me?

The custodian of the Meeting House has still not shown up to unlock the doors. I've left messages everywhere and still no one is picking up. The meeting begins in half an hour, and as my future prospects seem less and less appealing I start to think again of going to Mark's. It's the end of the day, Mark is no doubt ready to get high, and the dealers are about to turn their cell phones on. *Fuck it*, I say and start walking down 16th Street, away from the Meeting House, toward Sixth Avenue, toward Mark's. I can feel the adrenaline spark through my veins and the doomy clouds of my futureless future begin to streak away. Just as I approach Sixth Avenue I see someone on the north side of 16th Street waving. It's Asa. Neat as a pin, fit as a fiddle, and heading right toward me. *You going to the meeting?* he chirps, and I can't muster an answer. He looks especially crisp today in his usual uniform. *What's going on?* he asks, and as I struggle to come up with something to say to get away from him, he puts his freckled hand on my upper arm and says, *OK, let's go*.

By the time we get to the Meeting House, the door has been unlocked and someone is inside making coffee. The dusty schoolhouse smell mingling with the aroma of cheap, freshly brewed coffee acts as an antidote to the giddy, pre-high adrenaline of just minutes before. The obsession to use fades just as quickly as it had arrived, and while I watch Asa help the old guy who's setting up the meeting move a bench to the far wall, it hits me how close I just came to relapsing, and what a miracle it is that he materialized precisely when he did.

Jesus, I'm sick, I think. Unlike the people who can get sober on will-power, I need cheap coffee, church basements, serendipitous side-walk interventions, and relapsing cokehead dog walkers. But what is most discouraging is that all these things and more—Jack, Polly, Madge, Asa, The Library, my family, my remaining friends, the stag-gering losses and humiliations of the past few months, the empire of people I've hurt—are still, it seems, not enough to keep me clean.

People come in from their day, mostly nine-to-five types who can't make the midday meetings like the ones at The Library. They start filling the chairs and benches of the large room which doubles, de-pending on the hour, as a Quaker meeting house, a dance studio, and a gathering space for other programs of recovery. Chic, chatty, confident—these people seem a world away from the struggles that must have brought them here. *How the hell did they do it?* I wonder, as I remember how close I just came to picking up. If Asa hadn't hauled me in from the street, I'd be right now pressing the buzzer at Mark's apartment. Right now waiting for him to buzz me in and hand me a crack pipe. It was Asa and nothing else that kept me from using just minutes ago.

I look around from sober face to sober face and wonder again how these people found their way. How will I? I sense that just being here and in places like it will not be enough. I'm in the room but not of it. Present but not a part of. Saved, for a little while, but not sober. Not really. I come like a beggar to these meetings and I'm fed, yes, pulled in off the street even, as I was today. But it's clear that something beyond my own need and ability to ask for help will keep me here, involve me in what is going on, connect me to something greater than my addiction, and give me a fighting chance of staying clean and getting on with my life. But what?

The meeting begins. As the basket is passed and people toss in their bills, I raise my hand and say that I have eight days, and as I do I know that eventually, not today, and probably not tonight, but at some point soon, I will pick up. I don't know what I'll do with my life, if I'll ever have a full-time job again, another love, where I'll live or even if I will, but I will use again, this much I know.

The Mother Lode

My parents divorce the year I move to New York. I am twenty-one and they sell the deep-in-the-woods Connecticut house I grew up in and move to New Hampshire. They go there to save their marriage, but soon after they get settled, everything falls apart. It is my mother who leaves, finally, after years of threatening to, and in her flight back to Connecticut, as my father cancels credit cards and makes bank accounts inaccessible to her, she somehow lays her hands on a little pile of silver—ingots and coins they'd purchased as investments decades before.

A few years after their divorce is finalized, my mother gives me the silver to sell for her in the city. At the time, the market for precious metals is low and we decide to wait and sell later. The silver sits in the back of my closet for years in an old red and blue nylon knapsack I picked up in Scotland on my study-abroad semester in college. She asks about it occasionally but either I am too busy or it's not quite the right moment to sell. Eventually, she stops asking. The market crests and crashes dozens of times while the silver sits, unsold and unseen, in closets of apartments I move to in Midtown, the Upper East Side, Chelsea, and Greenwich Village. As I move, the silver moves. I forget it exists until I am packing up my things to leave One Fifth and see the familiar old knapsack. I don't remember, at first, what it holds but notice how unbelievably heavy it is when I pull it down from the shelf in the hall closet. It goes with the rest of my things to the studio on 15th Street, gets shoved to the back of another closet, and there it sits.

Meanwhile, my eight days become eleven and Polly's four become seven and then—after she joins Heather on a long, coke-crazed night—one. We raise our hands at The Library, count our days; people clap, encourage, and pass us their phone numbers. My routine calcifies: wake up, feed Benny, long workout at the gym, Library meetings at 12:30 and two o'clock, dog run with Polly, *Oprah*, Meeting House at six, diner dinner with Asa or others from the meeting, and phone calls to Jack, Kim, Asa, Jean, and Polly in between, before, and after. Once or twice a week I'll see Dave or Jean or Cy for dinner or a movie, but Jack has warned against straying too far outside the fold of recovery until I have ninety days. Bags of food arrive at least once a week from Jean, and when we see each other she'll ask if I enjoyed this or that and if there's anything special I'd like. I will never have much to say in response other than *Thank you*.

On Saturdays there is a 10:30 a.m. meeting that many people from The Library go to, and on Saturday evenings a big gay group that,

God help me, because Asa goes, I go to. The skinny boys with white belts are crawling all over the Saturday night meeting. Rafe is usually there, too, always says *Bill* in his particular tone and clocks me in his laser-like way, making it clear he sees me far more clearly than I see myself. Most of these guys talk about dance clubs and Fire Island, and they're all young and cute and skinny, and I don't belong. I feel uncouth and lumpy and unkempt and listen only for the differences in their stories, not the similarities. I'm gay but in this place I feel as if there's a manual for gays that covers everything from clothes, hair-style, and slang to eating, drinking, and using habits, and everyone in the room owns it but me. I tell Jack this one night on the phone and he asks me if there have been other experiences, other times, when I felt as if I never got the manual. When I think back to high school, college, book publishing, crack dens even—every world I entered—I felt exactly the same way: that there was a set of rules, a primer of some kind, that everyone else had read and understood but I had never seen. Like so many of my worries, Jack tells me, this one—right down to the word *manual*—is one of the bedrock feelings of most alcoholics and addicts. Again I'm relieved in some way, but also humiliated and annoyed that most everything I complain about he is able to label and place within both his own experience and the broader population of alcoholics and addicts. *You're just a garden variety junkie,* he tells me yet again and says good night.

At one of the gay meetings I meet, or re-meet, a guy named Luke whom I met a few times through mutual friends over the years and who, to my surprise, is sober. He's a screenwriter, my age, has a sober boyfriend, and has stories of using that make me wish we'd gotten sloppy together at least a few times. He feels like family from the second we reconnect, and even though he is only a year and a half sober, he seems like one of the Big Kids, like Madge and Rafe and Pam. Luke went to college with Noah and they know each other vaguely. The mutual friends, Noah connection, and similar stories of using make Luke one of the few people from the rooms who bridge both my old life and new. Everyone else is a world away from book publishing and my life with Noah, which is mainly a relief, but some-times, when I am trying to relate details of the life I lived and ruined to people like Polly and Asa, it can be frustrating. When I try to explain this frustration to Jack, he just laughs and says, *Honey, keep coming back* (an expression, minus the *honey*, people use in the rooms, usually when people counting days raise their hands and share).

So. The silver. It just sits there. I bump into it a few times while pull-ing shoes down from the upper shelf of the closet, or knock against it as I'm putting away some blanket or box. This is Mom's, I remind myself each time, not mine. I have a few thousand dollars in my ac-count—money remaining from a former client who repaid money I'd loaned her last year to cover an unexpected tax bill. Kim con-tacts the former client when I'm in Lenox Hill and miraculously a big chunk of cash materializes just as a deposit is needed for rehab. It is only in the last week that Kim has transferred the remaining money—just a little over two thousand dollars—into my checking account.

After the deposit at the rehab (which represents less than a quarter of the total bill, which they've agreed to let me pay back over time), the next big expense is the apartment. The deposit on the apartment and the broker's fee came from money I borrowed from Elliot—a guy I had an affair with a few years before, who became a friend. He lived with his exboyfriend a few blocks from One Fifth and they had, a few years back, broken up. The affair is short and boozy and ends weeks after it began on a weekend when Noah is away. Afterward, we become friends and see each other for dinner every few months or so. I don't see Elliot much in the six months preceding my relapse, but once I make it to White Plains he is one of the few people other than Jean who visit on a regular basis. He comes on the weekends to play tennis on the cracked, weed-choked asphalt slabs that pass for courts. We play for a while and walk the grounds. We don't talk much, but the distraction of the game and the easy air between us are welcome reprieves from the tormenting thoughts of my recent history and my all-too-near future. Elliot arrives each time with tennis racquets in hand and little gesture toward or judgment of the dark path that led me here. Elliot is exactly my age, exactly my height, similarly featured and colored, but has an enviable midwestern openness and ease that I don't possess. Elliot runs a highly respected nonprofit organization, we have virtually no one in common, and besides Dave and Jean and Julia and Cy, he is one of my few remaining friends. My once crowded life has dwindled to a few resilient stragglers. Elliot is one.

So Elliot lends me the money for the first month's rent, deposit, and broker's fee. I ask him because before I return to New York, he offers to lend me money if I need it. Some last scrap of vanity has kept me from going into my financial problems with him but he clearly detects trouble. At the time that he offers, asking Elliot for money seems out of the question, but weeks later he'll be the one person I think I can ask. I can't ask Dave for one more favor or helping hand, as he's at the breaking point already, and I can't risk losing Jean's friendship—especially not now when I have so few people left. I have a strong sense that if I asked her, it'd be curtains. Her wealth, I imagine, must be a familiar elephant in the room, a known animal brushing against most interactions. Now that I'm wiped out financially, it suddenly becomes, between us, an entire herd.

The first day Jean visits me in White Plains we go for a walk. As we walk I complain about how I'm not sure I can return to New York because I have no money, not sure I can stay in the rehab because it's so expensive, not sure I won't have to move in with my sister in Maine, and not sure I'll ever crawl out from under the mountain of debt that has risen since the day I relapsed two months ago. It's all I talk about because at the moment it's all I can think about. As we're walking Jean stiffens and goes quiet. She swats an invisible fly from her face and she doesn't turn to look at me when I ask her if she's OK. The elephant has its hoof on her throat and suddenly I recognize that the only way to make it go away is to name it. Loudly. So I blurt out something about how I'm suddenly poor, getting poorer by the second, and that I'm terrified. That I'm going to need to talk about being terrified with my friends, and since she's one of the few I have left, I need to be able to worry to her without her thinking I'm doing so because I want her to solve the problem. *So ditch me because I'm tedious, but not because you're worried I want you to bail me out.* I don't remember what she says to this but I remember her laughing, and that by the time we returned from our walk, the elephants had lumbered away.

So I return to New York, see the studio on 15th Street, and even though the rent is pretty cheap, I can't afford it. The landlord and broker need all that money. Since Jean and Dave are out, and because most of my family is broke, I ask Elliot. The first time in my adult life I've asked anyone for money, and Elliot's *yes* is as uncomplicated as if I'd asked him for a French fry off his dinner plate. As uncomfortable as the asking is, as grim as the circumstances are that bring me to the question, the yes is a miracle. The yes, with all its confidence and kindness, is like Jane's kiss on the street near One Fifth, or Jean's bags of food. It cuts through the plaque of shame and reminds me that somewhere underneath the wretched addict is a person worth being kind to, even worth betting on. And I do not look like a good bet, that much is clear from any perspective, but when I tell Elliot I don't know when I'll be able to pay him back, he just says, *I'm not worried. I know you will.*

With Elliot's money, May's rent is paid. I have no idea where June will come from. I'm eleven days sober, have a couple of grand in the bank, and with less than two weeks before it's time to pay next month's rent, I remember the silver. Of course, *the silver*. I'll sell the silver, pay the rent for June and July at least, and pay my mother back someday, somehow. At coffee after the Meeting House that night I ask Luke if he knows of a place that buys silver and he tells me about a guy on 25th Street between Sixth Avenue and Broadway. As soon as he says the address my stomach tightens: it's in one of Jack's off-limits trigger zones, just a few doors down from the office building where our literary agency had been. I don't say anything to Luke, but as I head toward home that night I think, I won't tell Jack and I'll just get it over with.

The next day, I grab my little blue and red knapsack and head up Sixth. The store is a combination pawnshop and rug showroom. It's huge and dark with great piles of carpets rising from the dusty floors and spider plants withering in the window. As I wait for someone to come out from behind the piles of rugs to help me, I imagine how many unseen rooms like this exist in the city, spaces behind doors I'll walk by a thousand times and never see. Since coming back, I've been amazed by how little I'd noticed before. Streets I'd walked on for ten years and never saw what was on them: pink town houses, eighteenth-century synagogues, ceramic shops, spectacular door-knobs, Italian bookshops. As with so much, I had been aware of so little off my narrow path or outside my own limited world. And there are so many worlds—fashion, academia, real estate, dance, educa-tion, firefighting, finance, advertising—each feeling, I imagine, like the center of the universe. All these separate and self-contained worlds making up entire cities within the city, coursing alongside and invis-ible to one another. *How is this occurring to me for the first time?* I wonder. How small my life and the world it happened within both seem now. What I know: book publishing, restaurants that serve vodka, crack dealers and crack dens. Bookstores, literary agencies, rugstrewn, book-crammed living rooms of editors and authors; gloomy apart-ments where people smoke themselves into shaky shadows, these I know. And now there are all the meeting rooms where I go each day and the diners and coffee shops we descend on in packs after. But these are just the tip of the iceberg. There are the rooms for sex ad-dicts and crystal meth addicts and debtors, and the rooms for all the people who love them—a whole empire of rooms filling regularly, every hour of every day and with no one paying or getting paid to be there. Invisible cities, invisible rooms we pass by until by way of desperation or desire or ultimatum they are revealed to us. Like this room—a dusty cavern with spider plants, Persian rugs, and now a knapsack filled with silver.

A middle-aged man with a trim beard, dark skin, and a bright, singsong voice comes out and says hello and can he help me. I unpack the silver and after he's inspected each ingot and coin he pulls out a calculator and begins to elegantly tap the keys until, after a minute or two, he turns the face of the gadget to me and on its screen is a figure just north of six thousand dollars. Nearly three months' rent, I calculate, and right away, without pausing, I say, *Deal*.

After he slowly writes out a detailed receipt and cuts me a check, I rush to the nearest Chase branch—the one at Sixth Avenue and 23rd Street—and deposit it into my checking account. I go to the teller instead of an ATM, thinking the money will make its way into my account faster. I hand over the check, grab my second receipt of the day, and head toward the door. I enter the small vestibule that separates the inside of the bank from the street. I've been here before, hundreds of times—it's the branch where Kate and I opened the business and client trust accounts for the agency—but suddenly I remember the last time I visited, over two months before, deep in the bender that landed me in the emergency room at Lenox Hill. I remember that I'd run out of drugs and exceeded my ATM limit for the day, so with passport and cash card in hand, I rushed to this branch. Rough from many sleepless nights and crashing from more than an hour without a hit, I withdrew three thousand dollars, stuffed it in the upper front pocket of my black Arcteryx jacket, and headed for the door. In my hurry I failed to notice that the zipper on the bottom of the pocket was unzipped, and when I stepped out of the bank into the vestibule, the cash dropped from my jacket. With air rushing through the doors on either side of me, the money flew everywhere. Hundred-dollar bills, mostly. I remember how, for a moment, it didn't look real and I was mesmerized. It looked like one of those game show challenges where people are put in a chamber of wind-tossed cash and they have thirty seconds to grab as much as they can. But when I saw a hundred-dollar bill fly out the door into the street I snapped to life.

Standing here, two months later, I picture my thin, wrecked, desperate self, scrambling to collect a windstorm of bills. I remember sweat pouring down my face, and the blasts of cold air coming in from the street. I remember a guy with a bike helmet on and two young women helping me collect the money. I remember putting the wad of bills back into the same pocket and its falling out again, but this time the guy with the bike helmet pounces and prevents the bills from flying. *You OK?* he asks doubtfully, and as I double-check the zippers I see my hands—stained black from scraping charred wire screens, blistered with lighter burns, and scabbed all over from nicks and cuts from dozens of shattered glass stems. I shove the money in my jacket pocket again, hide my hands in my jeans, and, not knowing how to respond, hurry to the street.

I try to remember where in the vestibule I was that day and how long it took to collect the bills. People—now in late spring clothes, not bundled for winter as they were then—pass in and out of the bank in front of me, and I try to picture one of them dropping three thousand dollars' worth of cash. Twice. I try to imagine what I would do and how I'd react. How on earth did I not get arrested? It seems so cartoonish and unlikely, so far away.

Further away is the memory of me and Kate meeting in this same space before sitting down with a bank officer to open the accounts we needed to start the agency. How many years ago was this? Four? Five? Three? I can't remember, and I can't see us then. It's too painful or too long ago, but in either case I can catch only the edges of that day, the conspiratorial air, the excitement and trust that passed between us. The hope.

I leave the little time machine bank vestibule and step out into the warm afternoon. It's almost three and I have three hours to kill before the six o'clock meeting at the Meeting House. I'm hungry and exhausted and think, fuck it, the Meeting House can survive with one less junkie tonight. I think this even though I'd agreed to meet Polly there. *I'm not a babysitter*, I say out loud, feeling the giddy rush of deciding to skip the meeting pushing away the heavy memories of just a few moments ago. *I'm no one's keeper!* I go on, declaring to the air like a lunatic.

As I walk home, I wonder how long it will take the check to clear, how long before the six thousand dollars will add to the two thousand in the account already and make eight. Eight thousand seems like an enormous amount of money. More than three months' rent. The apartment would be covered into the fall, and with bags of food from Jean, I'll be OK past October. The bank is at 23rd Street and Sixth Avenue. My apartment is at 15th Street and Seventh Avenue. Somewhere south of 20th and north of 16th I remember again that day two months ago, leaving the bank with three thousand dollars stuffed in my jacket, calling Rico from the street and telling him to meet me at my room at the Gansevoort Hotel. I remember him saying he was only a block away and how my heart raced as I hailed a cab to get there before he did, how his van was pulling up to the hotel just as my cab was, and how I hopped from one vehicle right into the other. From call to cab to van and back to my room took less than five minutes, some kind of record, and in the middle of the day, no less. Remembering the return to the hotel room, the wealth of drugs, the remaining cash in hand, and the night ahead starts my heart racing. I think again of the two thousand in my account. The two that will be eight. Following the thousand-dollar-a-day logic of those nights at the Gansevoort, three months' rent becomes eight nights high. Eights nights less the thousand I owe Rico and the thousand I owe Happy. Six nights high. If I call one of them now and pay back what I owe I'll still have a grand in cash to buy drugs. And I won't have to go to Mark's like last time and suffer through his jittery lectures and treacherous friends.

I arrive at my building, enter the lobby, and hit the elevator button. Somewhere between the lobby and the seventeenth floor, three months' rent becomes seven digits. Seven forgotten digits that bubble up from memory like a dark miracle that I dial on my new phone which, until now, has not stored or dialed any dealer's phone numbers. After a few rings, Happy picks up with a question, *Who is this?* I tell him.

Happy takes his time getting to the apartment. On the phone I let him know right away I have the money I owe him and that I need to buy a thousand dollars' worth of drugs. I give him the new address and he hangs up the phone. It's three in the afternoon and he shows up after eleven. I call him a few times through the afternoon and evening, but he doesn't pick up. I pace the studio and avoid phone calls from Polly and Jack while I wait with the two thousand dollars I ran back to the bank to get. Though eight hours pass from the initial phone call to hearing him knock on the apartment door, there is no turning back from getting high. It's like a switch has been flipped and I'm on autopilot. No phone call, second thought, or imagined consequence can keep me from doing what I'm about to do. Only Happy not showing up can keep me from using, and if he doesn't show up by midnight, I've already decided that I'll go to Mark's.

At eleven there's a knock at the door. There he is, looking exactly as he always has: white sweatpants, black hooded sweatshirt, Yankees cap, and large headphones around his neck. Without saying a word, he walks past me into the apartment and looks around. *Smaller place,* he says, in a voice that is both empty of and bursting with opinion. *Wondered where you went,* he adds with a hard emphasis on *went,* as I hand him the cash he doesn't count. He pulls out ten bags and two stems from the front pocket of his sweatpants and as he hands them to me says, *It's good,* and starts for the door. Usually two hundred bucks gets you two bags plus a third bag free, so I say, cautiously, *Aren't there five missing? Interest,* he answers, simply and without turning around, before he palms the door and steps into the hall. I watch him go and wait to hear the elevator open and shut before I go to the door and double-lock it.

From the first hit, which I load with as much as I once would have used in a whole night, there is something wrong. Something off. The drug tastes like medicine, and while, yes, there is a wallop of something blasting through my lungs and heart and brain, it's not the high I've waited for since three o'clock. After exhaling a huge plume of smoke, I light up and inhale another deep lungful. And then another. I pull so hard and inhale so deeply that on the fifth hit the stem pops apart from the excessive heat. I'm high but exactly where I started, still here and not there. And *there* is the only place I want to be, a place where no amount of this smoke can take me. Is it the drug or is it me? I can't tell what's wrong but something is. I call Happy and tell him that there's something not right with what he sold me and ask him if he'll switch the bags. I lie and tell him I'm about to start a period when I'll be ordering a lot more and this is not a great place to start. By one in the morning Happy shows up again. He's smiling, as if I've passed some test, and not angry as I thought he'd be. I've smoked down one bag and give him the remaining nine. He hands me back ten new ones that I can tell are colored and textured differently. He doesn't say one word from the moment he enters the apartment to the moment he leaves. I say *Thank you* as he goes and then lock the door, take a clean stem, and pack it to the brim. I can instantly tell the difference when I inhale the new smoke and the freight train I've been waiting for all day finally hits me. At last, the world cracks open and I fall through, leaving behind for a blessed second everything and everyone. I settle into the couch and, with eyes closed, hold on to what I know will be over soon. It will wriggle away as suddenly as it arrives, just as it always does, and I will, I know, sit on this couch for hours, burning my fingers and filling my lungs to court its return. But it never does. What comes instead is restlessness followed by an urgent need to get out of the apartment. What comes after that are two Asian guys—young, hip, bored, cute—standing in front of a white tile apartment building down the block from mine, who seem to be waiting for me. I ask them to come over and they do. I ask them if they get high and they say yes. I show them a stem and they ask what it is. I suggest they try, and they do. They both get naked and I join them and the hours pass as the three of us thrash around on the bed and stop and start dozens of times to get high and down vodka. At around ten in the morning I am convinced they are undercover cops or DEA agents who have tricked me into letting them into my apartment, and I demand that they leave. They are confused, ask for a stem and a bag of drugs, which I refuse, and at last they go. I sneak to the liquor store on Seventh Avenue and buy two half gallons of vodka and a bag of ice. I drink the first bottle quickly and close my eyes and fall asleep for a couple of hours. I have five bags left and I stuff a quarter of the contents of one into a pipe and begin to hope, like so many times before, that my heart explodes, that my brain erupts, and that the death dance can resolve, for once and finally, in death. I look across my small studio to the door that leads to the terrace and remember the first thought I had when I saw it, weeks ago, when the real estate agent showed me the apartment: if all else fails, there's that.

Wednesday becomes Thursday. Five bags become three. The lighter, bent down at an angle too far and for too long, pops, and its metal workings explode apart in my hand. It is the last lighter and it's now evening again. I scan a few drawers and pockets and find no more and realize I have to go out. I pour a vodka and look around at the apartment filled with glasses jammed with cigarette

BILL CLEGG

butts the Asian guys must have smoked. There are used condoms on the floor, a sheet nailed to the wall above the terrace door to block anyone seeing in, and empty beer cans and vodka bottles everywhere. The gloom of the wrecked room and the grim image of three strangers drugging and drinking and slamming into each other to create closeness or apartness or whatever each of us is running to or toward is too much to bear. And there is nothing new about it. It's like every other time getting high. And here I am again. I look at the terrace door. I look at the bags of drugs on the coffee table and think: Is there enough to get me on the other side? Is there enough to finish what I started two months ago? There's only one way to find out, I decide, as I put on my shoes to go get lighters.

Like every other time I've left a room with drugs, I worry it will be raided, and more than the fear of being arrested, I panic at the idea that the drugs will be seized, taken away, not used. So I tuck the bags in the front pocket of my shorts, put on a clean T-shirt, wash my hands to clear off the soot, and leave. The elevator man, the older of the two Serbian brothers who work the elevator in the building, mumbles something inaudible. I pray he can't smell the smoke I've been breathing for nearly forty-eight hours. I leave the building and immediately wish I hadn't. The sidewalks along Seventh Avenue are teeming with people. Cars streak by, sirens sound, voices come from all directions. I don't want to be here, but I need lighters and have no choice. I get to the bodega and ask for ten lighters, more than I need but I'm fearful I'll run out again. Once I have them in my pockets I walk back to Seventh Avenue, head south, and before I've turned onto 15th Street, I see him. Asa.

How he persuades me to come to his apartment I have no idea. I'm standing in his small studio living room listening to him talk to his sponsor, Lucy. I hear him say the word *Benadryl* and I can't imagine why. I go to the bathroom and run the water and flush the toilet while I draw as big a hit as I can. Immediately he comes knocking on the door. I pack another hit, light it, and exhale as I scramble unsuccessfully to find a window to open. The little room is dense with smoke, and when I open the door the drug clouds pour into the apartment like steam. Asa is calm and not confrontational but he asks me, gently, if I will give him the drugs. I say I should probably leave, but as I do I think I hear heavy footfalls outside his door. One part of me is aware that I am becoming paranoid, as I always do on drugs, and the other remembers the Asian guys who seemed to be communicating with each other last night in an intricate code of winks and hand signals. And then the shadows on the terrace that looked like men with bulletproof vests.

Asa has a box of Benadryl in his hand and says that Lucy suggests I take a few to kill the edge, soften the high, and help bring me down a little so I can decide what to do. This sounds good, so I ask for three and I swallow them down. I ask if he has alcohol in the house, and as I do I remember how we know each other—from the rooms—and I apologize. But I know that I need alcohol and I need it soon. *I need to go to the bathroom*, I say, and he seems genuinely stumped, so he turns his back and starts talking again to Lucy. I disappear into the bathroom and load up the stem a few more times. I feel a notch calmer as the hits push away some of the worry, but in its place comes something else. That old restless sexual energy that this drug unleashes. So I go back out to where Asa is and say I'm getting warm. I ask him if it's OK if

I take my T-shirt off and he just sort of blinks and says, *I guess so*. I'm feeling a bit bolder now than before, so after my shirt is off I pull out a stem and pack it in front of him and draw a hit. I exhale into the neat, attractive little studio. I pull a chair directly in front of where he's sitting on the couch and lean back and put my hands in my pockets. I push my shorts down my hips a little and flex my arms and think that something is about to happen. In the deluding inner sheen of the high, I think there's no way he won't be game to fool around. I've had a sense he may have a crush on me and by God if he does, here I am. It seems completely logical, and Asa the friend, the saving angel, the sober comrade disappears and in his place is just a beautiful nearby body that looks like the next place to go in my crack-mapped journey. He hands me another Benadryl and asks me again if he can take the drugs from me. Again, he's calm, not angry or pushy. But I can barely hear him for all my desire. He stays on the phone with Lucy and says to me, *You can stop now. You can stop and you can crash here and everything will be OK. This doesn't have to get any worse than it already is.*

Something in his tone strikes a nerve. *What if this could be over?* I think, and then remember the terrace off my apartment, the seventeen floors down to the asphalt of 15th Street. A few hours ago, that was the only way I could see to end this. Now here's Asa offering another way. But that way—the meetings and the diners and the phone calls and the sponsor and the off-limits trigger zones all over the city—that way is not working. Here I am with my shirt off, two and a half bags away from smoking a thousand dollars' worth of crack, hitting on and trying to relapse someone who has only extended to me kindness and patience and time. I am doing everything I can to seduce him into the very oblivion that nearly destroyed him years ago. Asa asks me where I got the money for the drugs and I tell him about the pile of silver but I don't tell him it was my mother's. Some alchemy of Benadryl, the mention of the silver, and Asa's patient tones spook the sexual weather away.

Confused and desperate for another hit, I tell Asa I need to take a shower. He gets me a towel, asks me not to smoke the drugs in the bathroom, which I agree to, and then, once the water is running, pack a fresh hit and try to force enough smoke into my system so I can figure out what to do. The water pipes creak as I turn up the hot water and through that noise I soon hear another noise—voices, men's voices, coming from the other side of the wall. Are they in the hallway? The next apartment? The dread of being under surveillance that has come in and out like a tide over the last forty-eight hours shows up again, suddenly and full force. There are voices coming from behind two walls now. I hear *Let's get him* and *Why are we waiting?* and I turn off the water to listen closely. Asa's at the door and says, *OK, that's enough, come on out.* And then I think: *He's in on it. These guys, whoever they are, are with him.* I scramble into my clothes, flush the toilet, and take another hit with what's left of the third bag. Thinking there may be drug agents and police on the other side of the door, I hide the last two bags, lighter, and stem in the medicine cabinet. *I'll say it's Asa's,* I think diabolically, pulling the cabinet door shut and confronting in the mirror what would be obvious to anyone: a desperate addict. Asa knocks, and his careful voice comes from the other side.

In a cramped, smoke-filled studio bathroom in Chelsea, one of three things is about to happen: arrest, returning home to a seventeen-story exit from everything, or giving the drugs to Asa and trusting that what he's saying is true. That I'll be OK. That this is just a stumble and not a fall. I look in the mirror again and see what I always see when I'm high: my eyes, dead and black and staring back as if they were someone or something else's eyes and not my own. I sway before the mirror and begin to feel the Benadryl crawl underneath the drugs and link hands with the sleepless hours of the nights before. I step to the door and open it. On the other side it's Asa, alone, no one else, no men in bulletproof vests wielding guns and handcuffs. I decide to give up. I know if I do, there will be no more voices on the other side of the wall. At least for now.

My eleven days become one and Polly's one becomes four. The eight grand becomes six and the messages on my phone are too many to count. June's rent is due in two weeks. After June is paid there will be $3,500 left in the account with four weeks until July's rent is due. How did I go from having nearly four months' rent covered to barely two? I know, I just don't want to remember. But as much as I try, the last three days keep flickering to life. The Asian guys I picked up off the street, got high with, and threw out. Which night was that? Tuesday? Wednesday? It's not clear. The voices behind the bathroom wall at Asa's. Asa. Taking my shirt off and trying to seduce him. And then the final deal he and I strike: that I'll give him the drugs if he allows me to smoke one more hit, which I do, in a chair, in front of him, while he sits on the couch and watches, cell phone and sponsor pressed to his ear. I give him the remaining bags and watch him flush them down the toilet. Watch him smash the stem and flush the glass. Afterward, Asa walks me home and spends the rest of the night on my couch. We wake up late the next morning, and after I feed Benny, he walks me to the corner of

Fifth and 10th Street so I can go to the 12:30 meeting at The Library. He rushes to class, and I promise I'll see him at the two o'clock meeting.

I can't bear the idea of walking into The Library and counting one day, so I circle the block a few times. My mother keeps calling, and I wonder if she knows that I've relapsed again. I have not yet listened to any of the messages. I call Jack and tell him what's happened. He sounds tired when he tells me to go to meetings all day and raise my hand. The rest can wait. Eventually, but not now, I will call Kim and Dave and Jean and Polly and Luke and everyone else who I suspect has left messages and who will have to decide whether to stick with me or step away.

I go to the meeting, but since I wait until the last possible moment to enter the building, by the time I get to the fifth floor the place is packed and it takes a long, uncomfortable minute to find a seat. Looking through the crowded room I don't see anyone I know. I then see Pam, who motions toward the far back wall where there is an empty seat. It's next to Annie, someone I met just a few days before. She's the one I saw that first day at The Library and was convinced I'd met somewhere before. At first I thought she was the girlfriend of Noah's screenwriting partner, but a week later, when I gathered enough courage to say hello, it turned out we'd never met. She has a little more time than I have and is, like me, not working and doing nothing else but getting sober. She's recently completed a two-year MFA program in acting, but she went on a bender two nights before her showcase performance, where the school invites agents and managers. Her acting partner had to go on with one of the professors reading from a script, and because the showcase is one of the requirements for getting a degree, she has not yet officially graduated. There was a messy period that followed the showcase disaster before she found her way into the rooms.

Hey, lambchop, she whispers as I sit down. Annie is wearing, as usual, a thrift store ensemble of Rickie Lee Jones-style beret, a big plastic-buttoned purple cardigan sweater, and denim overalls. *Long time no talk,* she says.

The meeting starts. At the break, I raise my hand and announce that I have one day and Pam gasps above the clapping, *Oh, honey.* In between the 12:30 and the two o'clock, I finally listen to my messages. It's a familiar series of regular check-in messages that, one by one, lose their carefree tone and crumble from concern to anger. My mother leaves three or four and the last one is a doozy. She is crying and she is angry and she shouts more than says, *You have stolen from me and you need to call me right away.* I haven't seen my mother since an afternoon last year when she left me in a restaurant after I brought up some difficult and never before spoken-about memories from my childhood. Since then we've barely talked and I have not seen her. I ask her, through my sister Kim, not to come to Lenox Hill while I am there, and when she offers to visit me in rehab and in the city after I return, again I tell her, through Kim, that I'd rather she did not.

Before the day in the restaurant I'd always been her faithful lieutenant in the ongoing war with my father. Never questioned her side of things, stood by her in the divorce, and generally agreed with her version of events, whatever they were. But with the marvels of therapy, a pushy counselor in rehab, and the miracle of suppressed memory, all that changed in the last year. Her tone with me—in voice mail messages, mostly—since that lunch has been conciliatory, careful, wounded. I cannot remember her ever being angry with me. We had always been on each other's side. Me, Kim, and Mom against Dad. It was fun when he was away on a trip, tense when he returned. He was the dark one, she the light. When I was thrown out of college he was the one who delivered the harsh lecture and she the one who comforted me afterward. When I skipped school she rolled her eyes and wagged a finger, but she was never hard or harsh or punishing. So this message she leaves, short though it is, packs a hard, jarring punch.

I'm standing on the corner of 10th Street and University, not sure whether to return her call or go to the two o'clock meeting. How on earth does she know about the silver? I run through all the possibilities and come up with nothing. Are there serial numbers on silver ingots and coins? Did some precious metals office call her to confirm the sale? Thinking about government agencies triggers the paranoia from the night before, and in addition to feeling hungover, defeated, and ashamed, I start to feel that old nagging dread of being observed. I turn to walk home, and before I get more than a few steps down 10th, I hear Annie call my name. She stands on the corner looking like a pint-sized host of some public access kids' TV show—red lipstick, goofy beret, lace-up Converse high-tops, jumbo overalls, megawatt smile. *Get over here, lamb, you're not going anywhere.*

Annie and I go to Newsbar, a small coffee and Internet café just a few blocks up University from The Library. She asks me why I look so spooked, and as I start to tell her about my mother, the silver, the rug guy from 25th Street, and the six thousand dollars, I notice two middle-aged guys in windbreakers sitting three tables away, listening to what I'm saying. Just then a woman with what looks like an earpiece enters the place, and I grab Annie's hand and tell her we have to go. *Now.* She doesn't blink or react, just says, *Gotcha, I'll follow you.* We rush to the street, and as we head toward Union Square, I notice Annie is still holding my hand. *I'm not crazy,* I tell her and she pats my arm. *Of course you're not, lamby,* she whispers, as if letting me in on a secret. *You're insane.*

When we get to Union Square I stop us in the middle of the steps on the south side and check and recheck to make sure there is no one within earshot. Still holding my hand Annie says, *OK, we're safe, now tell me what's going on.* So I tell her. Everything. My parents' difficult marriage, the buried memories from childhood, my mother leaving me in a restaurant last year, the time at Newark airport and after when I believed I was being followed by DEA agents, trying to kill myself after two months in hotel rooms smoking crack, the silver, calling Happy, the terrace off my studio and the returning thoughts of suicide, the voices at Asa's, and finally my mother's phone message. Annie takes it all in and then says, laughing a little and still, and tightly now, holding my hand, *That's one mother of a mother lode.* She pulls me down onto the steps to sit down. *I'm not going to even pretend I understood half of what you just said, but what you need to do right now is call your mother and listen to whatever she's got to say and then be honest and apologize. It's no more complicated than that. So let's go. Where's your phone?* If Annie said I needed to set my shoes on fire and sing Christmas carols I probably would. She has been sober only a little while longer than I have and has, from what I've heard of her share at The Library, seemed just as lost, but now, here, she seems like a Great Elder of sobriety.

I call my mother. She can barely talk she's so upset. She tells me that Asa called my sister, whose number I gave him weeks ago in case of emergency. He called to tell her I had relapsed but that I was OK. When my sister asked where I got the money from, he said he knew I had recently sold some silver. When my sister, who didn't know about the silver and assumed it was mine, tells my mother, she explodes. And now, she explodes all over again. *How could you do it?* she demands, sounding, within her rage, genuinely bewildered. *I don't know*, is all I have as a response, and *I'm sorry*.

As I'm getting off the call she says in the sternest voice I've ever heard her speak in, *Enough is enough, you've got to stop this. Stop it right now. Do you hear me? Enough is enough.* As much as I had dreaded the phone call, this last instruction, this line drawn, by my mother of all people—this girl-woman my sister and I took care of as kids, whom I've defended my whole life and avoided most of my adulthood—feels like something I've been missing for a long time but hadn't realized until now. Like how you don't know how hungry you've been until you see food, or how tired you are until your head hits a pillow.

Annie walks me back to The Library and hugs me goodbye. I agree to call her before going to sleep and rush into the building to catch the last half hour of the two o'clock meeting. I manage to get a seat next to Polly, who makes well-look-who-showed-up eyes at me. Asa is there, looking tired from being awake most of the night before. After the meeting he tells me matter-of-factly that he's spending the night again at my place and that he'll pick me up there to go to the Meeting House at six. All I can manage is *Thank you*.

Polly slaps me in the head and says, *What the fuck, Crackhead?* We walk to the dog run and I tell her what happened. She listens and nods and is in no way surprised. *Just keep coming back and next time, call me, OK? I promise you won't want to use once I'm through with you.* She comes over to my place for a while until Asa shows up. Asa and I go to the Meeting House and come back to my place afterward and eat quiche and roast chicken from the bags of food from Jean that arrived while we were out. While Asa unfolds the pullout bed from the couch, I call Jack to give an accounting of the day—the meetings, talking to Polly and Annie and Asa, apologizing to my mother, counting one day at The Library—to which he responds, *Do it all again tomorrow*. After I say good night and hang up the phone, Asa turns off the lights and we crawl under our respective covers. Benny curls against the door, as far from me as possible.

I can't sleep. Can't help but run through the events of the last three days. Everything that followed the phone call to Happy—the bad high, the good high, the Asian guys, the broken stems, the vodka, the ruined lighters, the paranoia, the thoughts of suicide—is familiar, follows the same desperate script of every time using. But what's different, what is completely new, is what happens after. I realize that from the moment I ran into Asa on the street twenty-four hours ago, I have not been alone. After Asa I'm with Annie and after Annie with Polly and now, again, with Asa, who is asleep on my pullout couch.

I lie in bed, awake, in the dark. I can make out the edges of the white sheet that I'd nailed to the wall above the terrace door to cover its small window. One of the corners has come off and I watch it flap against the door, making shapes and movements that remind me of the cops and DEA agents I was convinced were lining up on the terrace two nights ago. I curl against the window next to the bed and try to blink away the thoughts of what would have happened without Asa. I remember him sitting across from me at the New Venus diner on my first night back in the city, how I had no intention of going with those boys to dinner, how Jack made me, and how it was Asa who told me to meet him the next day at The Library, which was where I met Polly and Annie. How are these people, whom I didn't know less than a month ago, how are they now the most important people in my life? My mind races with how unlikely it all seems, how arbitrary.

The room and the city outside are quiet. I listen to the sound of Asa's rough breathing and look out the window to the Empire State Building. The old skyscraper goes dark at midnight, as usual, but as it does this time the remaining lights in the skyline appear to blink awake, shine with new energy, as if each one has agreed now to shoulder the heavy burden of lighting the city, pick up the slack as one of their own tires out, realizes that he cannot, could never, do it on his own.

Use

Polly has eight days and I have five. Though neither of us can put together longer than two weeks, we talk about what we'll do when we reach ninety. Polly may go back to teaching or working with animals. I have no idea what I'll do—little seems possible, and as my bank account thins and my debt thickens, the only solution seems to be to go live with my sister Kim in Maine. What I'll do there I can't imagine. How long she and her family would tolerate me is also unclear. Polly has a different predicament. Her sister Heather somehow lucked into their rent-controlled apartment on St. Mark's Place when she was in graduate school and the rent, by New York standards, is practically free. So there's less pressure on Polly to make money, but if Heather doesn't get sober it's not a place Polly's sponsor or anyone else at The Library recommends she remain. Her attachment to Heather is powerful—they are twins *and* using buddies—and up until recently, anytime I or anyone else suggests she move out Polly goes cold and swiftly changes the subject. But Heather continues to do lines of coke and stay up all night watching DVDs of *Law & Order*. Polly puts a few days together and, this time, becomes more open to talking about moving. By mid-May she begins mentioning—tentatively, cautiously—that she might look on Craigslist for apartments in Queens, which she's heard are cheap.

And then Polly disappears. She doesn't show up at either the 12:30 meeting or the two o'clock. I call and leave messages on her cell phone but get no answer. This goes on for days until her voice mail is full and stops accepting messages. I walk down St. Mark's and linger in front of her building, hoping to see her or Heather. Jack tells me not to buzz the apartment because I'm not even a week sober and there could be coke all over Polly's place. As much as I agree with his logic, there is no part of me that finds getting high with Polly appealing. There is no part of the prospect of coke in her apartment that triggers a craving. But I follow Jack's rules, even though I'm terrified she has overdosed. I call her sponsor, who says she hasn't heard from Polly but that someone from The Library saw Heather on the street, who said she's OK and to let her be.

So I do. The meetings at The Library for the rest of the week seem strange without Polly. The afternoons are more spacious. I go to coffee with Annie after the two o'clock meeting a few times, but it's odd not to go to the dog run, odd to be home for the beginning of the *Oprah* show at four o'clock each day. The weekend rolls around and Saturday morning, on a whim, I call Polly. Miraculously, she answers. *Hey, Crackhead*, she says, without the usual pluck, and I say, lamely, *If that's not the pot calling the crackhead black then I don't know what is.* She laughs but her voice is rough and weak. *You OK?* I ask, and after a long pause she says, *Nope.* She agrees to meet me at the dog run, and when she finally shows up nearly forty-five minutes late I see that she is, as she often is after using, still wearing her pajamas. She's got a sweatshirt over the tissue-thin, unwashed nightclothes, but I can see her collarbone jutting from her skin and her movements are labored. She looks as though she's lost ten pounds, and there weren't ten to lose. She has Essie's dog leash in one hand and a cigarette in the other, and when she sits down next to me I catch a strong whiff of alcohol, body odor, and cigarette smoke. I struggle not to react, but she's ripe and it's not easy to appear as if I don't notice.

How she smells is obviously the furthest thing from her mind. I've seen Polly after using a number of times, but something is different now. She seems startled by something more than the now familiar horror of having relapsed. I ask her what happened and she tells me that Heather came home with two eight balls Monday night and they used round the clock until Thursday night. On Friday, Heather's dealer comes by with another eight ball and the two of them dive in. After a few lines, Heather starts to complain of heart pains and lies down on the sofa. Polly is worried but does a few more lines. At some point, Heather passes out and Polly tries, unsuccessfully, to wake her up. She shakes her, splashes water on her face, and shouts her name, but nothing works. She checks for a pulse and feels Heather's heart beating in her chest so she knows she's alive. She must have overdosed, Polly realizes, as she does a big line to kill off her rising panic. When that doesn't work, she does another. There's almost an entire eight ball sitting on the coffee table, and when she thinks of calling the ambulance, she knows that when someone comes she'll have to go to the hospital with Heather. And stop using. She keeps doing line after line, thinking she's about to call 911, but each time the high doesn't last and soon she needs another line. She keeps thinking she'll call after one more. After two and a half hours or so of this, the eight ball is not gone, Heather is still unconscious, and Polly freaks out and finally calls 911. The paramedics come, get Heather to the ER, pump her system clean, and she stays the night. Polly leaves Heather at the hospital once the doctor says she's going to be fine. She goes back to their apartment, finishes the eight ball, drinks vodka, and takes sleeping pills until she passes out. Late that morning, Heather comes home, and soon after that, I call. And here we are, in the dog park. *Something has to change,* she says, shaking her head. *I chose coke over my sister's life.*

Out of the blue, I remember a small rehab called High Watch in Kent, Connecticut, which is an old Twelve Step retreat that has meetings all day and is, I think I remember someone telling me once, cheap. On the park bench in the dog park we call information and get a person on the phone. There's a bed open on Monday and the daily rate is, with help from Polly's parents, manageable. She reserves the bed, commits to staying two weeks, and the next phone call is to my mother. Without giving it more than a moment's thought, I dial her number, and when she picks up I explain the situation. She agrees to meet us at the train station near Kent on Monday morning. When she asks if I'll spend the night, I lie and say that I have a commitment at a meeting that evening and need to return to the city. Between the phone call on the bench at the dog run and getting on the train Monday morning, Polly calls her parents and tells them what's been going on. It's the first they hear that she's been using drugs, and it's the first they hear that Heather has, too. They live in California and don't see their daughters very often. Somehow Polly's years of unemployment have not sounded alarm bells loud enough to make them think there is a serious problem. She asks them for help in paying the fee at the rehab and they agree. Of course there is a huge blowup with Heather, who denies everything to their parents and tells Polly that once she's left for rehab she can stay there or move back to California, but she's not welcome in her apartment anymore. Polly goes anyway.

We meet early Monday morning on the corner of Fifth Avenue and 14th Street, and Polly arrives with a small duffel bag. A friend has agreed to watch Essie, and as we get on the Metro North train to Wassaic, Polly says she hasn't been out of the city in three years. On the ride up, she tells me terrible but hilarious stories of getting smashed before teaching kindergarten and being completely bewildered when the other teachers at the school don't want to meet her around the corner for a drink on their lunch break. She, like me, has a few airport stories. One of the most vivid is one from her college years, when she leaves a bar one afternoon, hammered, and shows up at JFK airport with no idea where she is going to go, just that she's going somewhere, anywhere. She sees that a flight to Sarajevo is leaving later that night and books a ticket. She gets there with little money, just enough to sit in cafés all day and have drinks bought for her. *I sat there thinking I was so interesting, drinking in cafés in a country going to war. People were going off to die and I was feeling glamorous, fascinating. As if somehow the war had more to do with me than them.* Her story triggers a memory of my mother's battle with cancer. I remember telling friends that she was dying as I drank vodka after vodka, as if her sickness was impacting me more than her. I cringe with shame when I think about that time and, later, when I turned up at the hospital the day of her surgery after I'd been up the night before smoking crack.

We arrive at the Wassaic train station and the only car in the lot is my mother's. I can see her through the windshield of her Honda station wagon. Only when she steps out of the car toward the platform to greet us do I realize that I have not seen her in over a year. Six years since her radical mastectomy and five years since she completed a year of radiation treatments, her hair has returned, much thinner and lighter in color than before. As Polly gathers up her duffel bag and says heavily, *Here we go,* whatever difficulties I have with my mother don't matter.

The rehab is beautiful, which none of us expects. It looks like an expensive bed and breakfast one would go to for a weekend get-away from the city. The women who admit Polly are friendly and the place seems mostly empty. We walk across the property to where Polly will be sleeping, and as she puts her duffel on the bed, it only then occurs to me that she won't be in the city for two weeks. Two weeks with no dog run, no Polly. I have a flash of panic about relapsing, that without Polly around I'll somehow be less able to keep from picking up. I hope none of these thoughts register on my face as I hug Polly good-bye and walk glumly away as if I'm leaving my daughter at college. I want people to like her, worry she'll be lonely. *Call me if you need to, anytime,* I say pathetically as I leave her room to go.

My mother takes me back to the station to catch a train that leaves less than two hours after Polly and I arrived. As she drives, we don't talk about the silver or anything else that's been hard between us. She tells me that when I was in college she threw my father out of the house after a particularly ugly drunken scene. She agreed to let him come home only if he completed a stay at the rehab where we just left Polly, which, apparently, he did. I'm surprised by the story. I knew things had gotten bad between them while I was in college, that his drinking had escalated, but I had no idea that he'd gone to rehab. I listen as she describes how hard that time was, but I'm reluctant to get too engaged. I'm just now talking again with my father, after not speaking for nearly a decade, so I'm cautious about getting too deep into the old familiar dynamic of listening to my mother complain about him. My father is an early riser, always was, so over the last few weeks we've been talking in the mornings. I've been meeting Elliot at the tennis courts along the West Side Highway before he goes to work, so I get there early to reserve a court and call my father. It feels as if I am getting to know him for the first time on these calls. As my mother talks more about my father's drinking, I get more and more uncomfortable and eventually I change the subject.

We pull into the train station and wait awkwardly in the car. She asks about Polly's sister and The Library, tries, like any parent, to get a glimpse of her child's life. I answer vaguely, reluctant to include her in any of it, and eventually just say, *Thank you*. It is quiet in the car for some time. *I'm happy I could help, Billy. I'm just glad I can be of use*, she says tenderly as the train pulls up and I reach for the door. *Me, too*, I think as I kiss her on the cheek, leave the car, and go home.

Goners

Jack asks me to meet him at a coffee shop on Irving Place. It's only a few blocks from my usual stomping grounds of Union Square, lower Fifth Avenue, and east Chelsea, but as I walk along the tall fences of Gramercy Park, it strikes me how small I've made the city again—how limited the terrain I travel, how predictable. As I'm about to cross up to Lexington from the top of the park I see a navy blue tracksuit with maroon stripes along the sleeves and pants. I see the tracksuit first and then the short, bearded, wiry, gold-ringed, Ray-Ban-clad kid wearing it. Lotto. Lotto is in lieu of Lowt, an old Jewish name given to Lotto by his old Jewish parents, who own and run a diamond store in the West 40s. Lotto was adopted as an infant, his parents are in their seventies, and he grew up in a town house on Gramercy Park that could double as an embassy. Last I heard he was at the Betty Ford Center in California. He's the kid I met over a year ago in Oregon at the rehab Noah and Kate sent me to. Then it was Lotto's ninth or tenth rehab. Now he's been to at least two more. In Oregon, Lotto resisted every suggestion, every instruction, and managed to alienate nearly every counselor and patient in the rehab. In clothes, language, and manner, he's hip-hop ghetto meets Italian mobster. He's the lippiest, most foul-mouthed, most confrontational kid I've ever met and also one of the funniest. In Oregon, we became friends. We'd walk the grounds of the rehab at night before curfew and he'd tell me stories of smuggling drugs into and busting out of therapeutic boarding schools up and down the east and west coasts. He was, then, twenty-one to my thirty-three. Now, both a year older and still, it seems—given that he's not at the Betty Ford Center, and I'm wearing shorts and a T-shirt on a weekday morning—not so much further along the road to recovery than when we last saw each other. I'd left the rehab in Oregon after completing five weeks in treatment; he left after going AWOL and secretly booking a ticket on my flight home to New York. *Surprise, surprise,* he had said at the airport, waving his boarding pass. *Time to get the hell home.*

Lotto spots me before I can say hi. *Yo, Billeeee!* he yells, more Gambino than Lansky. I notice that Lotto's wearing the usual amount of gold but less beard and that he's gained weight. He's graduated from whippet thin to wiry. His tracksuit, no doubt the smallest size made, still pools around his expensive running shoes and falls off his body like curtains. *You good?* he asks, and I say I'm just fine, that I have a few days sober and am making a run at ninety days. *Yo, I have ninety,* he says, *and I didn't need that joke rehab to get 'em. Really, Lotto?* I ask doubtfully. *Ninety?* He laughs and says, *Nah, but I will.*

I tell Lotto that I have to see my sponsor but he should meet me the next day at The Library. He gives me his new number—he's had two that I know of since we met in Oregon. Each rehab asks him to get rid of his old cell phone, as they did with me, so he doesn't have access to his dealers' numbers. We agree to see each other at The Library at 12:30 but it will be three days before I hear from him. *Let's get dinner*, he texts, and I suggest again that we meet at The Library. I don't hear from him for a few days, so when he texts and suggests dinner again, I agree to meet him at a place in the far West Village—more of a lounge than a restaurant. When I get there he's with three girls. All blonde, all look like they're in high school, all talking on or texting from their cell phones. *Looks like a party*, I say as I sit down, and Lotto smirks and says, *What else is new?* The girls are drinking champagne—*Of course they are*, I think. Lotto has a large bottle of Pellegrino in front of him. *Bubbly?* he jokes as he holds up the bottle. I nod yes and gesture toward the girls. He introduces me and they barely look up from their gadgets. A waiter comes, we order whatever we order, and when the girls all leave for the bathroom, Lotto tells me he's in love. *She's a good girl*, he says, and I ask which one of the three she is and he says, *Oh no, not these bitches, they're just friends. Tess is in art school and is in the studio tonight working on some sculpture or installation or something*. I ask him where he met her and he tells me the story of how he spotted her at Barneys, followed her out onto Madison Avenue, and asked her to dinner. I try to picture the scene and have a hard time seeing how Lotto pulls off this kind of move, but then again he has three girls at dinner tonight so who knows. *You'd like her, Billy*, he says seriously. *I know you would.*

The food finally arrives and the girls return from the bathroom looking a little more awake than before they left, which is my cue to eat quickly, throw a few twenties on the table, and go. I tell Lotto to meet me at the 12:30 the next day, that we can get coffee after. He gets up and extends his hand in the way that all young straight boys do these days. I ignore his hand and give him a hug instead. *Be good*, I say into his ear. *And meet me tomorrow.*

To my great surprise, he does—at 1:30, on the bottom step of The Library. I see him as I'm leaving to grab a coffee before going back to the two o'clock. Tracksuit, Ray-Bans, gold necklace, cigarette. He's just a kid but he looks like a sixty-year-old casino lizard from Atlantic City. *Where's my coffee?* he says laughing and starts walking to University before I even say hello.

Lotto tells me all about Tess. How she grew up all over the world, how her father is some kind of diplomat. He drops the names of a few very famous people who he says are to Tess *practically family*. Lotto hits his stride when famous people come into the picture. There is almost never a story that doesn't somehow come around to a celebrity. From the socialites he went to the therapeutic boarding schools with (*whores*) to the athletes who shop at the diamond store his parents own (*whoremasters*) to the rap stars who frequent the parties he goes to (*masters of all whoremasters*)—there are famous people. And always they are described as friends or practically family. This story is no different. But one difference is how he talks about this girl. She, too, has been to rehab, it turns out. *She just gets me*, he says, and shrugs. I ask if she goes to meetings of any kind and he says that she's figured out a way to use a little heroin on the weekends and not drink at all. *Booze was her problem, not drugs*, he says seriously. *And since heroin is not my thing, there's no temptation for me.* I listen to him and for a minute think he's joking. When I realize he's not, I tell him he's out of his mind. *We're good for each other*, he argues. *She keeps me away from coke and I keep her away from booze. She's getting an MFA and we're going to open a gallery together in Soho with my cousin Sam.* I honestly don't know where to begin; his earnestness is so palpable that I can't bear to say anything beyond suggesting we head back to The Library to catch the two o'clock meeting. *We can make it*, I say like a parent trying to make homework or going to the dentist sound like fun. Lotto's face pinches and by some miracle he actually follows me back to the meeting.

Lotto and I trade phone calls over the next few days. He says he'll show up at meetings but never does. He leaves a long message one night and tells me how glad he is we're friends, that we're in each other's lives, that it's fate that we should be on this journey together, and I know from the charged sentimental urgency in his voice that he's high. This is the last message I get for a week. And then, the day after taking Polly to Connecticut, while I'm doing laundry in the basement of my building, I get a call from his mother. Something has happened, she says, and could I come over to their house right away. It's late afternoon and I had been planning to go to the Meeting House at six. But instead I immediately start walking over to Gramercy Park. On the way, Lotto's mother, who sounds as exhausted and be-wildered as I've ever heard anyone sound, tells me what happened. Four nights before, Lotto and his younger cousin Sam were in his bedroom. Lotto had a bag of cocaine and Sam apparently wanted to try it. Lotto, according to his mother, tried to persuade him not to but he was persistent. So Lotto cuts him a line and within minutes Sam has a seizure and is soon unconscious. They call 911, and by the

BILL CLEGG

time the ambulance arrives he is dead. Apparently he'd taken several anti-anxiety medications that day, and combined with cocaine they caused his heart to fail. The family—Lotto's father's brother—had to be called and they and the police have agreed it's a no-fault fatality. Lotto's mother is telling me all this because they want him to enter a year-long treatment program in Northern California, some place a consultant they hired has strongly recommended. Lotto is, she says, refusing to go and threatening to kill himself.

I arrive at Gramercy Park just as Lotto's mother is finishing the story and ask her to remind me what the address is. *Yep, that's the one,* I mutter to myself as I look up at the enormous place. I expect Lotto's mother to greet me at the door, but instead it's Lotto. I had imagined him looking strung out, red-eyed, and shaky from all that's gone on and by his mother's description. But he's freshly showered, shaved (for once), and in jeans and polo shirt. I barely recognize him without the tracksuit, sunglasses, and beard, and see, for the first time, that underneath Lotto's usual costume, he's handsome. *Maybe this is what the girls see in him,* I think, and not just the cash and access to clubs and parties. Lotto gives me a hug and apologizes for his mother's calling. We go to the kitchen and he sits on the counter and starts talking.

Whatever grief Lotto feels is hidden behind a head of combed hair, a clean shave, and a steely tone. *I didn't know,* he says over and over again. *I didn't know.* His cousin didn't seem high, he says, didn't seem like he was on anything. *Who knew about the medications!?!? Jesus!* he bellows, his composure now gone. Lotto tells me that when Sam bullied him into trying a line of coke he didn't think it was such a big deal. *How was I supposed to know? HOW?!?* he yells across the kitchen. *How the fuck is this my fault!??! And now my mother has you up in my shit. Billy, don't even try to talk me into going to rehab. There aren't any left to go to!*

For a moment, as I run down the list of rehabs I know he's been in and out of, I think he may be right. *Have you been to this one in North-ern California your mom has lined up?* I ask, genuinely not knowing the answer. *No,* he says, *but it's a fucking cash machine like all the rest. You put the druggie in and they take the cash out. And there is no way I'm going for a year. No. Fucking. Way.* He tells me how his mother has called Tess and told her Lotto has left town, that he's in treatment again and not to call. Tess, in turn, texts Lotto that she needs to step away. *Too much drama,* she writes. *BITCH!!* he shouts. He punctuates what he's yelling with a refrain that goes something like *I'm going to walk out this fucking door and find a fucking gun and blow my fucking brains out before I go to rehab again.* It goes on like this for over an hour, and when I start thinking of Lotto in the city, shame-saddled with his cousin's death, heartbroken and suicidal, I think, *He won't live.* Which is what I say. *You're not going to live.* I tell him that he's going to be dead just like his cousin—not by a gun, which we both know he's not going to get, but by an overdose. And as I say this I remember Lotto on one of our evening walks in Oregon. He is describing his group of friends in high school standing on a corner in the Bronx trying to score weed, *Freezing our hairless balls off, all of us wearing these big puffy North Face jackets—blue, red, green, purple— we looked like a pack of Skittles.* He says this out of the corner of his mouth, deadpan, a smartass twenty-one-year-old sounding like an

old Catskills comedian warming up a room. I remember him showing up at the airport in Portland a year ago, waving his boarding
pass, how excited and lonely and lost he seemed. And here he is,
lost again, trying to put a tough face on a horrible tragedy, trying to
call the shots when his world, by his own hand, has fallen apart once
more. I start crying. It's the first cry in months, the first one since I
walked out the door of my life five months ago, since that relapse that
sent me headlong into a two-month suicide dive. I had, then, walked
out the door and into the city like Lotto is about to do. *I'm looking at
someone who is about to be dead*, I keep thinking, and then I think of his
cousin Sam, whom I never met but heard a dozen stories about. Sam
was two years younger than Lotto, an on-again, off-again partner in
crime since elementary school who somehow never got in trouble or
took things as far as Lotto did. Sam did well enough in high school
to go to a cushy four-year liberal arts college in Florida, where he
had just finished his sophomore year. This kid who, from a distance,
had a better chance than Lotto of making something of his life is now
dead. *We die*, I think. *That's what we do. Whether we want to or not that's
where this goes.* I think of Polly doing lines during Heather's overdose.
I think of me, less than two weeks ago, going to get lighters to do
enough drugs to jump off a seventeen-story terrace. Polly, Heather,
Lotto, me—we don't stand a chance. *You don't stand a chance*, I blub-
ber through tears at Lotto. *You don't stand a chance unless you go. You're
going to end up just like Sam. Or you're going to kill someone else you love
and end up in jail.* Lotto doesn't move or speak, just sits on that sleek
stainless steel counter.

Lotto's mother comes in. She gets me a tissue to wipe my eyes, but
I can't stop sobbing. If you only cry once every few years, it's not

pretty. This was not pretty. *Are you OK?* she asks, and I say, pointing to Lotto, *I will be if he goes to California.*

And he does. Though I'd like to think my tear-streaked speech in the kitchen is what pushed him to make the right decision, I learn later from his mother that she and Lotto's father threatened—convincingly this time—to throw him out, cut him off entirely, and let him fend for himself if he didn't go, and stay, for a whole year. He texts me the next morning: *Going to Cali. Wish me luck, brother.*

The next night, I relapse. Polly is still in rehab, Lotto will be tucked away in his eleventh or twelfth rehab in Napa Valley, and I'll be coming home from the Meeting House, thinking about Noah, work, money, all the things Jack has counseled me to stop thinking and worrying and grieving about. And then I think about getting high. I think about it and then I do it. It's after midnight when I call Rico. I use the occasion to pay him back the thousand dollars I owe him and buy a bag of crack. I smoke it down and at two in the morning go to Mark's. He's there with three other people—two middle-aged guys and a kid in his early twenties. I sleep with all of them and smoke their drugs, since I have reached my ATM limit and have access to no more money. *My, my, how the mighty have fallen*, Mark cracks when he returns to his bedroom to survey the scene. And I think, *I've always been down here, it's just more obvious now.*

I leave Mark's around noon, crawl into bed, blast the air-conditioning, and take a fistful of Tylenol PM. Polly leaves a message from the pay phone at High Watch. She's going to meetings all day and night, she says, and the food is good. She misses Heather and Essie and me but she'll be home soon. Heather, who has calmed down and called Polly to say she can still live in the apartment, is renting a car and picking her up next Monday. *I'm comin' home, Crackhead. You better be sober.*

I don't tell Polly or anyone else, including Jack, about the relapse. I keep it a secret, just like I used to with Noah. I think I'm doing it for her and not me. I think it's some kind of sacrifice so she doesn't begin to get the idea that staying sober is impossible. I don't want her to think what I'm beginning to suspect: that none of what works for Jack and Asa and Luke and Annie is going to work for me. I'm like Lotto, without the wealth, without the endless safety nets of rehab after rehab. I'm like Sam and like I imagine Lotto would be if he hadn't left for California: a goner.

Done

First Monday in June. Polly's two weeks in rehab are up and Heather brings her back to the city in time for the two o'clock meeting. She comes in just before it starts and sits down across from me. She looks younger, brighter. I'm so used to seeing Polly in her pajamas or in unwashed sweatpants and T-shirts that it's jarring to see her in clean jeans and a blouse, her hair washed and skin clear. At the break, when Polly raises her hand and announces that she has seventeen days, the place goes wild. Later, when she shares about her time away, Pam and others sob and sigh with what can only be described as joy.

At the dog run afterward, Polly tells me that Heather has promised to slow down, and if she uses, not to use in the apartment. Polly seems hopeful, but I can't help but doubt that whatever promises Heather has made she will surely break. And soon. Now that Polly has some clean days together, I look on the bright side and think maybe we're both out of the woods, finally. I haven't told her about my relapse and don't plan to.

Our schedule of the 12:30, two o'clock, and dog run resumes. Jack has insisted that I take a service commitment at a meeting, so I make coffee and set up the chairs at the Meeting House on Wednesday nights. There's another guy who shares the commitment with me—a gentle fellow in his early forties whose story is very different from mine. His story reminds me of my father's—years of drinking and a slow, steady narrowing of a life until the loneliness causes enough agony to instigate change. For my father, it wasn't until his mid-sixties, when he was living alone in a small house in New Hampshire, twice divorced, with children who didn't speak to him and friends and siblings who had, one by one, gradually disappeared. What is bewildering to me is that my father didn't get sober—instead he switched from scotch to beer—but he still went through the kind of change that I see happen in the people who do. It began, at least from what I can tell, with a young couple who lived nearby. Dad got to know the husband because he also had a small plane at the nearby landing strip. One thing leads to another, and the couple invite my dad over for dinner. Sometime soon after the dinner, the wife is diagnosed with a serious cancer and given less than a year to live. They find out that there are experimental treatments that take place in Boston and all of a sudden their lives are in chaos. Whether he offered or they asked I don't know, but my father begins watching their dog—a poodle, of all things—while they are away. He gets very attached to the dog and it begins to stay over at his place for longer and longer stretches. As the wife becomes weak from the treatments, she is no longer able to drive herself to Boston for her frequent doctor's appointments. The husband is a commercial airline pilot, as my dad had been, so there are many times when he is simply not available to drive her. My father steps in and begins driving. This goes on for several years until, eventually, the woman dies. I remember my father mentioning the couple and their tragic situation during one of the first conversations we have when I'm back in New York from White Plains. By this time, her death was near. I remember being baffled by and jealous of his instinctive care for these strangers, particularly since, until now, he's had very little to do with my life or with any of my three siblings. My father and I speak two or three times a week that spring and summer, and there isn't one time when he doesn't mention these people or their poodle, which I think has basically become his. Before this, conversations with my father usually involved patiently listening to him complain about the president (it never matters which one), Congress, the health care industry, or an old favorite, the Kennedys. But now, most of the whipping boys have vanished. Not all, but most. In their place are detailed accounts of this woman's decline, the toll on her husband, and the latest attempt to reverse what appears to be irreversible. And questions. About my days, how I fill them, and recent developments with Polly and Asa and Jack, all of whom I've described to him in detail, the first people in my life since grammar school I've talked about with him or even mentioned. During this time he also becomes increasingly involved with my younger siblings, whose twenties are drawing to a bumpy close. He makes sure they have insurance, lawyers for legal troubles, money for night classes. And my nephews, his grandsons— he attends every birthday in Maine, flies his small plane to recitals and sporting events even. It doesn't happen overnight, but phone call by phone call, action by action, he becomes part of our lives, a member of the family—the father, the grandfather and friend he never was. That he still drinks, albeit far less than before, is none of my business (Jack's phrase, not mine).

The Wednesday setting-up-the-meeting commitment takes all of twenty minutes before the meeting, and yet I bring it up in every conversation, every description about my routine, every discussion about getting sober. People who address the United Nations or perform open heart surgery no doubt talk less about what they do than I did about those twenty minutes of flipping light switches, brewing coffee, and arranging chairs once a week. After tennis in the mornings with Elliot, or at dinner with Jean at Basta Pasta, I go on and on. I even tell them about the commitments I don't have yet. After ninety days, Jack says, I need to chair a meeting. There are ten different meetings a week at The Library—speaker meetings, topic meetings, meditation meetings, et cetera—and I wonder and worry about which one I'll get and if I'll be confident enough to sit in front of the group and lead. Whenever I try to talk to Jack about this stuff he cuts the conversation short with *Worry about which one when it's time. Get ninety days, and then let's talk about it.* So until then, it's mostly Jean and Elliot and, amazingly, my father who I talk to about this stuff. And, of course, Polly.

Only a few days after Polly returns home, Heather starts using in the apartment again. And more people than before seem to be using with her there. Polly shares about what's going on in meetings and talks to me about it at the dog run, but she still can't imagine moving out. Not only does she not think she can afford to move, but also she's worried that if she does, Heather will overdose, either accidentally or on purpose. In the last few days, when the subject of moving out comes up, Heather has threatened to kill herself if Polly leaves. It's a strange development, since less than a month ago Heather was demanding Polly move out, but as Annie reminds me one afternoon over coffee, Heather is losing her running buddy. Polly is getting sober and Heather isn't, and Heather's mad. That they are twins is easy to forget. Heather is stocky whereas Polly is rail thin. Heather has a coiled, angry energy that seems as if it could spring and strike at any moment. Polly is someone who looks more likely to hurt herself than anyone or anything else. Polly has Greenpeace and PETA stickers on her knapsack. Heather has a skull tattooed on the back of her neck. I know how difficult it is getting sober on my own, but living with a using buddy—and a twin, no less—who has dealers and drug addicts in and out of the apartment is unimaginable. Polly may have talked about it, but it's only now that I'm really beginning to recognize how tough what she's trying to do is. *That Heather is a strong undertow*, Annie says. *It's a good thing Polly was a champion swimmer in college.*

Polly keeps sharing about Heather, keeps showing up to meetings, and continues to walk dogs in the neighborhood to cover her portion of the rent. May winds down and as it does I think, *These have been the longest two months of my life.* Not because they've been the hardest but because it seems that so much has happened, so many new people have come into my life, and even more have left. I'm hopeful but I'm also tired. I didn't count on relapsing when I first came back to the city from White Plains. Didn't count on how expensive those relapses would be. Money is tight. With the last relapse and money needed for one of the lawyers handling my settlement with Kate, I've wiped out what would have paid June's rent. I'm trying to sell the only Eggleston photograph that's of any value in a portfolio I have, but so far have had no luck. Dave's friend, a respected art dealer, is doing her best—as a favor to Dave—to unload at least that one, but there have been no bites. On the bright side, an envelope arrives with a preapproved credit card and, on a lark, I send back the papers with a signature and a few weeks later a credit card appears with a $17,000 line of credit. From a cash advance that I get with this card I pay the June rent. It takes a number of visits to the ATM to advance that much cash from the credit card, and when I finally have $2,500 I deposit the money in my checking account and write a check to the landlord. *One more month of shelter,* I think, as I drop the envelope in the mailbox, and I'm genuinely grateful as I do.

During, in between, and after my meetings, I still think about getting high, still get cravings. I make my phone calls, share at The Library about it, but still feel as if I'm a sitting duck. Less than two weeks after my last relapse, I pick up again. It's like all the other times. A memory of getting high, a sudden craving, the world narrowing to one desire. I can't remember much about that day, the events or thoughts preceding the phone call to Happy. I remember using alone and then not alone. Someone I don't know materializes, the way these people, these people precisely like me, always do. We run out. It's nine in the morning. He says he has a connection uptown. I give him two hundred dollars, he leaves and doesn't return. It's a long, grim day and I scrape the stems and screens that I have, smoke them until they resemble charcoal, and eventually give up. There are a few beers left in the refrigerator. I drink one down, take a few Tylenol PMs, and lie in bed and wait until Happy or Rico turns his phone on.

There is no doubt in my mind that I will call to get more. I can get a few hundred dollars from the credit card I advanced the rent money from. It's mid-afternoon and the sun is pulsing on the other side of the drawn blinds. The old sheet nailed to the wall above the terrace door flaps with the air gushing from the wheezing air conditioner.

I wait, fall asleep for a little while, wake up at seven or eight, and even though I know the dealers are open for business again, I don't call them. Later, I think. I'm exhausted. There's a phrase I hear in the rooms all the time—*Sick and tired of being sick and tired*—and it couldn't diagnose more acutely how I feel. I go out to the terrace, look down to 15th Street, and again think about jumping. *Why do I always want to die?* I think impatiently. I always have, as long as I can remember, and never as much as when I'm coming down from a high, nearing the ruin of consequences that wait. It's so predictable, so selfish, and so weak. I go back inside and down the last beer—an Amstel Light, of all things. It doesn't feel like an end but it will be. Perhaps not *the* end, but *an* end.

I sleep through the night without waking and begin the day as I've done most days since April. I go to the gym, get to the 12:30 meeting early, raise my hand, and count one day for the last time. I don't remember who is there that day, but I do remember staying for the two o'clock and, after, going to the dog run with Polly. The dogs race in circles, hump each other, bark. The guys in the tracksuits make their phone calls and we sit in the middle of it all, me with one day and she with over three weeks. *Look who's on top now, Crackhead*, she teases, and I laugh, for what feels like the very first time.

Later in the summer, a month after Polly is back from rehab, The Library closes for a day. It's a Monday and the closing is either for a holiday or for a renovation of some kind. Polly and I agree to meet at Dean & Deluca at noon for a coffee and then walk east to a meeting at one o'clock. Walking up University I can see Polly sitting on a stool in the window. Before I get to the door I know something's wrong. There is the angle of her slouch, her hair falling in her face, and the surest sign of all: her pajamas. *Motherfucker,* I say or think and rush inside. *Motherfuckingmotherfucker!* I shout as I get closer and see for sure that she's a wreck, that she's been using. *Are you kidding me?* I ask as I approach her on the stool. Usually when Polly relapses I react in the way she usually reacts with me—with disappointment, fear, even, but always with compassion, and always quick with a plan to get to a meeting.

This time I'm furious. But not as furious as I am when she says, *I'm giving up. Sobriety isn't for me. I had a long talk with Heather this morning and it's what I decided.* I cannot believe what I'm hearing. *HEATHER?!!??* I bellow. *Are you kidding? You're now taking advice from Heather?* She just looks at me. It's not a conversation. She's barely in front of me now. She's already back in the apartment. Of course she looks terrible, of course she hasn't slept all night. But what she's saying is not part of the script. She's supposed to get back on the horse, go to a meeting with me right away, and announce that she has one day. *I'm done,* she says, more matter-of-fact than defiant. *I'm sorry, but I'm done.* I don't know what to say. We sit in the window and stare at each other and two things cross my mind: (1) I'm jealous that when we leave she will return to an apartment just a few blocks away to drugs, and (2) I'm sure she's going to die. Not someday, not even soon, but now, today, right after we part ways. I know she's going to die and I know that there is nothing I can do about it. She's not as strong as Heather is, not as tough, can't do the kinds of drugs she does. Do I call the police to raid Heather's apartment? Is it better for her to be in jail than to be dead? What if Noah had done that with me? I'd be in jail now. But am I now so much better off? If I'd gone to jail I'd probably have a lot more than a few weeks sober by now. And then, right there, before I say another word, I pray. Jack is always telling me to pray and when I balk he usually just says, *Whatever you're doing isn't working, so you might as well try.* So now, for Polly, I do. To whom or to what I don't know, but to something: *Tell me what to say. Tell me what to say so she doesn't die. Please.* But no words come and I eventually say what my friend Lili said to me months ago after she found me deep in a bender at One Fifth: *You want to die, die. You want to live, call me. But until then, leave me out of it.* And just as I say these same words, Polly's up off the stool, out the door, and back on the street. She's gone. Just like that.

I go to the meeting in the East Village and the only one there I know is Pam. I raise my hand, announce my day count, and wonder if Polly doesn't have the right idea. After the meeting I tell Pam what's happened and she just shakes her head in her sanguine, maternal way and says, *Sometimes you have to let them go so that they can come back. In the meantime, you pray they don't die.*

After the East Village meeting I go home, fall asleep, and the next day can't bear to go to the 12:30 meeting. *But what if Polly's there?* I think, and rush out the door to get to The Library on time. Polly's not there. I stay for the two o'clock and Polly doesn't show. She doesn't turn up at the Meeting House either. For the next few weeks I go to every meeting, hoping she'll appear. I see her once, on the street. She's coming up Fifth Avenue, walking Essie and smoking a cigarette. She's in her sweatpants, all angles and jutting bones, moving at a snail's pace. She looks like the Grim Reaper's girlfriend. We cross each other on the sidewalk and when I say hi she puts her hand up to wave me away. I keep going.

Asa tells me to pull back and let Polly hit her bottom. Jack and Annie and Luke do, too. But what if her bottom is death? What if there is something I can do that could keep her from dying? At one point Asa recommends I go to an Al-Anon meeting. *I drive people into those meetings,* I joke. *I don't actually go there myself.* Asa shakes his head.

Life goes on, my one day becomes a few days and then a few weeks. There is a night after dinner on Sixth Avenue when I say good-bye to Cy and look down toward Houston and wonder what Mark is up to. I walk down into the trigger zone and stand on the corner of Sixth and Houston and see that his lights are on. Shadows pass in front of the window and my heart races as I conjure scenarios of what is transpiring there. As if I have to imagine. The same thing is always transpiring there. I cross Sixth Avenue, cross down to the south side of Houston, and step toward the building. *Fuck it,* I think, like I always do at this moment, and head toward the door. But before I press the buzzer, I think of Polly. What if she calls me when I'm in there? What if she hears I've relapsed again? What if I don't make it to the meeting tomorrow, stay up for a few days, and miss her when she comes back in? What if my picking up gives her another excuse to keep using? It's narcissistic, I realize as I'm thinking it, but I can't help but ask myself: *What if my picking up results in Polly dying?* The logic is suddenly so plausible, so powerful, and so likely that it stops me in my tracks. It stops me less than ten feet from the buzzer I've pressed countless times over too many years and with the same grim results. I've never been this close and not gone in.

I turn around and start walking north on Sixth Avenue, away from Mark's, where I never set foot again. I call Jack and leave a message on his voice mail. I tell him I've gone into the trigger zone and come out clean.

Over the next few weeks there are a dozen or so times when the thought to call Happy or Rico or go to Mark's happens in the way that it always has. The idea sparks and with it a craving to use and then the plans to figure out how I can. Each of these times I think of Polly or Lotto or someone in the rooms counting days who I've given my number to, and each of these times I stop long enough to call either Jack or Asa or Annie, and by the time I do the urge passes. And then, miraculously, the cravings disappear. The thoughts still come—I expect they always will—but the craving doesn't follow. The desire to use or drink vanishes as stealthily as it used to arrive. I won't even notice it go, just that it has.

Pink Cloud

It's the Fourth of July and Elliot and I go for a hike on Bear Mountain. We hike and walk for a few hours and find our way to a ridge that looks south down the Hudson River to Manhattan. *It looks like Oz*, Elliot says as the ridge of buildings appears, floating on the horizon like a crown. I remember thinking the same thing in Dave's car three months ago on the drive from White Plains. That car ride now seems a lifetime away.

Elliot and I return to the city just as it's getting dark. The elevator man, the older of the two brothers, is smiling when we enter the lobby and we ask why. *The roof is open!* he says loudly, as if we should know why this is cause for celebration. *For the fireworks!* Of course, the fireworks, the Fourth of July. We get off the elevator on the twentieth floor and rush to the roof. The building is the last tall building on Seventh Avenue before the acres of town houses and low buildings of the West Village begin to spread south of 14th Street, so the view from the roof is breathtaking. We see the long lit riverbanks of New Jersey, the huddled buildings that make up what's left of the financial district, the Met Life tower north of the Flatiron, and the tallest of all, the Empire State Building, celebrating in red, white, and blue lights. Never has the city looked so festive, so possible. Fireworks begin to explode up and down the Hudson River, south of Battery Park, and across town above the East River. I have never seen so many fireworks at once, and the two of us stand there, stunned. We kiss. Not for the first time since our affair several years ago and not for the first time that day, but in a way that makes it clear that something is beginning, or has begun and is now being acknowledged. It is one of the great kisses of my life. Jack warned me against getting involved romantically until I had ninety days, but it's a suggestion I fail to take. The worry is that if there is heartbreak or romantic upset in those ninety days, one will relapse over it. Maybe because my heart was already broken, and Elliot came in like a friend and stayed as something more, it was different. I don't know. I wouldn't recommend it to anyone else, but I also don't regret it.

Two days after the Fourth of July, I arrange to meet Asa at Mary Ann's, a Mexican restaurant in Chelsea. Oddly, it's the restaurant my girlfriend Marie took me to on our first trip to New York together, the summer after I graduated from college. When I go to the bathroom I look in the mirror that could well be the same mirror I looked at all those years ago. Twenty-one then, thirty-four now; jobless then, jobless now, I think, and then say to my reflection, *Nothing's changed.* I look closer and see the creep of wrinkles around my eyes and along my brow, and the more-than-a-few gray hairs above.

Some things *have* changed, I think, and then again as I return to the table and see two glasses of tap water.

I've asked Asa to dinner to tell him about Elliot. I'm nervous because I know he has developed feelings for me. I know this because he told me so a few weeks earlier—after a meeting, in my apartment—before he kissed me. I kissed him right back and for a little while, we kissed. It was a mistake, I knew it, but it felt good, and as with all the other mistakes that felt good, I had no power to stop this one before the damage was done. Asa had become my life raft and I had clung too tightly. I called him all the time, followed him from meeting to meeting, talked his ear off, and only now had begun to listen. After the kiss, I told him I didn't and never would have romantic feelings for him and that I was sorry if I'd led him to believe otherwise. *And let's face it*, I pointed out, trying to make light of the event but also reminding him of the obvious, *I'm hardly a catch. Among other things, I have less than three weeks sober and I can't stop relapsing.*

What I said didn't matter. Our relationship was never the same again. By then, Luke, Polly, Annie, and a few other people from the rooms had come into my life. Jack had, for weeks, perhaps expecting this very thing, encouraged me to spend time with and call people other than Asa. *Spread the neediness*, he said. *There's plenty to go around.* And I did.

After the food arrives, I tell Asa about Elliot. The Fourth of July hike, the rooftop fireworks, the kiss, the whole shebang. *So you're seeing him now? He's your boyfriend? Is that what this is about?* he asks, gesturing to the burritos, the nachos, the restaurant. As I say yes, Asa pushes his chair back, crosses the dining room, and shoots out the door. I chase after him but he waves me away, shakes his head, and disappears down 16th Street. By this point I have lost a lot of people—clients, friends, colleagues, Noah—but watching Asa rush down the street away from me is one of the toughest losses. I didn't, and still don't, have anything to compare it to. How do you thank someone for saving your life? How do you apologize for needing him too much? For not being stronger when it mattered? If I had the words I would have said them. But that night I have only his name, which I shout uselessly as he hurries down 16th Street, his red hair and pale skin disappearing into the night like they had the first night we met.

Not long after, I get a phone call from Dave's art dealer. There is an offer for the Eggleston photograph she is trying to sell for me, and it's for what she's asking. Even better, she thinks she has a buyer for two more, and even though their value is a bit less, the prospect of those two selling as well is like winning the lottery. With less than a thousand left in my bank account, and tens of thousands of dollars now piled up on credit cards, the timing of her phone call couldn't be better. She eventually sells all three, and with that money I am able to stay in the 15th Street apartment.

Annie and I go to Coney Island. Neither of us has been there before, and it's the day of the annual Mermaid Parade.

We eat the creamiest, most delicious gelato imaginable and watch guys in drag and girls who look like guys in drag prance and jiggle on and alongside floats made of everything from macaroni to marshmallows. On the ride home we sit down next to a woman who moves, dramatically and with great sighing, to the end of the subway car bench. When she's not looking, Annie mimics her gesture and it is, this little impromptu impersonation, the funniest thing I have ever seen. We laugh so hard the woman leaves the car at the next station and we howl all the way back to the city. Later that night it occurs to me that I haven't thought about drinking or using in weeks. I open a journal I've been keeping since White Plains and write: *Coney Island with Annie today. No cravings for weeks. How did this happen?*

Before the summer is over, almost two months since that grim day in Dean & Deluca, Polly calls. It's morning and I haven't left for the gym yet. At first, I think I'm imagining her name on the screen of my cell phone—I have so many times. I pick up. She asks me to meet her at the dog run, and I say I'll leave immediately. I peel out the door and run down 15th Street, past Sixth Avenue, past Fifth, all the way to Union Square. I manage to call Jack as I huff and puff toward the dog run and leave an excited message. And, like the last time I saw Polly and a few other times since, I pray.

To whatever forces have kept me sober this long, I pray for the right words. *TELL ME WHAT TO SAY!* I yell as I run. *Please.*

I arrive at the dog run and Polly is sitting on our usual bench. Essie is waddling nearby. I don't need any words because she has the ones that matter. *I need help,* she says, not looking particularly hungover or strung out, just tired. *Will you take me to a meeting?* she asks. *Are you kidding?* I answer. *I've been waiting my whole life.* And though the words are lazy and said playfully, as I say them I know they're true. I know in that instant that everything that has happened—every last lucky, lonely, destructive, delusional, selfish, wretched, insane, desperate second of it—has made this moment on the bench with Polly possible. I'm sober enough to show up, addict enough to be asked. I'm one of her kind and she's one of mine and there is no one in the world who can help us but each other. I tell her about the night on Houston and Sixth Avenue in front of Mark's apartment, how I stepped away and she was the reason. *Nah, Crackhead, it would take a hell of a lot more than me to keep you from the pipe.* We laugh, the way addicts laugh about the agony of their using in the only way that makes it bearable: with each other.

Soon after that morning, Polly and I move all of her belongings into a truck driven by a scruffy cute guy from the rooms, someone neither Polly nor I know. Polly shares in a meeting that she's moving and that she needs a truck, and this guy materializes and offers not only his truck and his driving skills but his hands and back as well. He and I spend hours shoving boxes and chairs and bookcases into the small one-bedroom apartment in Astoria Polly finds on Craigslist.

Heather comes by while we are moving Polly out and without a word walks in and out of the apartment, around the truck, and alongside us as we haul bags and furniture down the hall and into the street. I worry she is going to let me have it before we're finished, but just before the three of us pile into the truck, she turns to me and says without looking me in the eye, *Thank you.* Tailgate shut, Polly jammed in the front seat between me and the cute guy driving, we start to roll down St. Mark's Place. *Wait!* Polly shouts. *I forgot something in the apartment.* Before the truck comes to a stop, she is nudging me to let her out. I hesitate, afraid she's changed her mind, that once she gets out she'll never get back in. *C'mon, it's just gonna take a minute,* she says, more wistful than impatient. I let her out and watch as she keys the lock to the building door and disappears inside. Something unfamiliar plays on the radio and the stranger next to me taps the wheel. Minutes pass and my eyes are closed when Polly climbs in next to me. She's shaking, her eyes are red from crying, and there is nothing in her hands retrieved from the apartment. *Go,* she croaks-more-than-speaks. *Before I change my mind, go.* And so we do. It takes most of the afternoon to move Polly into her new apartment. Neither of us ever sees the cute, generous guy again.

On the last night of summer, at the end of Labor Day weekend, Elliot and I play tennis. It's a beautiful night—crisp, clear, and the sky is crowded with clouds that look like enormous waves crashing against a shore. After we play, we walk up the West Side Highway to the pier and collapse on the grass. The sky turns pink above us. The air is chilly and the green and red lights of New Jersey blink across the water. As the sun dips lower, the pink darkens against the clouds, and everything—the city, the river, the people around us—appears to shrink against the magnificent sky. Neither of us speaks. In a few minutes it will be dark. In the morning, summer will be over. I am happy, I think—for the first time in my life, happy. I'm sober, sur-rounded day and night by other sober people, the urge to drink and use has left, finally; I have just enough money in the bank to pay the rent and send tiny checks to the many people and places I owe, and I'm with someone I have no secrets from. *I wish I could stop time,* I tell Elliot. *If I could, I would stop it right now, under this great pink cloud.* We shiver in our damp tennis clothes and huddle into each other for warmth. *I know,* Elliot whispers into the darkening night. *Wouldn't it be wonderful.*

Shoulder to Shoulder

On a Sunday night in September, I raise my hand in a meeting and say that I have ninety days. It is at the Meeting House, and Polly and Jack are there. Luke and Annie are there, too, along with a few other people from The Library. Though I have left messages to tell him when and where and asking him to please come, Asa is not. At midnight that night, when the Empire State Building turns its lights off as it always does, it is officially a new day, and the day after that another and the day after that another and so on and so on until a year, and then another and then another and then four, and as I write this now—five years, eight months, and two days. And with the help of the rooms, the people in them, and the power their words and actions and courage have shown me—a power that is unquestionably greater than myself, greater than my desire to use, to drink, and to die—tomorrow will, likely, be one day more.

Before the end of the year, Jean invites me to a party. It's a dinner for someone important, and it's large and seated and in her apartment. Jean's had lots of parties since I've come back to New York, and with each one she has said, *Don't worry, it'll be a bore anyway*, but with this one she says, over dinner at Basta Pasta, that she wants me to come, that her daughters are coming and that she'd like me to be there. Of course I say yes. The dinner is a month away, and I worry about it from the moment she asks. All my outings with Jean this year—theater, music, movies—have been one-on-one, and the few suppers at her apartment have been in the kitchen, with Paul, her chef, cooking and chatting behind the counter. I haven't been to one party or social function that hasn't been a sober gathering of people from the rooms, or a small group of very close, very supportive friends. It's only when I think about going to this party at Jean's that I recognize fully how protected these months have been, how sealed off. Jean's parties, even on a good day, are not for the faint of heart. But as a first outing, after hiding inside a sober cocoon for half a year, it is downright terrifying. I keep imagining people asking one question: *What do you do?* And when I imagine what I say in response, I come up with nothing. *I was in book publishing, and now . . .* In the rooms it's not uncommon for people to be out of work or taking time off to get sober, so answering that question in the past tense there is easy. But at this party, I imagine the group will be a little less fluent in the language of falling apart.

On the night of the party, I arrive late so I won't have to navigate the cocktail hour for very long before dinner. I don't ask Jean who she has me seated next to, because I don't want her to worry. But of course *I* worry. During cocktails I talk to Jean's daughters, who are always friendly. At dinner I sit next to an exquisite middle-aged woman, dressed in a perfect suit and deftly arranged scarf. Just as she introduces herself, a waiter comes and asks if we'd like red or white wine. She places her elegant hand and long fingers over the top of the empty wine glass next to her dinner plate and says, *I won't be drinking tonight.* After I blurt, *Same here,* she places that same hand on my shoulder and says, *I gather you've had quite a year. Welcome to the rooms.* How many times had I been convinced there was a dark conspiracy of intricately placed people observing, entrapping, stalking, and circling? So many. Now, with this kind, sober woman sitting next to me in the thicket of a challenging dinner party, I experience the flip side of this paranoia—the opposite of all that wild-minded dread, the feeling instead that there are forces conspiring on my behalf, placing people in my way at precisely the right moments to guide me on whatever path I should be on. Like a blubbering imbecile, I grab her hand and say, *You have no idea how happy I am that you're here.* She asks what meetings I go to and she knows The Library well—a former sponsee of hers goes there regularly. *Madge?* she asks. *Have you heard of her?* It turns out she was—pedigree of pedigrees—Madge's first sponsor. It was a beautiful dinner.

Early in the summer Annie and I begin to meet every Saturday at various meetings. We try one and then another and always get together for coffee after. She graduates from The Library before I do. In September she gets a job teaching performing arts to kids in the Bronx during the week. Three years later she arranges to perform a showcase for the faculty at her graduate school and, at last, receives her MFA. Once she goes back to work, Saturdays become the only time I see her. Aside from the occasional Broadway musical and dinner at the Carnegie Deli, they still are.

It won't be until November that I begin to think about going back to work, and when I do, I am—out of the blue—offered a job at a literary agency. The very thing I puzzled and panicked and stressed and moaned about since the day I returned to New York all those months ago—a job, work, my career, money—solves itself without my doing a thing. *I told you so*, Jack gloats on the phone when I tell him. *All you had to do was get honest, get sober, and offer help to a few addicts and alcoholics along the way. The rest took care of itself.* I accept the job but with two requests: that I start in March instead of right away and that I'm free to leave the office every afternoon to attend a two o'clock meeting. They agree, and until that first day of work I spend the remaining months as I have since April: gym, three meetings a day, dog run with Polly, *Oprah*, and seeing as many alcoholics and addicts in recovery as I can find.

After the dinner at Mary Ann's, Asa drifts away. Still, I call him on my anniversary every year to thank him for helping me get sober and ask him to call back and let me know how he's doing. For the first few years he does, and we exchange messages for a while until we give up and another year passes. This year I call and don't hear back from him. I call a few more times, and still nothing. I give up and weeks later I overhear someone say they heard he had gone out, that he was drinking again. I call him right away and leave another message, but again, not a peep. A few weeks later I decide to call from the BlackBerry I've been given at work and not the cell phone he's used to. Just as I hoped, he picks up. I don't recognize his voice. It's different—quicker, tighter—and by the sound of it anything but happy to hear from me. He does not ask how I am or what's going on in my life. He does not ask one question during the entire phone call. He tells me he's drinking and using coke recreationally and that he's happier, more confident, and having more sex than he was when he was sober. He reminds me that coke and booze were never his problems, heroin was, and he's able to manage it. He tells me that the meetings are a cult and require the people who go to them to agree that they're defective, and he doesn't have any use for that kind of thinking anymore. When I finally get a word in, I ask him to be careful and awkwardly remind him that buying coke is illegal and that I don't want him to get arrested. This sets him off and he yells that doctors and psychiatrists are breaking more laws than dealers and tells me not to call if I'm only going to lecture him or try to persuade him to get sober or go to a meeting. *Don't call me,* he says, and it feels like a punch. *Don't call me,* he says in the voice that is not the voice I knew—the one that coaxed me off the street, charmed drugs out of my hands, told me how the rooms and the people in them saved his life, talked me to sleep on the phone the night after my first relapse, told me not to give up, and asked me, the night we first met at the New Venus diner, to meet him at The Library the next day.

I am in the lobby of a movie theater on Third Avenue and 11th Street when Asa hangs up. Soon after, Cy arrives. *You OK?* she asks. *You look like you've seen a ghost.* It takes a few seconds before I can answer. I still can't believe what I've just heard. *I'm not sure,* I say, *but I think I just have.* I have not seen or heard from Asa since.

Heather shows up at The Library later that year. She raises her hand and counts one day. She relapses, returns, and relapses again. She has the same gift her sister has and when she tells her story—plainly, powerfully, honestly—everyone strains to hear. Polly's parents come to town, and we all go to breakfast at the diner on Seventh Avenue and 15th Street. Heather shows up half an hour late, high, belligerent, shouting about her boss, taxes, stingy tips, and until the bill is paid no one but she speaks. She comes back into the rooms, counts days again, and then disappears. Eventually she loses her job and, not long after, the rent-controlled apartment on St. Mark's Place. Polly allows her to move into her apartment in Astoria and sleep on the couch under one condition: no alcohol or drugs in the place. For the most part, she's complied.

There is a time, later, years later—after I've completed, with my sponsor's help, an unflinching review of my behavior before getting sober—when I begin to face the people I did harm to. Some I haven't seen in a long time—six, eighteen years—and some I may have seen the day before. One by one, I sit before them and read what I spent days writing—describing the harm I caused, offering to make the wrong right, if possible, and asking what I left out—and each time, when it's the moment for the person I am addressing to respond, what each one says is nothing I expect. Each time, I walk away feeling—at the edges—gratitude, relief, compassion, but at the center what can only be described as love. For a while the world will appear more as it is and less as I make it, and I will have a new courage to face the remaining wreckage of the past. I was an active addict and alcoholic for over twenty-three years. The list of people I harmed is long, and I have only scratched the surface.

Seven months after our Labor Day evening on the pier, Elliot and I break up. There is a night when it is clear that it is over, and I name it, and then cry for the first time since that morning in Lotto's kitchen. I cry uncontrollably, outlandishly, and Elliot, as he had when we were together, sits by my side, holds my hand until I can pull it together. We don't see each other for over a year, and then slowly, gradually, we begin to meet again as friends, as we do now, on tennis courts, with racquets in our hands, and between us, a speeding ball, a net.

Noah and I get back together. Something I give up wanting suddenly arrives, again, and with much hope. But it is clear from the very start—though it takes us both a year to accept—that in order to work, our relationship needs me to be an active addict and alcoholic, that the thing we thought tearing us apart all those years was actually what was holding us together. Without that dark glue, we come apart. I learn from him later, after we break up, that there was more to the dark glue than I knew. Of course he had his own battles, of course he struggled with his own demons that had nothing to do with me. I was too mired in my own to see, too invested in his being what I needed him to be to recognize him as he was. But all that comes out later, in fits and starts, and even then it takes a long time for me to believe.

Not so long ago, Noah and I run into each other at the Knickerbocker. Cy and I show up there, late, after seeing a movie nearby. Noah is sitting across from the bar, at a corner table, with his boyfriend. I haven't seen him for months, though we've spoken and e-mailed and in our way stayed in touch. He doesn't see us at first, and for a long time remains undistracted from his very engaged, very focused conversation. When he sees us, he quickly stands to come over. He crosses the room—this room that held so many of our best and worst nights—and slows before reaching our table, recognizing something as he does. He stops and turns to the side slightly, gesturing to the bar, to the restaurant, out to the street, and back to us. *Hi, Bill*, he says, a big smile on his face, holding out his hands as if to contain every last awful, ridiculous inch and minute of our shared history. *Hi, Noah*, I say. And we laugh, finally.

Lotto gets kicked out of the rehab in California. Somehow a stolen car is involved, but he will avoid arrest and prison and end up—after a year and a half of living at home and relapsing and finally being cut off from financial support—back in another rehab in Georgia. This one sticks. He stays there for a year and continues on in a nearby sober-living community for another year. I will get one message in all this time that fills me in on the ups and downs. A few months ago I see him on the street with a tall, tough-looking friend of his from Georgia. He has two years sober and is in town to visit his parents for a few days before going back. *My addict ass can't be here long*, he says in the same Mulberry-Street-meets-boarding-school voice. *And when it is, I bring protection*, he laughs, nodding to his muscled buddy. He tells me the women in Georgia are hot but lazy, and about a meeting down the street from the apartment he's just moved to. *It's a club. We have a flat-screen TV and a pool table, and it's seltzer and fucking Pepsi but it's cool.* Before we say good-bye, he gives me his cell phone number—the same one he's had for the last two years.

Some kind of record, I say, and we both laugh. As of this writing, his phone number has not changed.

Annie gets married. The wedding is less than a week after Noah and I break up, over a year after I've been back at work, and the ceremony and the reception take place on a sloping field next to a lake in Ithaca, New York. I drive to the wedding with Rafe, the wildly articulate guy from The Library who never quite becomes a close friend in the way Annie and Luke have, but whose knowing looks and *Hi, Bill*s have become a steady, counted-on part of my recovery. He agrees to be my sponsor when Jack moves upstate to teach at a small college. Rafe and I stop for lunch on the way, during which my sister Kim calls, upset because my younger brother has been the cause of another drunken brawl and, after, an ugly scene at my mother's house. I feel helpless. I know what to say and how to act with other addicts and alcoholics, like Polly, but I have no clue what to do for my brother or how to help my family. I tell Rafe about my family, my struggling brother, breaking up with Noah, being single, without romantic possibilities or entanglements for the first time since high school—and he listens. I tell him I feel lonelier and more alone than I can ever remember feeling. He reminds me that feelings aren't facts (another one of Jack's old expressions that I used to cringe at but now cling to), and that I'm sober, which means I may be low but I'm not lost, powerless but not useless. *Stop feeling sorry for yourself*, he snaps, and not for the first time suggests the simple, surefire solution for self-pity that on my own I always forget: *Call another addict with less time sober than you.* And so I do.

I check into a hotel that is also one of the tallest buildings in Ithaca. I am assigned, because of some accident in the booking, a large suite on the top floor, and it seems like the emptiest room I have ever seen. My friend John, who moved to Asia a few years before and whom I'd mostly lost touch with, calls from Saipan the next morning and we stay on the phone for hours before I leave for the wedding. I tell him everything that's happened over the last two years—returning to New York after rehab, relapsing, The Library, reaching ninety days, Elliot, starting a job at a literary agency, getting back together with Noah and ending it, finally, just days ago. I tell him, as I look out the window to the hills that surround Ithaca and rise shoulder to shoulder against an enormous blue sky, that I'm thirty-six, a year and ten months sober, and on my own. At the reception later, surrounded by Rafe and Polly and Annie, at a table crowded with seltzers and Diet Cokes and coffee cups, I know that I've never been less alone in my life.

Asa arrives late, as the procession music begins, and leaves early. We wave to each other as he's being seated, but after Annie kisses her new husband and the rice is thrown, he disappears. I look for him at the reception after, but he is gone before I have a chance to say good-bye.

Polly and I walk down to the lake and sit on a dock as the sun goes down. She is wearing a green dress and her loose hair shines in the late daylight. She looks healthier and more beautiful than I've ever seen her. She has a year and four months sober that night. She has just over five years now. *Here we are, Crackhead*, she says, the way she always does. We look out over the lake. Wind skims the surface, swallows dart and swoop above the shimmering water, and the first stars stitch the sky. The dock sways beneath us, laughter sparks above the thumping music of the reception, and neither of us makes a sound as the sun finds its way home, again, behind the formidable hills of Ithaca. I know exactly what she means. Here we are.

Close

I had the best gin and tonic in the world in the lobby of the Mandarin Oriental Hotel. My friend John says these words as we're sitting on the terrace of a house we've rented on a small island in Thailand. It's early January and we've come here for a month to work—him on a book project and a magazine article, me on a book I've been writing for two and half years, the one you are reading now. We've spent four weeks working from morning to night interrupted only by meals cooked by two shy women who arrive in the morning and leave in the evening and blush when we praise and thank them for the delicious food. It's dinnertime now. Fading sun and stars commingle in the early evening sky as the women load plates with curried vegetables and steamed rice.

I've told John I've booked a room at the Mandarin Oriental in Bangkok on the way back to New York and he tosses a memory of a gin and tonic he drank in his early twenties into the air as casually as he would a receipt in the trash. But I catch it and hold on. This drink he consumed decades ago now sits on the dinner table between us, and nothing else holds my attention—not the last panels of light sliding along the rippling sea below, the flickering candles, the magnificent food. Nothing exists but the drink—its sleek vessel of glass, its magic contents, and the legendary hotel it was consumed in. Over the next four days I imagine the perspiration on the rim of the glass, the thrum of hotel lobby glamour, the garnish of the greenest lime. On the morning I leave for Bangkok I finish a draft of the book, type the last lines, the ones you just read. I send the document to my editor by e-mail and a few hours later ride a longboat to Phuket, where I catch a plane to Bangkok. John will arrive a day after I do and we have planned to meet in an overpriced restaurant along the river to celebrate our last night in Thailand.

When I arrive in Bangkok I hail a cab in front of the arrivals terminal. The driver is young—twenty-five, maybe thirty—and after I tell him which hotel to take me to, he asks the following questions: *You like boys? You like girls? You like drugs?* My answer, without thinking, without thought of any kind, as reflexive as a leg shooting straight after a doctor's tap on the knee, is this: *Yes*. When we pull up to the hotel the driver scribbles a number on a piece of paper and hands it to me. *Tonight*, he says. *You call tonight*. I nod and take the paper and put it in my pocket. What am I thinking as I get out of the taxi with this number, the first of its kind I've held in almost six years? Nothing. I am thinking nothing.

The lobby of the Mandarin Oriental. It is thrumming, as I had imagined, but it is modern and familiar and Americans are everywhere. I am taken to my room, where a middle-aged man in a hotel uniform shows me the bathroom, the various electrical outlets, the bar, which I see has only Smirnoff vodka, and the balcony overlooking the river. He takes my credit card and looks at my passport. I sign something and he leaves. It is now late afternoon and the sun is like a chunk of molten lava hanging in the sky and the air around it is hazy and orange. From the balcony I see boats crowding the river and dozens of hotel guests pacing the terraces below. Bangkok seems caught in something heavier than air, everything and everyone pushing sluggishly through the thick atmosphere. Planes labor across the sky so slowly they seem about to drop from exhaustion.

The ice bucket above the bar is full. The butler buzzes my room to find out if I need anything. I ask him if they have Stolichnaya and he says he'll go see. On the bed my phone buzzes to signal it has received an e-mail. I don't go to it. It buzzes again and I lean against the desk and wait for the butler to return. Ice is bursting from the bucket. I've never seen ice so abundant, so refreshing. I fill a glass. A thick, low glass, the kind my father drank scotch from when I was a kid. There are no limes in the place but there is a fruit basket and in it an orange that I slice a small wedge from. I squeeze a bit of juice onto the ice and shove the rind between the ice and the glass. No butler. No Stoli. My phone buzzes again and I grab the bottle of Smirnoff and pour the drink. There it is. Vodka not gin. Orange not lime. Smirnoff not Ketel One. Smirnoff not Stoli. By no means the best vodka in the world. By no means even the second best. But it's here. And no one else is. No one is watching. No one is waiting for me and it's been almost six years. A drink, just one, on the balcony of the Mandarin Oriental Hotel. Why does this feel necessary? Why has it seemed inevitable since John uttered those words four days ago? I do not know. But it does. And so I pick up the drink, put the glass to my lips, and swallow a mouthful of vodka. It tastes like poison. Cold, foul, thick. Is it because it's Smirnoff? Is it because there is an orange and not a lime? A balcony and not a lobby? Or is it because I haven't had a drink in so many years? Agitated, I drink more. I pour a second and a third, and the vodka tastes no better. I don't feel anything more than a gathering heaviness. A slowness like the air around me. A dulling. In the room I pour a fourth and return to the balcony. Six floors up. I palm the piece of paper. It's too soon to call. It is not night. How many drinks until it will be late enough to call? I can see the fuzzy mural of the near future: the cab ride, the cash machine, the bag of crack or its equivalent, the stems, the lighter, the skin, calling for more, bottles of vodka, the dizzying crash. I don't want it but I want it. But want feels more like acceptance of a kind of sentence. There is no turning back. I've begun something that will be finished, and as I look down the six stories to the terrace and alley below, I know that death is where this will go. Hours ago I sent off a manuscript about early recovery, how difficult getting and staying sober is, how it cannot be done alone. Alone, I down most of the fourth drink. I don't bother with the orange now. Dying in Bangkok. It feels suddenly like the most logical, inevitable outcome. The cabdriver, the phone number, this terrace, this drink, the coming night and all it will entail—each piece clicks into place, the intended path becomes visible. It's clear now. The book is finished, my use expired. A new slow wind moves warm air across the balcony and lights blink across the river from hotels and apartment buildings. My death will remind people how serious addiction is, how lethal. Death will be useful.

I finger the scrap of paper. I finish the drink, which tastes just as awful as the first. My phone buzzes again. Before I pour a fifth drink, before I call that number, I go to the bed and check the phone to see who has been sending me messages. *Hey, you around? Free to talk? What's up? Can we talk?* Four messages—each one from my new sponsee. The one who relapsed while I was in Thailand, the one who has seen me at The Library every day for months and because of that asked me to be his sponsor. The one who, more than anyone else I've met, reminds me of myself in early sobriety. The determination to appear in control, the relentless relapsing, the recurring courtship with death. There he is, reaching out from the other side of the world. And here I am, about to pour a fifth vodka. About to call the number in my pocket.

I look again at his messages. So persistent, so willing. Finally, after months of relapsing and dodging his former sponsor, he is asking for help. Asking *me* for help. Reaching out to end the agony he's thrashed around in for years. Agony I know, agony I had been released from. I close the phone and put it back on the bed. And just like that, it's over. I'm done. Whatever started days ago on the terrace with John and led to four vodkas in this hotel room has stopped. I rip up the piece of paper, grab my hotel room key, and head for the door. I walk through the lobby and out to the front drive and into the street. I call my brother. It is morning in Maine where he lives and I leave him a message. I tell him an almost-truth. I tell him I almost picked up, almost drank, almost used. I walk until I find a guy selling large bottles of water. I buy one and dump half of it on my head and down the rest in a few long gulps. I walk through the hurdy-gurdy streets of Bangkok, past the bars with boys and girls for sale, past fruit stands and T-shirt vendors, past the empty streets in the now shut business districts. I walk until I am about to collapse and signal a tuk-tuk, a cross between a moped and a rickshaw, and tell the driver the name of the hotel. When I enter the room for the second time that day I am as far from wanting a drink or a drug as I can be.

The next night, with green and red and white fireworks streaking above the river, I tell John every part of the story except for the drinking. I expand the almost-truth I left on my brother's voice mail. I tell him I read my sponsee's messages and didn't drink, and as I do I feel that old distance return, that old barrier rise up between me and the people who think they know me. He suspects nothing, is an arm's length from where I sit, but word by word he recedes further and further away.

After I return to New York, I tell the same story to everyone at The Library and I tell the same story there twice again. The story of how I almost picked up. The story of how close I came. How close. It's the story I tell my brother, my sponsee, my family, Rafe, and everyone else close to me. I tell this story and in the space it creates between me and everyone else, a second self, a hidden one, returns. And with it the fear of being found out. The little thread of almost true gathers and braids with other threads and soon the thread is a rope and from the rope a noose that chafes and tugs, just like it always had. But no good can come from telling this, I remind myself. No good at all. I can't worry the people in my life—my family, my clients, my friends, my colleagues. I can't put the threat of relapse back on the table again, it's not fair. But I know it's not them I'm thinking of, it's me. I'm afraid of losing what I have—respect, trust, success, financial security, love; afraid of not getting what I want— more of all these things. Again, as it once did, fear shoots through every thought, every action, every minute. I sit in The Library and hear people—newly sober, long sober—talk about how once they lived in fear and now do not. They say things like *The truth will set you free*, and I think they are speaking directly to me. My sponsee, the same one whose messages stopped me in Bangkok, refuses to count days in meetings. I beg him to come to The Library and raise his hand and he refuses. *I'll go to meetings*, he says, *but I won't count days. I don't want people to know I relapsed. It's no one's business.* I tell him, again and again, he needs to come clean in the rooms, to be seen and heard there, to let people help him. I say these words and it's as if they are coming from someone else's mouth and throat and are meant for me.

A friend, not someone who struggles with drugs and alcohol, is embroiled in a complicated situation, a house of cards of deception and secrecy involving many people that is toppling in on him, and one night he comes to my apartment in desperation. There seems to be no solution, and for a while I get caught up in the faulty logic that delivered him to this mess. At first the situation appears just as hope- less as he describes. And then it's clear. The truth is the only answer, the only chance of moving ahead toward any sane future. When I say this he responds as if it is the last and least likely solution. Cit- ing all the imagined consequences—what will be lost, what won't be gained—he rejects the idea, and I do everything I can to convince him it's the only way. *The truth will set you free*, I say cornily, passion- ately, and again a voice that is mine and not mine is speaking to me.

In February I go to Miami for a long weekend. It is just after the breakup of an almost-year-long relationship and getting out of New York seems like a good idea. It is the weekend of the Academy Awards and I invite the friends I am with to my room to watch the show. After they leave I begin to clean up, collect the dirty dishes, the empty glasses. I notice a glass of white wine. It is full and untouched and perspiration beads on its rim. I pick it up and take a sip. Just like that. The sip of wine is in my mouth and down my throat and I recoil as if bitten by a snake. I spit the remaining wine out of my mouth and sit down on the couch as if the sip had happened to me, as if I am somehow its victim. I don't want more but I know I am in trouble. I leave the room, take the stairs down to the lobby, head out past the pool, the boardwalk, and onto the beach. Halfway between the boardwalk and the ocean, I drop to my knees and lie down face-first in the sand. Six years ago, at the rehab in White Plains, just a few nights before returning to Manhattan, I lay down in a muddy field under a raining sky and asked for help. I was lost then. I am lost now. I don't have a plan or any answers. I am powerless and fearful and into the damp sand I ask for help. *Help me. Help me, God.* The answer almost six years before was the faintest streak of light in a sky crowded with rain clouds. The answer now is the roar of the ocean, thumping music from the hotel lounges, and the sound of teenagers shouting in Spanish from the boardwalk.

There is a phrase I've heard at The Library and in other rooms hundreds of times. It's a phrase that sounded loudly in my ears in the months after Bangkok, after Miami: *We are only as sick as our secrets.* I missed not being sick. Eventually, weeks later, I call Annie. We hadn't spoken in months. An occasional text, a voice mail here and there.

She picks up on the first ring and I tell her everything. *OK*, she says after a short silence. *OK*. We talk for a long time and as we do I feel the noose loosen, the rope go slack. As the call ends she says, *Stay close, lambchop*. And I do. I tell Luke and then John and Kim and Cy. I tell my brother and my parents and I tell Polly, who will respond without words but with the tightest hug. I tell my sponsee, who, two days later, turns up at The Library, raises his hand, and announces his day count. Three days later he does it again, and at the end of the meeting he is surrounded. I tell Rafe, who says, among other things, exactly what Annie had said and what Jack, years ago, used to say: *Stay close*.

Later, three months from that sip of wine in Miami, I will raise my hand in a meeting I rarely go to in Midtown and say, shakily but with great relief, *I have ninety days*. Three days later, at The Library, with Polly in the seat next to me, her hand on my back, I raise my hand and tell everyone in the room what happened. And now I'm telling you.

Five and a half years and then one day. For me, there are no finish lines. No recovered, just recovering. My sobriety, that delicate state that can, for years at a time, feel unshakable, is completely dependent on my connection to other alcoholics and addicts, my seeking their help and my offering it. I went to an island for a month where there were no rooms where alcoholics and addicts gather to stay sober. If we learn at the speed of pain, the painful lesson here was that I need those rooms, those addicts and alcoholics. I need them like oxygen. No matter how good, how sober, how in control I feel. There are many programs of recovery. Paid, free, anonymous, not anonymous. I don't name here which one I go to because I don't want that program held responsible for anything I do or say or write. I don't want anything to get in the way of your finding it if it can help you. Alcoholics and addicts create enough obstacles to getting sober and I don't want to add more.

If you are struggling with drugs and alcohol, go to the rooms where alcoholics and addicts go to get and stay sober. These rooms and the people in them are your best chance. Listen to them, be honest with them. Help them—even if you think you have nothing to offer. Be helped by them. Depend on them and be depended on. And if the only thing you can do is show up, do it. Then do it again. And when it's the last thing you want to do and the last place you want to go, *go*. Just go. You have no idea who you might be helping just by sitting there or who might help you. I've heard many alcoholics and addicts describe a voice that tells them to drift, to detach, to follow their own counsel and cut off. It's the same voice that told me I could be on an island for a month without meetings; suggested that a drink was better than all others—*the best*—because it happened to be in a hotel; that no good could come from telling the truth and that death was useful. In my experience only one thing has been able to quiet that voice: other alcoholics and addicts in recovery. Their voices have been louder than the one that lies, louder than my own. They have, one day at a time, guided me toward honesty, usefulness, and they have saved my life. Together, they stay sober. Together, they end years of agony and isolation. If you are struggling with drugs and alcohol, they can help you, too. Find them now.

Acknowledgements

Thanks to Pat Strachan, the wisest eye, for ongoing editorial guidance; Michael Pietsch and David Young for continued support; the Dream Team at Little, Brown—Michelle Aielli, Amanda Brown, and Heather Fain—for unflagging excellence; Raffaella DeAngelis, Tracy Fisher, and the foreign-rights team at WME for being the best; Robin Robertson and Luiz Schwarcz for their rigor and care and for their friendship; Julia Eisenman, Jill Bialosky, Chris Pomeroy, Jay Knowlton, Joey Arbagey, Adam McLaughlin, Jonathan Galassi, and Kelle Groom for their time and their meticulous notes; Cy O'Neal for thieving, for movies, for more; Shaun Dolan for never blinking no matter what; John Bowe for being in the next room; Jean Stein for every magnificent voice mail and for having faith; my family— Mom, Dad, Kim, Brian, Matt, Ben, Lisa, Mark, Lillian, and Sean— for encouragement, love, and for defying gravity; Van Scott for all the days, and Jennifer Rudolph Walsh—great force, friend, agent, boss—for everything.

Thanks most of all to all the drunks and addicts who helped me get and stay sober and all those who still do.

penguin.co.uk/vintage